Duffus Hardy

Through Cities And Prairie Lands

Sketches of an American Tour

Duffus Hardy

Through Cities And Prairie Lands
Sketches of an American Tour

ISBN/EAN: 9783744753777

Printed in Europe, USA, Canada, Australia, Japan

Cover: Foto ©Andreas Hilbeck / pixelio.de

More available books at **www.hansebooks.com**

THROUGH CITIES
AND PRAIRIE LANDS

THROUGH CITIES

AND PRAIRIE LANDS.

SKETCHES OF AN AMERICAN TOUR.

BY
LADY DUFFUS HARDY.

BELFORD, CLARKE & CO.,
CHICAGO, ILL.
1882.

TO

MRS. WILLIAM HAYWOOD,

IN TOKEN

OF MY AFFECTIONATE REGARD,

I DEDICATE

THESE PAGES.

CONTENTS.

CHAPTER I.

ACROSS THE ATLANTIC.

Our Good Ship *Sardinian*—At Sea—Our Companions—Their Amusements—The Theorist—The Phantom Ship—Our Last Night on Board.................................... 1

CHAPTER II.

QUEBEC.

Land again—A Quaint Announcement—A Gastronomical Exhibition—A Pleasant Fireside—The Convent—The Heights of Abraham—Wolfe's Monument—French and English Canadians 13

CHAPTER III.

MONTREAL.

The Stolid Indian—Mount Royal—Sir Hugh Allen's Home—The Banks—The Windsor Hotel...................... 27

CHAPTER IV.

THE CAPITAL OF THE DOMINION.

River Travelling—Trail of the Fire King—Ottawa—Parliament Buildings—The City—The Home of our Princess......... 35

CHAPTER V.

FROM CITY TO CATARACT.

On the Train—The Thousand Islands—At Kingston—Toronto—The Government House—Arrival of the Princess Louise—"We expect the Moon"—Niagara Falls............... 46

CHAPTER VI.

THE EMPIRE CITY.

New York—Fifth Avenue—Madison Square—The Elevated Railway—The Cars—The Shops—The People—West Point 59

CHAPTER VII.

TO THE PHŒNIX CITY.

We Start—Our Car—Our Dressing-room—Chicago—Its Park—The Palmer House................................... 72

CHAPTER VIII.

WESTWARD HO!

Our Travelling Hotel—The Prairies—The Emigrant Train—Bret Harte's Heroes—Reception of General Grant in the Wild West—"See, the Conquering Hero Comes"—The Procession 80

CHAPTER IX.

ACROSS THE ROCKY MOUNTAINS.

Our Fellow-passengers—Unprotected Females—Prairie Dog Land—A Cosy Interior—Cheyenne—The Rocky Mountains—"Castles not Made by Hands"—Ogden........... 91

CHAPTER X.

THE CITY OF THE SAINTS.

Salt Lake—Our Mormon Conductor—Mormon Wives—Their Daughters—Their Recruits—Their Agricultural Population 102

CHAPTER XI.

AMONG THE MORMONS.

Society—A Mormon Wife's View—The Shops—Amelia Palace—The Tabernacle—The Organ—Endowment House—A Mormon Widow—Currency in the Old Days—The Elders Hold Forth.. 114

CHAPTER XII.

ACROSS THE SIERRAS.

Ogden Station—Bustling Bedtime—Boots—An Invasion—A Wedding Aboard—The American Desert—The Glorious Sierras—Cape Horn—Dutch Flats—"Here they are!"—A Phantom City... 129

CHAPTER XIII.

THE GOLDEN CITY.

The Streets—Kaleidoscopic Scenes—The Stock Boards—Wild Cat—Bulls and Bears—The Markets—The "Dummy"—Lone Mountain... 142

CHAPTER XIV.

THE OLD MISSION.

The Windmills—The Golden Gate Park—The Seal Rock—The Cliff House—The Mission Dolores......................... 155

CHAPTER XV.

SOME SAN FRANCISCO WAYS AND CUSTOMS.

Street Architecture—Curiosities of Climate—Brummagem Baronets—The Sand Lot—The Forty-niners—"Society Ladies".. 162

CHAPTER XVI.

THE FLOWERY KINGDOM.

A Visit to Chinatown—Its General Aspect—A Tempting Display—Barbers' Shops—A Chinese Restaurant—Their Joss House—Their Gods...................................... 175

CHAPTER XVII.

A WORLD UNDERGROUND.

The Pawnbroker's Shop—The Opium Dens—The Smokers—A World within a World—The Women's Quarters...... 187

CHAPTER XVIII.

CHINESE AMUSEMENTS.

Gambling Dens—Theatres—An Acrobatic Performance—New Year's Visits—The Bride—The Hoodlum—A Scare—The Matron's Pretty Feet 197

CHAPTER XIX.

CHRISTMAS ON A CALIFORNIAN RANCHE.

Old Friends—The Ranche—Christmas Day—Salinas Valley—A Magic City—A Californian Sunset..................... 210

CHAPTER XX.

IN THE VALLEY OF CARMELO.

PAGE

Monterey—The Ruins of the Mission—The Spanish Inhabitants of the Old Town—The Moss Beach—The Lighthouse—The Pebbly Pescadero—Good-bye 221

CHAPTER XXI.

ON THE BANKS OF THE BAY.

New Year's Visits—The Gentlemen's Day—Local Attractions —Berkeley College—Saucelito—In Arcadia—Among the Woods and Flowers—A Fairy Festival.................. 231

CHAPTER XXII.

IN THE FOREST PRIMEVAL.

Pleasant Retreats—Californian Trees—Cañon and Forest Scenery —Duncan Mills—A Stormy Evening—The Redwoods— Farewell to the "Golden City."........................ 243

CHAPTER XXIII.

THE SILVER STATE.

Snowed in—Indians—Journey to Denver—A Forage for a Supper—"Crazed"—Domestic Difficulties—Colorado Springs —Cheyenne Cañon—The "Garden of the Gods"—Ute Pass—Glen Eyrie 258

CHAPTER XXIV.

BRICKS AND MORTAR.

The Road to St. Louis—The Kansas Brigands' Exploit—Picturesque Population—Mississippi River—Washington—The Capitol—Public Buildings—Society—A Monument to a Lost Cause—Mount Vernon........................... 278

CHAPTER XXV.

THE QUAKER CITY.

Baltimore—Its Stony Streets—Druids' Park—A Stroll through the City—Aristocratic Quarters—Washington Monument—Philadelphia—General Aspect—Picturesque Market Street—Fairmount Zoological Gardens........................ 292

CHAPTER XXVI.

SUMMER AMONG THE GOTHAMITES.

A New York Summer—How they meet it—Airy Customs—Coney Island—Rockaway and Long Branch—A Mountain Village—Ellenville—View from "Sam's Point"................. 302

CHAPTER XXVII.

THE "AMERICAN ATHENS."

Aboard the *Massachusetts*—A Perambulation—The Electric Machine—An Easy Way of committing Suicide—Boston—The Cars—The Common—The "Glorious Fourth of July".... 314

CHAPTER XXVIII.

FAREWELL VISITS.

A Visit to Longfellow—The Poet's Home—Dr. Oliver Wendell Holmes—Newport—A Fashionable Watering-place—The Old Town—The "Cottages"—Homeward................ 325

THROUGH CITIES
AND
PRAIRIE LANDS.

CHAPTER I.

ACROSS THE ATLANTIC.

Our Good Ship *Sardinian*—At Sea—Our Companions—Their Amusements—The Theorist—The Phantom Ship—Our Last Night on Board.

T is the gray dawn of a July day; we are up with the sun, nay, before the sun, eager to start on our first Atlantic voyage. In order to avoid the hurry and bustle of a crowded Liverpool hotel, I and my companion, for we are two, had resolved to start by the first train, and go direct on board. Therefore, at six o'clock on this bright July morning, we arrive at Euston Square station, and there find a host of friends, who, in spite of the early hour, have gathered to bid us "God speed." They are all gift-laden; one brings books and bonbons, another a basket of rich ripe strawberries, then a patent corkscrew and telescope is thrust into my hand, and last, though not least, just as the train is mov-

ing out of the station, one late arrival breathlessly gasps "good-bye" and flings a packet of pins, a box of matches, and a cake of scented soap in at the window.

At Liverpool the little steam-tug was in waiting to convey us to the vessel, which lay a short distance from the landing stage. It was a lovely July day; the sun was blooming, like a flower of light, in the bright blue skies, the tiny waves danced and murmured joyously as they ran rippling along the shore, and the soft balmy air, laden "with the briny kisses of the great sweet mother," greeted us with invigorating breath as we steamed across and stepped on board the good ship *Sardinian,* ready to face the fearful ten days which we had so often anticipated with shivering and shudderings at our cosy fireside.

There was a hurried hand-shaking. "Good-byes" and parting words resounded on all sides of us, uttered in varied shades of feeling, some with a choking sob as of friends who would never meet again, others with hearty cheerful voices, as though they were bound for young life's first holiday. Presently stentorian lungs shouted "all for the shore," departing friends and relatives swarmed down the steep wooden wall of the vessel; we all rushed to the side, nods and smiles "that were half tears" were freely exchanged, last words were shouted from one to the other, and amid the waving of handkerchiefs and echoing voices, the little steam-tug which had brought the passengers on board went shrieking and snorting back to the shore, and our great ship steamed majestically up the Mersey, out towards the obnoxious Irish Channel; some weak-minded mortals started with a hazy idea that if the Channel treated them too roughly, they could, if they pleased, land at Moville, and so bid "adieu" to the horrors of the sea for ever; but that was a cowardly idea which I never encouraged for a moment.

My first idea was to take a survey of my fellow-passengers. There were plenty of them; as a rule they were mere commonplace specimens of humanity, such as nature turns out by thousands, with no distinctive mark, but merely labelled "men" and "women." There were exceptions of course. One was an elderly hard-featured man, bronzed and weather-beaten, with keen, gray eyes, which looked as though they could detect a spot on the face of the sun without the aid of glasses, and so searching that, like the east wind, they could reach the marrow at a single blow. But my attention was most attracted by a very young and very beautiful widow; beautiful, so far as grace of form, regularity of feature, and soft colouring was concerned, but the beauty of her face was utterly destroyed by its expression, which may be briefly catalogued as "evil." She looked like a woman who had got a story, and not a pleasant one. No accompanying friends had bid her "good-bye," or "good speed." She was alone, but she did not seem lonely. She carried a child about a year old in her arms, and marched up and down the deck, looking neither to the right nor to the left, till the gong sounded and we all went down to dinner; but before the table could be satisfactorily arranged the question arose, "What was to become of the baby?" At last a young Scotchman volunteered to immolate himself on the altar of beauty, and held out his arms for the child; she gave it without a word, and he disappeared up the companion-way, holding it upside down, which awkwardness may perhaps be excused, considering that was the first time he had officiated in the capacity of dry-nurse.

The gilded glories of the saloon were a surprise to me, as this was the first time I had been on an Atlantic steamer. Of course, in common with the world generally, I had *heard* of the luxurious arrangements and admirably served table on board those magnificent vessels; but I had yet to learn how luxury and comfort combined could make that floating world a pleasant ten days' home. The dreaded voyage turned out delightfully. The Irish Channel behaved beautifully, literally "it broke into dimples and laughed in the sun," as its rippling waves ran dancing round the prow and along the black sides of our vessel, gurgling and murmuring in smothered tones as though they were enjoying a joke, exulting in their hidden strength, knowing that their pleasant playful mood might pass and their tiny wavelets grow into mountains and uplift us in their giant arms and toss us up to the moon, or crush our huge iron-hearted home like an eggshell, and swallow us all up. On we went, cutting a rapid way through the calm waters; the daylight and the land together faded from our sight, the stars came out, and as the silent night closed slowly around us, merry laughing voices sank into quiet sober tones. We seemed to realize the fact that we were alone on the wide world of waters—the same living restless waters whereon Christ had walked, and whose waves he had bidden "Peace, be still." We retired to our cosy little state-room early, and slept as we had never dreamed we could sleep on our first night at sea, our slumbers soothed, not broken, by the musical "Yo, heave, ho!" of the sailors; and the steady monotonous "thud, thud" of the engine had a by no means unpleasant effect on our drowsily unaccustomed ears. When we awoke in the morning we found ourselves, not tossing, but gliding calmly over the "wild Atlantic waves," which were rolling round us on all sides as far as the eye could reach, a world of palpitating waters, unruffled and smooth as the bosom of a lake. For three days this calm continued. The masculine element grew turbulent and rebelled against this unnatural state of things; there was something wrong about it altogether; even the "rolling forties," from whom some show of spirit was expected, forgot to do their duty, and allowed us to ride over them without a protesting blow; their wild white horses were stabled in the caves below, and with all sails set, a brisk breeze following in our wake, and the briny kisses of the "great sweet mother" on our faces, we scudded along at the rate of fifteen knots an hour. We female passengers thoroughly appreciated the stormless sea, and paced up and down the deck chatting and exchanging harmless confidences; the gentlemen tried to beguile the time with ring-toss and shovel-board. When they grew tired of such harmless occupations they got up a walking match, or ran half-mile races round the deck, and, indeed, in every way did their best to scare away ennui, and make the monotonous days and hours pass pleasantly; for after the first novelty of the scene is over, skies of eternal changeless blue and calm summer seas are apt to grow monotonous, and a thunderstorm or a howling hurricane, "warranted harmless," would have created a pleasant diversion. However, on the whole, time passed pleasantly enough; we were all sociably inclined, and lived on strictly communistic principles, in a general exchange of civilities. Everybody was welcome to the belongings of everybody else; we used each other's chairs, rugs, wraps, and even made occasional walking sticks of one another's husbands, and when we had nothing else to do indulged in a game of speculation concerning the "widow," who held herself aloof, in a state of as complete isolation as though she had been on a desert island; she accepted courtesies without a word of thanks, or refused them with an impatient gesture, till the chivalrous spirit of the gentlemen flickered and died out, and as she resented any offer of assistance, she was left to stagger about the deck at her pleasure. The child was the pet and plaything of everybody on board; the mother seemed willing to ignore its existence, and gave it only a kind of wooden automatic attention at best. Nothing attracted or interested her, and the beautiful dark face became a weird strange mystery to us. We grew accustomed to see the tall lithe figure pacing silently to and fro like a shadowy ghost in the gloaming; for long after the daylight faded and the evening closed in she continued her monotonous round, like a perturbed spirit that could know no rest.

We had a theorist on board, too, who by a sheer habit of aggravation kept us lively. His theory was *starvation*. Nobody ought to be sick, nobody ought to be hungry;

he pounced upon everybody with an appetite of even the most moderate dimensions.

"My dear madam," said he in deprecating tones, addressing an elderly lady who was modestly picking a chicken-bone, "you are committing an outrage upon nature; she doesn't require that chicken-bone."

"I must eat to support life," said the lady apologetically.

"Bah! you can support life on the backbone of a bloater; as I say, you are outraging nature, forcing things upon her that she doesn't want, and she will revenge herself by disturbing your digestion and depressing your spirits."

"My spirits are always depressed; I don't know what it is to be cheerful *now*," she answered in a lachrymose tone.

"Of course not. An overloaded stomach acts like a weight to keep the spirits down. Look at me," he added, slapping his ample chest and outstretching his brawny arm, "*I'm* strong and healthy; I nourish myself upon—next to nothing, and I'm never hungry—never depressed."

"Ah, sir!" she answered, shaking her head with a tear in her eye, "if you were in my place you'd never be anything else; but you don't know what it is to lose your life's partner."

"Don't I? Why, I've buried two! This is my third venture." He jerked his head towards a fair, pale little woman, whose appetite was evidently under his control. "Why, when I first married my little wife there," he added, regarding her affectionately, " she used to eat three meals a day; now she is reduced to one."

"By the time you have reduced her to half a meal, perhaps, she'll give you a chance of experimenting on a fourth," suggested my companion; which observation our theorist did not choose to hear, but sauntered on, threatening one with apoplexy, scaring another with visions of sudden death; investing everybody with the "ills that flesh is heir to," the one inheritance that nobody is in a hurry to possess. Lobster salad was alive with horrible nightmares, and delirium tremens bubbled in the glass of sparkling Moët and Chandon. On all sides his theory was greeted with good-humoured derision, and occasioned much merriment, and though there was little wit, there was much laughter among us. At last a living contradiction to his theory stepped out from the companion-way in the person of a fair-complexioned young Englishman, a perfect athlete, broad-chested, strong-limbed, a "crisp and curled Antony," brimming over with the healthful vigour and vitality of young manhood; he could run, row, leap, ride, and in every manly sport had kept to the fore.

"Look at me," he said, "*I* eat four square meals a day, and, perhaps, put more roast beef out of sight than anybody here; but do *I* look like a wreck? Just feel my biceps."

"My good fellow," said our theorist, regarding him with grave compassionate interest, "you have a good constitution; you are doing your best—but—you have not had time to ruin it yet."

Our vessel carried a hundred and fifty steerage passengers, with whom we had many a pleasant chat on the forecastle deck; some hoped to ply their trade in the cities, some were going up the country. "We can get plenty of land there, and never a stiver to pay for it," said one burly man, with a large family of small children. Somebody suggested that the United States offered a wider field and less difficulties. "That may be," he answered, "but I don't want to cut myself adrift from the old country; I mean my children and their children after 'em, please God, to grow up under the British flag. The stars and stripes are very well in their way, but the Union Jack's good enough for me." That was the general feeling among the emigrant classes; the vast uncultivated lands of the United States might offer better fortune, but they would not cut themselves adrift from the "old country."

Our captain read prayers in the steerage night and morning, but we first-class sinners had a religious service on Sundays only. Every evening such sailors as were not on duty gathered in the forecastle, and the captain gave them an extemporaneous sermon, in forcible homely language best suited to their comprehension, and allowed them to indulge in a goodly sprinkling of Moody and Sankey's hymns. It was a strange and rather a weird scene, that narrow forecastle, with bunks all round, the long oak table, lit with tiny oil lamps, flickering up in the swart grimy faces of the men, as they united their voices—and with all their hearts, or at least with all their lungs—in praises or thanksgiving, as they tramped on their "March to Canaan's Land" or lingered round the gates of "Jersusalem the Golden."

In a pleasant desultory fashion the eventful days passed on, the smallest thing affording us great diversion ; once a shoal of porpoises gambolled beside the vessel, tumbling and rolling over one another in their fishlike frolics ; then a school of whales passed within a quarter of a mile of us, uplifting their huge heads, and creating a series of waterspouts by the way. Our route was so far north that no other vessel had hitherto crossed our path ; we seemed to have the sea all to ourselves. One morning the exclamation went round, "A sail in sight ;" we flew to the bulwarks, but nothing was visible to our unaccustomed eyes ; we watched, eagerly straining our eyes in the direction indicated ; by degrees a kind of phantom ship, with all sails set, loomed upon our sight ; it seemed to hang suspended on the very edge of the world between sea and sky. We watched it breathlessly ; but it came no nearer, no clearer. Shrouded in mist, like a spectral illusion, it remained a few moments in sight, and then disappeared as mysteriously as it came, and once more we were alone on the wide desolate sea. That evening we had a splendid sunset ; the whole of the western skies were draped with crimson, lighted up with flames of gold. We watched its kaleidoscopic glories change ; one brilliant colour fading into and amalgamating with another, till the whole horizon was a gorgeous mass of rose-tinted purple and green and gold, which presently broke up, and drifted and re-formed till the pale dim skies were filled with floating islands of fire. We literally felt as though we were sailing "into the land beyond the sunset seas, the islands of the blest."

On the evening of the eighth day we sighted Father

Point, and sent up a rocket to summon a pilot from the shore; three rockets, red, white, and blue, went whizzing through the air in answer—" coming." In another moment a white light, like a gigantic glowworm came creeping along the face of the water, nearer and nearer, till the plish-plashing of oars brought a cockleshell of a boat alongside, and the pilot, with the agility of a cat, climbed up the huge black side of the vessel and leapt over the bulwarks on to the deck.

Our pilot embarked, we were soon on our way again. After the long uneventful days and nights, the slightest occurrence amused and interested us, and that day, to our unoccupied minds, seemed crammed with adventures. As we paced the deck chatting and laughing, some warbling or singing snatches of old songs, we were startled by the appearance of a huge black mass, which seemed to grow mysteriously out of the darkness, with many-coloured lights swinging in the empty air. It was the steam-tug which had come off from Rimouski for mails and such passengers as desired to go on to Lower Canada; the lights swung from the shrouds and rigging of the vessel, and shone down with a weird effect upon the bustling scene below. There was a general commotion; impatient friends had come on board to meet their relatives; one after another eager faces swarmed over the bulwarks, and welcoming exclamations and hearty handshakings and embraces followed their appearance; the pleasant greetings of the genial happy voices cast a momentary cloud over our spirits; our thoughts flew homeward; we knew it would be long before familiar faces and friendly voices could give *us* greeting, and we half envied our fellow-passengers their welcome to what to us was an unknown land. But in the unknown there is always a mysterious attraction, and before the little steam-tug was well out of sight, we were again buoyantly pacing the deck, with never a thought or care beyond the present. It was a lovely night; the stars, such big blazing stars, shone down like angel's eyes through the dark-blue sky; the waves sparkled and danced beneath the light of the planet Jupiter, which shone like a baby moon upon the dark face of the water. We were all too nervously excited to care for rest that night. We lingered long upon the deck, and at last disappeared one by one down the companion-way, our captain's cheery voice assuring us "we should sight Quebec in the morning."

CHAPTER II.

QUEBEC.

Land again—A Quaint Announcement—A Gastronomical Exhibition—A Pleasant Fireside—The Convent—The Heights of Abraham—Wolfe's Monument—French and English Canadians.

HE next day we were up early, and went on deck in time to see the first rosy flush break from the east, and creep over the cool gray dawn. It deepened, and widened, and spread, till the golden sun rose slowly and took possession of the pale blue skies, casting his lance-like beams to the right and to the left, tinging all things above and below with his heavenly alchemy, but concentrating his light, like a crown of glory, on the beautiful city which loomed slowly upon our sight out of the shadowy distance.

With straining eyes we watched to catch the first view of Quebec. We had heard of it, read of it, knew of all the vicissitudes it had undergone, had looked upon its pictured beauty scores of times; but now the reality was before us, and the picturesque beauty of its appearance fully realized, if it did not exceed, our expectations. How few things in this world ever do that! Something was no doubt owing to the extreme beauty of the morning, the clearness of the atmosphere, and the glowing sunlight that gilded the tall spires, flecked the sloping housetops, till the china roofs sparkled and flashed like a world of broken diamonds. Slowly we steamed up the St. Lawrence towards our goal. It was good to see land at last. The soft, picturesque river scenery spread like a panoramic view on either side of us—luxuriant, grassy mounds and meadows came down to the water's edge, pretty villages were dotted about here and there, with a background of swelling hills, which rose higher and higher till they were lost in the pine forests beyond. The distant jingle of the church bells broke pleasantly on our ears after the long monotonous plish-plashing of the waves. On our left rose Pont Levis, a busy place or collection of houses, churches and manufactories, creeping up a lofty hill almost as imposing to look at as Quebec itself, and with a tolerable amount of historical associations too, though they have been swallowed up in the more prominent facts of its more beautiful and picturesque neighbour. It was at Pont Levis that the military authorities bided their time, and held their discussions and arranged their manœuvres before carrying them into effect; and it was there that General Wolfe waited and chafed impatiently for the gray dawn which gave him victory and death.

We disembarked at Pont Levis, and were ferried across the river to Quebec. There our pleasant party drifted away in different directions, some going north, some going south; there was much handshaking, many good wishes, and hopes to meet again. We were very sorry to part with our theorist, who, with his delicate young wife, went on his homeward way to Maine, where we promised to pay them a visit before our tour was ended. At the landing-stage, a forlorn-looking place in a most dilapidated condition, we were surrounded by a clamorous crowd of Irish and French, who made a raid upon our small baggage, and struggled manfully as to who should bear it off. However, while we were looking helplessly around, we were rescued by the timely advent of the hotel proprietor, who, through the thoughtful kindness of our captain, had been notified of our arrival, and had come down on the look-out for us. He thrust the rabble to the right and to the left, handed us into a *calèche* which he had in waiting, and in another moment we were bowling along through the lower market-place, on our way to the St. Louis Hotel. With reckless speed we rattled up the steep, stony streets, the breath almost jostled out of our bodies, and clutching one another wildly in our endeavour to keep steady,—on across the upper and more aristocratic market-square, which is surrounded by large, handsome shops, past the puritanical-looking Cathedral, a plain, barnlike building with a tall tapering spire, and were at length deposited safely at the door of the St. Louis Hotel, a commodious and comfortable place enough for a temporary resting-place. We were at once shown into a room on an upper floor, having a beautiful view of the town and river. We looked down upon a congregation of towers, turrets, steeples, and housetops, with the Laval Museum standing out the chief feature below, and the Convent of Gray Nuns standing square and gloomy on the hill above. Having taken a brief look around, we inquired:

"When does the dinner-bell ring?"

"Sure thin, there's no dinner-bell at all!" answered a stout Irish lass.

"How shall we know when it is dinner-time?"

"Oh, yez'll know; 'e 'ollers."

She disappeared, leaving us slightly puzzled as to who would 'oller. We waited a few minutes, and then sure enough, he did "'oller." A pair of stentorian lungs shouted through all the corridors, "Dinner! dinner!" The voice dwindled away, and went wandering in ghostly echoes to remote corners and distant chambers, circulating the fact in this most primitive fashion that dinner was served. Having eaten and drank for the last ten days under difficulties, never being quite sure that our soup would not find its way into our pockets, or our chicken fly into our faces, and obstinately refuse to be driven into our mouths, it was pleasant to find ourselves comfortably seated at a table that wouldn't turn a somersault on its own account, or send the crockery flying about our ears. There were specimens of many nationalities at table, with a fair sprinkling of the gentle Canadians themselves; and here began a gastronomical exhibition. As a rule (of course there are exceptions) people did not eat, they *bolted;* flung their food into their mouths, and sent their knives after it to see that it was all right. Seated opposite to me was a round, bullet-headed man, like a monk, "all shaven and shorn," with large ears, which seemed to grow out of his head, not on it, and a large loose mouth, that looked as though it could never tighten, and had no idea of ever shutting itself firmly; but oh! so much went into it! He surrounded himself with the whole bill of fare, and then "fell to," demolishing one thing after another, till I fancied he must have a fit of apoplexy or—burst. He handled his eating utensils with such marvellous dexterity, that when his knife flashed in the air and disappeared down his throat, I watched for it to come out at the back of his head; but no! it always came back. Well, they are used to playing with edged tools this side of the water, and provided they do not compel me to join the game I am content.

The next morning we received a visit from the Sanitary Inspector (who had been introduced to us when he boarded our vessel for our bill of health). He came accompanied by his wife and daughters on hospitable thoughts intent. We were quite at home with one another in half an hour, nay in ten minutes, and in their pleasant home we spent many evening hours. It was a musical household; the young daughters, with fine contralto and mezzo-soprano voices, warmed our hearts with some of the sweet home songs which we thought we had left behind us. Our captain, too, while he was on shore, occasionally dropped in and enlivened us with the patriotic ditties in which our souls delighted. Our mutual favourite was the thrilling ballad of the "Slave Ship." He would bring his hand down with a crash upon the ivory keys, and send a shrieking shiver through the chords as he triumphantly announced:

> "There's always death to slavery
> When British bunting's spread."

His face beamed as though his individual hand was striking slavery dead. When not patriotic he was intensely moral, and the lesson of "Mrs. Lofty's jewels" was so vigorously driven into our brain, we ought to have been dead to the dazzle of diamonds evermore.

On the first day of our arrival we sallied forth to see the town. The picturesque fascination of its first appearance, which took us captive as we first steamed up the St. Lawrence, lessened on a closer acquaintance. "Distance lends enchantment to the view" in this as in many other cases. It is a delightfully old historic city, full of incongruities, and marvellous in its general aspect of griminess and decay. The ancient buildings do not seem to be enjoying a hale and strong old age. They have a gray, worn look, as though they felt their mournful position, and grieved that no hand was outstretched to save them from the ruin into which they are fast falling. It seems as though time had robed and crowned this quaint old town with historic fame and interest, and then turned away and left it forlorn and half forgotten; for it has all the appearance of a bankrupt estate, with little life or money left in it. Its glory has departed, there is no doubt of that, and the good folk are trying to destroy its picturesqueness as fast as they can. We feel this as we stroll through the long straggling up and down streets, their china or slate roofs glistening in the sunshine. The houses, some old, some new, represent every style of architecture or non-architecture under the sun; no uniformity, no regularity anywhere. Some are built of red brick, some of gray stone, with odd little latticed windows breaking out in unexpected places. Some modern occupants of ancient homes have discarded the tiny twinkling panes, and replaced them with huge squares of plate glass and other "modern improvements," marring as much as possible the quaint picturesqueness of the old, without imparting the imposing aspect of the new. The wooden pavements are in a generally rotten condition, and the roads when they are not cobble stones are full of ruts, holes, and pitfalls, which makes us sigh for Macadam and all his host.

We pass through the Governor's garden, where a huge placard warns " not to pick the flowers." But never a flower is in sight ; only a growth of dank, long grass, and a thick undergrowth of weeds of the wildest ; *they* flourish luxuriantly enough. We pick our way over the stony pathway, and reach Dufferin Terrace, a splendid promenade, which is and will remain for centuries a noble record written in stone of Lord Dufferin's administration in Canada. It is fifty feet wide and a quarter of a mile long. It runs from the fort of the citadel, on the edge of the quaint old town, on the one side, and has a wide extensive land and river view on the other, perhaps one of the loveliest views in all Canada, for as far as the eye can see on all sides there is a well-wooded landscape of undulating hills and valleys dotted with toy villages and tiny towns, with the beautiful river lying like a sheet of silver below, winding and widening till it seems to fade in the far horizon, and is lost in the vast ocean beyond. Leaning over the fanciful iron railing we look sheer down a hundred and twenty feet into Champlain Street, the St. Giles of Quebec, and out over the lower town. Here on this splendid terrace the Quebeckers take their evening promenade when the sultry day is over, for if there is the slightest breeze stirring, it is sure to be found here. Standing back, at about the centre of the terrace, is the monument to "Wolfe and Montcalm," situated in a small square plat, "which is a garden called," but which in reality is like the rest of the public gardens here, a mass of tangled weeds and briars. The renowned general himself looks as though he was rather tired of standing there, and would gladly descend to that oblivion into which all men great and small must sink at last. It is only a question of time. He is doing his best to get away from men's eyes, and is crumbling to pieces as fast as he can. Already he has no features to speak of, and his clothes are crumbling from his back. He has stood there so long that few people care to look at him now except strangers, and they make such scornful remarks upon his generally dilapidated appearance as would make his stony brow blush for shame if the stony heart could feel! Would not all great men prefer to live in the memory of their countrymen till their names become household words in every home rather than be libelled in stone and left to the gaze of unborn generations, to whom their deeds or their works are as a tale that is told,—long past, half forgotten in the greater mass of great works which have succeeded them?

We are not sorry to turn our backs upon the dismal effigy of our hero and get into one of those delightful waggons which are the pride of Quebec, easy, light, well hung; while they serve all the purposes of an open carriage, they shield you most effectually from the sun or the rain, being open all round, and provided with stout waterproof curtains, which can be drawn or left undrawn at pleasure. In the course of half an hour we find ourselves on the Plains of Abraham, where we can indulge in a little poetic dreaming of our hero, and the days that are dead and gone. Standing there and looking round on that historic spot it is easy to send our imagination travelling back to the gray dawn of that misty morning long ago. There are Montcalm's troops encamped around, sleeping securely on that lofty and seemingly inaccessible height, their dusky Huron and Iroquois allies hanging like a ragged fringe upon their rear. Noiselessly and with muffled oars Wolfe and his gallant soldiers cross the river from Pont Levis, and with catlike silence and agility climb the steep sides of the cliff, gaining a foothold wherever they can, hanging on by straggling bushes or jagged edges; one after another in stealthy silence they creep, they swarm upward; no clink of sword nor clang of armour warns the sleeping adversary of their approach, till in the gray dawn of the morning they gather, a grim and silent army, on the Heights of Abraham in the midst of the enemy, who are startled from their sleep. We fancy we hear the bugles ring out, and the hurrying to and fro, as the dust and fury of the battle begins. It does not last long, not very long; a few hours decides the fate of the picturesque old town. Wolfe is wounded; a gray mass is seen flying eastward. "They run, they run!" a voice is heard exclaiming. "Who, who run?" asks the wounded general. "The French, sir." "Thank God!" he cries, and falls back dead. An obelisk marks the spot where he fell.

Having admired the splendid view from those lofty plains, we turn on our way back to the town. The suburbs of Quebec are very beautiful, being studded with elegant villas, surrounded by gardens all abloom with bright, sweet-scented flowers, that fill the air with perfume. The Foye Road is especially remarkable for its collection of palatial residences. Every man appears to be his own architect, for each house differs from the other, and all are built with more or less originality of design, some highly ornamented, others remarkable for their elegant simplicity. It would be difficult to classify these dwellings with any recognized style of architecture. It is strange to observe how entirely the French and English Canadians keep apart. There is no intercourse between the two. On the side of the French, at least, there seems to be an undercurrent of the old hostility still flowing, though it is never brought actively to the surface, for they are a law-abiding, peaceful people; in their collisions with the Irish, it is generally the Irish who make the first hostile move. They will not learn English nor allow it to be taught in their schools. You may walk for miles through this British Colony and never hear the sound of your native language; if you venture to inquire your way you will be answered in a kind of French that is not spoken in the France of to-day. They cling to the ancient French of their forefathers, with no innovations or modern improvements. The upper classes of both nations keep as much aloof from each other as the lower. It is seldom you meet a French family in an English drawing-room, or an English family at a French reception; for those little social dissipations do occasionally take place, though, as a rule, life seems to flow on in a dull, sluggish fashion in this quaint, historic town. Religion is the only thing that seems to keep itself lively, for the air bristles with church spires, like drawn swords flashing in a holy battle, pointing upwards. Week days and Sundays, and, at it seems to us, at all times and hours, the bells ring out their musical, rhythmical chimes. The Cathedral has a splendid peal of bells, which play "The last Rose of Summer" and some other English melodies with exquisite sweetness and precision. It was pleasant to hear the old home tunes clang out beneath the blue Canadian skies.

Through the kind interest of our new friends we gained entrance to the Convent of Gray Nuns. By a low arched doorway we entered a small stone hall, with a staircase on one side and a narrow aperture on the other, where the face of an aged nun appeared as she received or gave messages. We received instructions to go upstairs, and went; we passed locked doors and chambers barren of furniture, except, perhaps, a few bare benches; we could find our way nowhere, and after lingering for awhile in these empty chambers, haunted by the ghostly echo of our own footsteps, a door opened and a voice bade us enter. In another moment we had the pleasure of presenting ourselves to the reverend mother, who was seated in a light, airy room, the first of a semicircle of nuns, who were saved from contact with us worldly folk by a partition of wooden railings, which reached from the floor to the ceiling. There was no space through which we could even shake their saintly hands. Conversation under these circumstances was difficult, originality was impossible; we could make no semi-confidential inquiry or insinuating remark with those twenty pairs of smiling eyes upon us, each keeping guard over herself and her neighbour, and all being under the "right eye" of their "Mother Commander." Any idea we might have entertained of digging below the surface and getting a glimpse of conventual life perished on the spot. They had evidently no intention of extending their favours further. A view of their bare-benched chambers and of themselves was considered privilege enough. "The secrets of their prison-house" were closed from our unhallowed eyes. Once only in living memory had the convent been unreservedly thrown open to the eyes of the outer world, and that was on the occasion of the visit of the Princess Louise a few weeks previously. Even the simple event of our coming must have created some little excitement, for we were advised that many of the nuns then present had not seen a face from the outer world for forty years until the Princess came amongst them.

In reply to our few commonplace inquiries or remarks, they tried eagerly (speaking all at once or echoing one another) to assure us of their perfect happiness and content, so earnestly indeed as to make us doubt the fact. Yet they certainly had a look of peace and content; not the content that is born of the fulness of joy, or is the result of a happy, busy, useful life, but the peace that is born of sorrow, or of inward struggles and battles, fought out in loneliness and silence; for human nature robbed of her rights will chafe, and struggle, and rebel, till she is broken down and taught to waive her rights in this world that she may grasp a higher right in the next. For that she waits.

The luxurious comfort and bright, sunny aspect of the Father Confessor's chamber (he is the only male allowed upon the premises) was a striking contrast to the nuns' bare chambers. He was a small, wizened old man, with the simplicity of a child. Whether he possessed the "wisdom of the serpent," I query—though how that interesting reptile has proved its claim to wisdom I fail to comprehend. He showed us his photographs and his sample curiosities with as much pride as a child shows its prize picture-book, and attached as much importance to the most trifling things. He was the proud possessor of the skull of Montcalm, and all that is left of that heroic general grinned at us with socketless eyes from beneath a glass case where it reposed on a velvet cushion. "Alas! poor Yorick." He pointed out where some teeth had been extracted without the aid of dentistry; they had been stolen by some British tourists to whom he had exhibited his treasures. He had been spiritual adviser to that world of lonely womanhood for forty-five years, and very rarely went abroad. Well, we took our last look of him, of our friends, the Dufferin Terrace, and the quaint old town, with much regret. We had taken our berths on board of one of those palatial river steamers, which are indeed like four-story houses afloat, replete with the most luxurious accommodation, with balconies running round every story, elegant drawing-rooms for the ladies, smoking and billiard-rooms for the gentlemen, and a capital cuisine for everybody's benefit. Slowly we steamed up the St. Lawrence, keeping our eyes fixed upon the gilded spires and steeples of Quebec till the haze of distance shrouded them from our view.

CHAPTER III.

MONTREAL.

The Stolid Indian—Mount Royal—Sir Hugh Allan's Home—The Banks—The Windsor Hotel.

E were roused at a most unearthly hour in the morning, the bells were ringing, the engine shrieking, panting and struggling like a refractory steed who rebels against the will of his rider; but it was brought to a standstill at the landing-stage at Montreal, and we were turned out only half awake among droves of bellowing cattle, bleating sheep, and generations of grunting pigs, from the huge sow, half a ton weight, to the tiny squeakers a month old. We dodged the horns of the cattle and scrambled into the hotel omnibus as best we could. Then we took breath and scanned the scene around us. All was or seemed to be in a state of "confusion worse confounded," men and cattle seeming to be inextricably mixed together. The shouts of the one and the bellowing of the other shook the air, and filled our ears with discord. A posse of Indian squaws and "bucks" stood leaning along the wharf, watching us with expressionless eyes and immovable stolidity of countenance. They might have been statues of bronze for any signs

they gave of life. If the playful earthquake had paid a sudden visit to the shore and swallowed us up, I doubt if they would have moved a finger or quivered an eyelid. They all wore ragged red shawls or striped blankets wrapped round them, their dark faces and black beady eyes looming out from a mass of thick unkempt hair. This was the first time the untamed savage on his native soil had crossed our path, and I must say they were the most revolting specimens of the human race. It is simply impossible to regard them as "men and brothers," and the more we study the nature, character, and capabilities of these people, the more firmly we are convinced of that fact. Civilization, with its humanizing principles, may struggle with the difficulties, but it will never overcome the inborn blindness of the savage race. They have not the power to comprehend our codes, nor to feel as we feel. Much has been said of their treachery and cruelty, but oppression creates treachery, and that they have been oppressed and hardly used, driven from their native hills and plains to a strange world, which is as a sealed book to them, of which they neither know the letters or the language, nobody can deny. Regarding their cruelty, it is a quality native born, and directed not against the white race especially; they are cruel to themselves, to one another, and delight in lacerating and torturing their own flesh, regarding (as did the Spartans of old) the endurance of bodily pain as a virtue, courting it as a good rather than avoiding it as an evil, as we more civilized folk are apt to do. This is not meant as an extenuation of the Indian's malpractice, who in reality only carries out the instincts of his nature.

The dog, poor brute, cannot help being mad, but it must be got rid of. Looking on these people, with their low brows and the animal expression on their expressionless faces, we felt there might be some truth in Darwin's theory after all.

Our Jehu cracked his whip, and his bony steeds began to move slowly through the noisy throng. The wharf was swarm.ing with a busy population loading and unloading the many trading vessels which were drawn up by the river side. We passed under a crank of squeaking pigs, which were being swung through the air and lowered on to the deck of the vessel, protesting with all their swinish lungs against such unnatural elevation.

There is a slight rise in the ground as we wind our way from the waterside, but on the whole, the city is built on a flat, level piain, lying where the St. Lawrence and Ottawa rivers meet, stretching away, and widening through handsome squares and streets till it reaches the "mountain." It runs round it, covers its feet with pretty villa residences, but never attempts to climb or disfigure its green sides with bricks and mortar. There are no building-plots to let there, for Montreal is proud of its Mount Royal, and keeps it for the pure pride and glory of it. Sir Hugh Allan, the head of that splendid line of steamships bearing his name, has built an elegant and palatial residence there at the foot of the mountain. I am by no means sure that he has not encroached upon it, and planted his greenhouses in its arms, and sent his garden creeping up its soft velvet sides. But Sir Hugh is a benefactor to the city, a pleasant gentleman, and a great favourite with every class of people; no doubt if he even wanted a slice of the mountain he might have it, especially if he was willing to pay handsomely for it. This beautiful " Mount Royal " is much more than its name indicates. It is a perfect sylvan retreat, full of shady groves and bosky dells, luxuriant in its growth of wild fruits and flowers. Fine trees, with gnarled bark and wide-spreading, leafy branches, stand here and there in shady groups, while whole colonies of birds are singing the summer day through. There are whole battalions of nut trees and straggling blackberry bushes skirmishing round, each struggling to get a sight of the sun, eager to be the first to ripen and fall into the hands of the young children who come "a blackberrying" in the golden autumn days. There is not a single barren spot on the whole mountain; it is one garden of green, with tiny rivulets of living water, laughing and gurgling as they fall from its grassy crown to its moss-covered feet, which stand on the fringe of the city.

This is not one of the mountains which taxes your energies from the beginning, and makes you pay everlasting toll in the shape of aching limbs and weariness of spirit, using the sun's rays as a kind of airy razor to scrape the skin off your face and peel your hands till you can scarcely prod its rugged sides with your alpenstock. After much trouble and tribulation, with your clothes dragged off your back, the result of the hauling process common to your guides, you reach the top at last, and stand blowing like a grampus on its bald, white head, while you look round upon the wonderfully wide and extensive prospect you have risked so much to see. The sun laughs in your face, withdraws his forces into cloud-land, and flings a white misty veil over the world below. You see nothing but mist, mist everywhere; your very brain seems to get frozen and foggy; but what does that matter? you come down exulting that you have scaled the precipitous mountain. But you will not own, like Sir Charles Coldstream, that you found "nothing in it." Well, Mount Royal is not one of these. Like a vain and beautiful woman it likes to show itself off to the best advantage, and has a capital smooth road, where you can either drive in cosy carriages or walk on foot through a pleasant winding way, through leafy shade and blooming flowers, till you reach the top. You can return by another road, which lands you about three miles from the town.

The city is never out of sight during the whole progress up the mountain. But from one special point, which is always indicated to the traveller, there is a remarkably fine view of the entire city and its surroundings. There is the broad river, studded with green islets, spanned by the famous Victoria Bridge, certainly one of the handsomest, and they say the longest and costliest, in the world; beyond it the opposite shore stretches away, breaking into small towns or villages till it is lost in the distance; while beneath our feet the city itself lies clearly defined under the deep-blue skies. The white, gray, or red tiled roofs of the houses, church spires, convents,—square and ugly in massive gray stone,—public buildings, and Cathedral towers rise out of a forest of green, for the houses generally are surrounded by gardens, and the wide streets are bordered on each side by grand old trees, the relics of the ancient forest, on whose hoary head the city now stands and holds its place among the first cities of this Western world. The trading portion of the town, where commerce in every imaginable form is briskly carried on, is lined with handsome shops, hotels, and banking-houses. As we passed by one of the most important of these latter we were stopped by a vast crowd, which thronged the doorway and surged and overflowed across the street, and effectually blocked all progress. A placard was on the door, "Stopped payment," and a sea of human faces, waves of excited, desperate passions sweeping over them, surged round us. On every side we read signs of wrecked hopes and ruined lives. Some, with sullen, despairing faces, went silently on their way; others gesticulated fiercely, with threats and curses "not loud but deep." Some hysterical women were in tears; others crept out of the crowd with white, wan faces, broken down and crushed utterly; they had no voice even to complain or bemoan. Gradually we made our way through this mass of miserable people, and went on through the populous streets, across fine squares, past handsome monuments, all of which are kept in perfect order and neatness. In the centre of the square which bears her name stands a splendid statue of Queen Victoria robed and crowned—you find her picture or her bust among the most cherished household gods of every family.

Everywhere in this beautiful city there are delightful promenades; on either side of the spacious streets are elegant villa residences, with tastefully arranged gardens, a light, fanciful railing only separating them from the footway, and sometimes not even that. You may enjoy a perfect feast of the beauty and perfume of flowers as you saunter beneath the trees which border the footway, their overhanging branches forming a perfect shade and bower of green. Here, as in many other Canadian cities, three-fourths of the population are Catholics, and their churches and Cathedral are among the finest architectural buildings in the city, where churches of all denominations abound. Christ Church Cathedral (Episcopal) is, they say, the finest specimen of English Gothic architecture in America. It is built of Caen and Montreal stone. From the centre of the cross rises a spire 224 feet high; the choir stalls are splendidly carved, and the nave is supported by columns carved in imitation of Canadian plants; but an adequate description of the churches, convents, or museums, here and elsewhere, would each require a volume to itself, and those who require that special kind of information will find it in every local guidebook. Going the general round of these places forms no part of my programme. Such special descriptions are only needed for special objects, and nine cases out of ten are both wearisome and uninteresting. In their Continental experiences people rush through miles of picture galleries, and visit scores of churches, believing it to be their duty so to do, but at the end of the day few have a distinct impression of any perfect thing. The mind reflects only a confused mass of gorgeous colouring, stained glass windows, groined roofs and arches, all mixed up together, and when they sit down to think things over it is with the greatest difficulty they summon one distinct picture before their mind's eye.

2*

Last though not least among the attractions of Montreal, is the number of its commodious hotels, among which the Windsor stands pre-eminent. It is built at the highest point of the city, under the shadow of the mountains, and for comfort and luxurious appointments is second to none, either on this side of the Continent or on the other. The charges here, as in all other first-class hotels, vary from two and a half to five dollars per day, inclusive, according to location of rooms. This is most moderate when compared with our home charges, where the extras and sundries swell the bill till it is ready to burst with its own extortions.

CHAPTER IV.

THE CAPITAL OF THE DOMINION.

River Travelling—Trail of the Fire King—Ottawa—Parliament Buildings—The City—The Home of our Princess.

HE journey from Montreal to Ottawa is for the most part dull and uninteresting. We have half an hour's train through a rough, ragged country, laden with straggling bushes, rank grass, and charred tree stumps ; then we take the boat and steam along the river, a broiling sun overhead and flat barren country on either side. There being nothing attractive or interesting in the surrounding scenery, I betake myself to the general saloon, which is a perfect bazaar, with knick-knackeries of all kinds, and books and newspapers for sale. I invest a dollar in literature of the lightest kind and ensconce myself on the most comfortable lounge I can find, and in rather a limp drowsy state try to keep myself awake.

My companion, aglow with the delights of travelling, rejoices in the inconveniences thereof, and sits broiling in the sun, which seems inclined to have no mercy upon anybody. It glares down with its fierce, fiery eye, breathing a hot sultry breath over everything everywhere. The land on either side is a plain of brown dried-up grass ; a few lean, hungry cattle are straying hither and thither, browsing on the dry breast of mother earth. Brown barelegged children wade into the river ; some cast off their rags and leap in, splashing about, laughing as they play at "catch-who-can." When they are tired they come out and lay themselves out to dry in the sun. The water has a sultry, sleepy look. It is as clear and still as a glass mirror, but we wake it into fury as our iron steed tramps through it ; it hisses and runs after us, snarling with its white foam lips as it closes in our wake, and under the blazing sun our vessel steams on. The deck blossoms with umbrellas, which look like gigantic toadstools growing out of scores of human heads. Some put cabbageleaves in their hats and hang silk handkerchiefs down their backs, as a kind of protection from the sun's keen rays ; but they will not sit down ; they wander in and out of the saloon, like evil spirits that can know no rest ; they like to get bronzed with the sun and sultry air, and as a rule are not satisfied till the skin peels off their faces and the tips of their noses require a bag for protection. I lean back on my luxurious lounge in a rather sleepy state, and am fast drifting away into a land of dreams, when I am roused by the loud prolonged sound of the dinner-gong, and we all crowd down, helter-skelter, to the dining saloon, where our captain, a big burly man, sits at the head of the table, with sundry roasts and fancy dishes smoking before him. We speedily spoil our appetites, and leave but a mere wreck of bare bones and skeletons. One dish contains Indian corn cobs about a quarter of a yard long, looking white and tempting with their granulated covering. Believing they are some stuffed delicacies, I ask for a small piece. A smile goes round, and I receive a whole one on my plate. What am I to do with it? I glance at my neighbours. Every one is holding a cob with his two hands, and, beginning at one end, nibbles along as though he were playing a flute till he gets to the other, repeating the process till the cob is stripped of its pearly corn. I don't think it is worth the trouble of eating, though it is considered a great dainty on this side of the Atlantic.

About two o'clock we reach Carrillon. The rapids bar our progress up the river; a train runs alongside the vessel; we are soon seated in a comfortable car, and have a two hours' railway journey through what was once a magnificent forest, but is now wild waste land, a terrible fire having swept over it some few years ago, destroying and devouring all before it—farm-houses, flocks, all animate and inanimate things—leaving here and there groups of tall spectral trees, standing weird and ghostly in the summer sun. Here it had feasted greedily and left nothing but charred roots and fantastic tree stumps straggling over the ground. One spot on the line of that terrible fire was pointed out to me as having once been a flourishing farm; but the fire fiend swept down upon it in the night, when the inhabitants were all in their beds asleep. The man rushed out with his wife and child and crouched down in a potato field, trusting that the storm of fire might pass over them; but the red-tongued flames came leaping along and drove them into the river, and all night long he stood up to his neck in water, supporting his wife and child. The great white moon shone out serene and peaceful in the calm blue skies. Not a breath of air was stirring, not a sound was heard but the tramp of the fire king as he roared on his blazing way. In the morning they were saved, but the terrible flames had licked the life out of all wayfarers who had barred its progress, and left their blackened skeletons grinning in the sun. After a rush of two hours through this weird, wild scene, we reach Grenville. There we take boat again and steam on till we find ourselves at Ottawa, about six o'clock in the evening.

The approach to this city, the capital of the Dominion of Canada, is by no means imposing; the face of the river is covered and its mouth filled with sawdust; it is stifled, and has scarcely strength to flow, it could not burst into a smile, or ripple under the most tempting of summer suns. Immense booms of timber, which have been floated down from the "forest primeval" hundreds of miles away, float still on the river surface till they are hauled up to feed the hungry mills, mechanical giants, whose rasping jaws work day and night crushing these sturdy "sons of the forest," cutting them in slices and casting them forth to be stacked in huge piles along the river-banks miles before we reach the town. There is no bustle or confusion on our arrival there. On the quiet little landing-stage two or three lumbering vehicles are waiting; we are escorted to one of these by our chivalrous captain, who carries our hand baggage, and superintends the removal of the rest. A little girl, about ten years old, follows us, with a dog almost as big as herself, and looks up at us shyly.

"My little lass, ladies," observes our captain, his face

wrinkling and his eyes twinkling with smiles; "she comes down every evening to 'meet father.' It wouldn't seem like coming home if I didn't find Nellie here."

With a proud fatherly air he takes the child's hand, the dog trotting behind them as they ascend the stony hill towards a gray cottage of rough-hewn slate, which he has pointed out to me as "home." We turn on towards our destination in Nepean Street, where we find ourselves so comfortably located, that instead of staying a few days, as we originally intended, we resolve to remain some weeks.

Through the good offices of Mr. Leggo, a popular and most enthusiastic Canadian, we made the acquaintance of Lieutenant-Colonel Dennis, one of the oldest pioneers of the state. Those gentlemen were like animated encyclopædias on all matters regarding Canada; from them we received more information in a few weeks than we could have gained on our own account in a year.

Our first day in Ottawa was spent in visiting the Parliament buildings, which occupy a plateau of about thirty acres on the loftiest point of the city and nearly two hundred feet above the Ottawa River; they are surrounded by beautifully laid out gardens, and seem to be growing out of a bed of soft greensward of velvet smoothness. They are composed of cream-coloured Potsdam stone, the ornamental part being of Ohio and Arupois marbles; they are built in the Italian Gothic style of the thirteenth century, and I am told they are the most beautiful specimens thereof in all America, perhaps in the world. Their elevated position, with their long lines of pointed windows, massive buttresses, and numerous pinnacles and towers, silhouetted against the bright blue sky, are objects of imposing and majestic beauty for miles around. In the front centre stands the Victoria Tower, one hundred and eighty feet high, and surmounted by an iron crown. The chief entrance to the building is through the broad-pointed arches beneath this tower; the royal arms are above the doorway; in the grand Senate Hall there is a very beautiful statue of the Queen, and the vice-regal throne is flanked by busts of the Prince of Wales and the Princess Alexandra. In the most remote, as well as in the most populous districts, the features of the royal family are duly represented. The Canadians are the most loyal of all British subjects; they lower their voices with solemn reverence when they speak of "Her Majesty, the Queen," to whom they never refer as "the Queen," pure and simple; they give her a whole string of titles and adjectives, like the tail of a paper kite, and set her sailing in the heaven of their imagination, as though she were beyond the range of humanity altogether. They seem to regard royalty, not as an upper branch of the human family, but as a higher and holier species; any adverse or quizzical criticism of them or their doings would be met with severe reprimand, if not positive maltreatment. We cannot help wondering how the loyalty of the Canadian people manages to exist, for it has been half-starved, or fed only upon the crumbs flung from the state table. It must have lived on its own robust strength or the clinging patriotic spirit of the Canadian nature, rather than from any consideration or care it has received from the home government. It is certainly the most beautiful, the most fertile of the

British colonies, and lies nearest to the mother land though it seems farthest from her care.

Much has been said, much has been written on the subject of Canada; we have learned its geographical position, the length and breadth of its lakes and rivers, the extent of its vast forest lands, the height of its mountains, etc., but the figures dazzle the mind, and bring no realization of the fact. Nothing less than a personal visit will enable us to comprehend the wonders of this luxuriant land, which is surrounded and encompassed with its own loveliness. The primeval forest still holds its own in the vast solitudes, sacred as yet from the increasing encroachments of man, its immense inland seas, and fruitful rivers winding through scenery the most picturesque, the most sublime; to say nothing of its vast unexplored lands and mineral resources, and the wide tracts of rich uncultivated country, watered by springs and rivulets which have been flowing in their living liquid beauty since the days of Paradise. We hear sad tales of poverty and misery in the old land, of scanty crops, wasted labour, and ruined farmers, who, after all, are only tenants on the land they live on; the small farmer who labours there, on another man's land, may here become a land-owner. There is no room for great farming operations or agricultural enterprise in the limited cultivated land of the old country, every rood of which is occupied; there is no room for new comers,—the great tide of human life, which is rising every hour, must roll on towards the great cities, and perhaps starve there, for each city is filled with its own people, who work at their different trades, and in their turn overflow into the country, drifting, heaven knows where. There is small chance of rural folks gaining their bread in the old land. Here in the New World there are, not thousands, but millions of acres of rich fertile soil waiting for the magic pick and the ploughsnare to turn it to a veritable "Tom Tidler's ground;" only scatter the seed on its broad fair breast, and it will pulsate with a new life and swell the seeds with its own fulness till they burst and blossom into a wealth of golden grain, and "the hand of the sower gathereth a rich harvest."

The governing powers, in their desire to get the country well populated, are willing to make most liberal terms to forward this object. They are ready to give a grant in perpetuity of one hundred and sixty acres to all or any who are willing to make a home there, with the power, of course, of extending their possessions as their means increase. There is an abundance of wood for building purposes, the rivers and lakes teem with fish in great variety, and the earth gives forth such a variety of wild fruits, strawberries, raspberries, grapes, gooseberries, and huge trees of red luscious plums, and butternuts, we feel that in summer-time, at least, we could live as the birds do, on sunshine and sweet fruits.

We had heard much of the extremes of temperature, of heat and cold, especially in Ottawa, and prepared ourselves for broiling; well, it was warm, the sun blazed, the hot winds blew, and the dust of this most dusty city whirled and swirled around us, got into our eyes, our ears, crept insidiously down our throats, and seemed struggling to turn us inside out; but we clutched our mantles around us, and butted against the wind, screening ourselves from the sun's fierce rays as best we could. It is not often that the sun and the wind have such a tussle together. However, we reached home at last in an uncooked state, feeling not much warmer than we should do on a summer day at home, though the temperature is much higher, and the hours are marching to the tune of 90° in the shade. We had spent the whole day in wandering and driving about the streets of Ottawa, till we gained a very good idea of its external appearance. It has numerous fine churches, and its town hall, post office, and all the municipal buildings are substantially and massively built in an attractive and fanciful style of architecture. As for the rest of the city, it is in a perfectly unfinished state; it is as yet only a thing of promise, though it has the making of a very fine town in the future; but however fast it marches, it will have to keep growing, and work hard too, for another century at least, before it reaches the level of its magnificent Parliament buildings. The streets are wide and long, stretching away out of sight; they are cobble-stoned and roughly wood-paved for the most part. After passing the principal lines of shops in Sparkes Street, the houses seem to have been built for temporary convenience only, and crop up here and there in a direct line, leaving wide spaces of waste land between, as though they were in a hurry to see which should reach the end of the long street first, the end that seems to be creeping back to the primeval forest, which civilization and time has left far behind.

Ottawa itself is neither picturesque nor attractive, being

built on perfectly flat ground. It looks like a timber yard, and smells of sawdust. The Ottawa river has as many long thin arms as an octopus, and they run meandering inland by a hundred different ways; here, they meet in a vast tumbling mass, falling over huge boulders and broken stony ground till they are dignified by the name of the "Chaudière Falls;" lower down, their headlong course is stopped, and they are utilized and made to turn a huge sawmill where a thousand steel teeth are biting through the grand old trees, tearing them into slips, digesting and disgorging them on the other side; in vain the water foams and groans, crashing its rebellious waves together—man is its master, and will have his way. Just over the bridge is an extensive match factory, employing six hundred children from six to twelve years old, swarming on all sides like busy little ants, measuring, cutting, dipping, and filling the boxes as fast as their tiny hands can move. There is, on the opposite side, a pail and tub factory, all for exportation; long galleries, filled with tubs and pails from floor to ceiling, enough to scrub the world clean, and turn it inside out and begin again on the other side.

Rideau Hall, the home of our Princess, lies on the outskirts of the town, and is by no means a regal-looking mansion; it is a long low building of gray-stone, standing on rather elevated ground, and has a pleasant view of the town and river from the lawn and flower garden, which encloses two sides of it; the approach is through tolerably well timbered grounds, not of sufficient importance to be called a "park." The Governor and Princess

Louise were away, and the house was undergoing repair—it looked as though it needed it. There was nothing to distinguish this from any second or third-rate country house at home, except the one solitary and rather seedy-looking sentinel who paraded before the door. The people of Ottawa speak most enthusiastically of our Princess; every one has some kind memory or pleasant anecdote to tell of her. It is said that when Her Royal Highness held her first reception, she appeared in a plain high dress, expecting, perhaps, to find fashion "out of joint" in this far-away place; but the Canadian ladies came trooping "en grand toilette," with fans and diamonds, trains and laces, like living importations from Worth himself. At the next reception matters changed, and the royal lady appeared in all the splendour of the British Court receptions.

CHAPTER V.

FROM CITY TO CATARACT.

On the Train—The Thousand Islands—At Kingston—Toronto—
The Government House—Arrival of the Princess Louise—"We
expect the Moon"—Niagara Falls.

ROM Ottawa to Toronto is a tedious journey, in consequence of the many changes, from rail to river, river to rail again. The train is waiting for us as we reach the station; it is a hot, sultry morning, the warm air, sand-laden, comes in short, fitful gusts and is stifling rather than refreshing; the sun blazes down from a copper-coloured sky—everything is sun-dried, sun-baked; the city glows like an oven; the stony, shadeless streets reflect the burning rays, and blind the eyes with their white dazzling light; one might cook eggs upon the housetops, and set bacon to frizzle in the sun. It is an undertaking to cross the blank space from the omnibus to the platform, many a sunstroke has been got with less provocation. In a limp, dusty condition, tired before the day has well begun, we take the first vacant seats we come to—there is little choice, for the car is half full already, and more people come trooping in, till it is filled to overflowing with a miscellaneous mass of human-

ity of all sorts, sexes, and sizes: there are women with babies, women with bundles, and baskets of fruit, crockery, and cabbages; two elderly ladies, in corkscrew curls, carrying a pet cat in a basket and huge bunches of flowers, come timidly in, smiling and giving a recognizing nod to everybody with the information that they "have not been in a train for twenty years, and consequently are a little nervous." Hobbledehoys trample on our skirts, and stumble over our feet, and one young tourist, evidently got up by his tailor in stereotyped tourist fashion, for his first outing, struggles into the car under a weight of walking-sticks and fishing-tackle, and commences operations by fishing my hat off, and in the confusion of disentanglement and blushing apologies, all his belongings come rattling about my ears. The bell rings, the train moves slowly; everything moves slowly in Canada—whether it is that the red tape stretches from the mother country and ties their hands, or public spirit languishes, or private enterprise is sleeping, it is difficult to say. The Canadians are a most loyal, kind, and hospitable people. Conservative too, with the worst kind of conservatism, they are content with things as they are, and so long as matters go smoothly in the old grooves, they will not trouble to make new tracks. They want waking up; if they were once possessed with the restless, ambitious, go-ahead spirit of the United States, they would soon be even with them; at present they are a century behind.

We rattle along through a not especially interesting country; here and there we come upon undulating woodlands, with pretty farmhouses lying amid their cultivated lands; but there are whole acres lying idle of rich land, which has only to be tickled with a ploughshare and fed with a scanty meal of grain, and it is ready to burst into laughing fields of golden corn; meanwhile masses of gaudy weeds flaunt their flags in the sun, and straggling brushwood spring aggressively from the ground, and such a glorious growth of thistles as would delight a race of donkeys—no better could be found anywhere. Meanwhile we amuse ourselves, each according to his or her fancy. One woman sucks oranges all the way, another "clucks" and makes zoological noises to amuse her rebellious offspring; the young tourist looks unutterably bored, and plays the "devil's tattoo" on the window; somebody perfumes the car with the odour of peppermint drops. The old ladies enter into a conversational race, and discuss their private affairs in a most audible voice, taking the whole car into their confidence. We catch snatches of a domestic tragedy, blithely borne by the chief sufferer, who dwells upon every revolting detail with great gusto, as though she revelled in the telling; next to enjoying other people's miseries, some people love to gloat upon their own, the excitement following the tragedy overpowering the tragedy itself. Every time the train stops, as it does with a jerk, they clutch each other wildly, and pelt everybody with questions, "Was it a collision?" or "had the boiler burst?" During their excitement the cat wriggles out of the basket, and a general scrimmage ensues before the poor beast can be recaptured.

At ten o'clock we reach Prescott, and there take the boat for Kingston, hoping to catch the four o'clock train for Toronto. Our luggage is soon aboard, and in the course of a few minutes we are seated under an awning on the deck of a palatial river boat; here the river broadens and joins the Lake Ontario. We rejoice at leaving the dusty train and baking city behind, and set ourselves to enjoy the fresh genial breeze, and watch for the first glimpse of the thousand islands. We are soon in their midst. It is like a dream of fairyland—the perfect day, warm sunny atmosphere, and fresh cool breeze dimpling the face of the water; the luxuriant islands, as we thread our way among them, seem to be floating with us—they are everywhere, before, behind, and around; some are large, some small; some are inhabited only by waterfowl, some by men of literary and artistic taste, who make their summer home there; but they are all clothed in a luxuriant growth of green, trailing low down to the water's edge, white willow and silver birch coquetting with their own shadows fluttering on its surface. After a few delicious lotus-eating hours' floating on this romantic world of land and water, we reach Kingston just in time to miss the train—everybody misses that train, it is a delusion and a snare, nobody was ever known to catch it, even by accident. I believe the captains and hotel-keepers are in collusion to keep the tourist in Kingston for the night. The best hotel, The British American, has poor accommodation, the table being ill-served and the viands ill-cooked.

We brought splendid appetites to bear on greasy chops, tough steaks, and soup so weak it had scarcely strength to struggle down our throats. The meals were served at most unearthly hours—dinner at twelve, supper at five o'clock. It is a large, old-fashioned town, with a capital fruit and vegetable market in its centre, and fine houses with walled-in gardens; the tallest and gaudiest flowers sometimes climbed up and took a peep at the world outside: a good old-world city, wrapped up in itself and its people; no doubt comfortable enough to live in, but no attractive features to interest the passing stranger. It seems to be an isolated, self-centred place, with nothing to do with the present and no stirring associations with the past. We were not sorry to find ourselves in the four o'clock train en route for Toronto. The cars were clean, and not overcrowded; boys came along, peddling books, papers, hot cake, rich ripe fruit, and "real English walnuts." We were tired, and lounged back in our seats, watching the panoramic landscapes fly past us, and listening to the sweet voices of two young Canadian girls who were singing hymns, nearly all the way. Towards eight o'clock there was a stop of twenty minutes for supper, and a capital supper we got—salmon, trout, cutlets, sausages, fruit, coffee, iced milk, and all for the modest sum of fifty cents!

The sun sets in a glory of crimson, purple, and gold, fading and changing, one colour amalgamating with another, till the western skies are dressed in gorgeous crimson plumes, and the lake is illuminated, glowing red in the reflected light, and the opposite shore seems veiled in the purple mist of dreamland. Slowly the twilight falls, the moon rises, and presently we are speeding by full moonlight along the shores of the Lake Ontario.

It was nearly midnight when the lights of the City of

Toronto loomed upon our sight. Our engine bell began its musical ding-dong as we slackened and steamed slowly into the station, and soon we were on our way to our hotel. Thanks to the delightful baggage system here, as all over the United States, luggage is no trouble to its owner. The arrangement is simple enough : your luggage is taken from your house by the expressman, who checks it to your destination wherever that may be, giving you little brass numbered checks in return ; a similar check is strapped on each of your boxes. About an hour before you reach your journey's end, an express agent boards the train ; you give up your checks, and tell him where to send your luggage. On your arrival, or very soon after, you find it there ; there is a specified charge for each package. The loss of passengers' luggage is unknown ; and by this easy arrangement, much loss of time, trouble, and temper is saved. You may carry as much as you please, and from the time you leave England it is no trouble to you, until you return to Liverpool,—then your vexations begin anew.

We put up at the Queen's Hotel, about three minutes drive from the station, and facing the lake, though it stands back a few hundred yards from it. We found it a luxurious hotel and perfect home, being an extensive but not a monster hotel, large enough for the most complete arrangements, but not too large to be comfortable. It is three or four stories high, and has a balconied and verandahed front with pretty climbing plants trailing among the lattice work. The Governor, Mr. Macdonald, and his two charming daughters, at that time had a suite of apartments here, having vacated the Government house for the occupation of the Princess Louise and the Marquis of Lorne, who were expected in a day or two to open the Dominion Exhibition. Toronto was much excited on the occasion. The Misses Macdonald took great interest and delight in beautifying their already beautiful home, for the reception of their royal guests. The day before the arrival we accompanied them on a last visit of inspection to see that every arrangement was complete, and add any little finishing touches their refined taste might consider necessary.

The Government house is a massive square stone building, approached by handsome iron gates, and is surrounded by tastefully laid out flower gardens, soft velvety lawn, fanciful conservatories and green-house filled with rare exotics. We get the key from the head gardener, and enter the house: there is no sign of life, not a creature is visible; we saunter through the corridors, up the stairs, and through the vacant chambers, attended only by our own shadows; our tread falls noiselessly on the soft carpet; once or twice a door slams, and an echo wakes up and tries to follow us, but is smothered by the way. The rooms are all in perfect order, prettily arranged, fresh, airy, and beautifully clean, not a speck of dust is to be seen anywhere; everything seems to be in a waiting stage —eider-down beds, spring mattresses all bare, waiting to be made; wardrobes waiting to be filled; fires waiting to be kindled. There is no sign of silver or linen anywhere. We inquire, "Why is this?" and learn, that when the Princess travels, like some visitors to the sea-side at home, she finds her own plate and linen! The royal servants are expected to take possession every minute; as we are leaving the house, they are beginning to arrive with the baggage in advance. Meanwhile the city is all agog with expectation, people come flocking in from all parts of the Dominion. The hotels and refreshment houses are full to overflowing; eager sight-seers throng the streets; we enjoy our gape among the rest. It is a pretty bright town, with long wide straight streets, bordered on either side with fine old trees,—a striking contrast to the blank stony aspect of Ottawa,—and is calculated to show off at the best advantage on such a festive occasion as this. Triumphal arches, covered with a glory of green, bright-coloured flags, and wondrous devices, span the streets on every side; we come upon troops of merry children singing "The Campbells are coming," "Rule Britannia," and "God save the Queen," with all the might of their strong young lungs; great is the excitement of the child-world—they are to muster ten thousand strong to greet the Princess on her arrival to-morrow.

We are roused early in the morning by a general hubbub and a conflicting choir of young voices, and look from our window upon a transformation scene. The whole space between our hotel and the railway, at which point the royal party are to alight, is cleared of lumber, and newly swept and garnished; and on either side, rising one above another, rows of seats have been erected to accommodate ten thousand children, leaving between them a wide avenue for the progress of the vice-regal party. The children are already beginning to assemble;

they are all dressed in light colours, generally in white, with broad gay-coloured sashes, worn crosswise from the shoulder, each school wearing a different color, and having its own special flag fluttering over it. At first the schools seem to be all mixed together in inextricable confusion; teachers and trainers dash frantically about, gathering their wandering flocks together; but long before the slow swinging engine bell heralds the approach of the royal party, each school occupies its proper space and all is in order. From our balcony we watch the train come wriggling like a great black snake into the station. We are not near enough to distinguish faces, but a company of gayly dressed midgets seem to slip out upon the platform, and stand silent in the sunshine. There is a momentary lull. We look down the long lines of children's faces, rising tier upon tier ten thousand strong; they are so arranged that their colours blend harmoniously together, they look like an animated flower garden; a wave of excitement sweeps over them, suddenly ten thousand snowflakes seem fluttering in the air, ten thousand hands are waving tiny white handkerchiefs; the choir of distant voices begin to sing "The Campbells are coming, Hurrah! hurrah!" and soft as the sound of an echo, the old familiar air reaches our ears, swelling louder and louder as it is caught up by one section after another, nearer and nearer, till the whole ten thousand voices fill the air with one great volume of sound. Meanwhile the newly arrived visitors progress slowly along the avenue, and "God save the Queen" and "Rule Britannia" follow in quick succession, the children's voices quickening to a race, so eager are they to finish before the Princess is out of hearing. As she reaches her carriage, there is a clapping of hands and roar of welcome; but she keeps in the background, leaving all the honour and glory to her husband, the Governor-General of the Dominion. Troops of rifles, and engineers line the streets, and a general festivity takes possession of the city; squibs, crackers and illuminations finish up the day.

The short time we are able to devote to Toronto passes too quickly; everybody is hospitably inclined, and every day there are luncheons, kettledrums, or dinners to be attended: all are strictly arranged on the "home" principle; in fact the people here are more English than we are ourselves, and scrupulously avoid any peculiarity of the adjoining states,—you may hear Americanisms in London, but never in Canada. The people are lavish in their liberality, but the city carries its economy farther than we care to follow it. On our way to a friend's house one evening, we found the town wrapped in darkness; we could neither see the names of the streets nor the numbers of the houses; we lost ourselves, and at last came upon a dark gray figure carrying a bull's-eye—it was a policeman, who courteously convoyed us to our destination.

"You see, ladies," he said, apologizing for the Cimmerian darkness of his beloved city, "the moon is expected, and we never light the streets when we expect the moon!" So when the moon is on duty the gas-works have a holiday. Toronto is beautifully situated amid stretches of well-wooded cultivated land, and spreads its wide skirts along the shore of Lake Ontario, where there should be a splendid promenade—but is not; for between the lake and the tall rows of handsome houses the railway runs close down along the water's edge, marring the prospect with its array of ugly sheds and cattle pens, while heavy goods trains are shunting and shrieking in the face of the town from morning till night: thus the opportunity of making one of the finest promenades in the Dominion is lost. From Toronto we steam across the lake to the village of Niagara, where a train is waiting to carry us on to the falls about half an hour further on. We all watch from the windows, eager to catch our first glimpse of the world's great wonder.

I quote from my companion's note-book on the spot. "There was a break in the wood, a flash of white, a cloud of spray tossed high above the tree-tops; then the dark woods closed again. That glimpse, flashing upon us and passing before we could fully realize that the great tumbling mass was indeed Niagara, can hardly be called our first view of it. . . . It was dark when we reached the Clifton house; the roar of the falls filled our ears, we stepped out upon the balcony, and there was a sight we can never forget. It was a moonless night, and in the dusk we could only obscurely trace the vast vague outline of the two falls, divided by the blurred mass of shapeless shadows which we learned was Goat Island. As we looked upon them silently, and listened to the ceaseless boom like distant thunder, which shook the ground beneath our feet, across the snowy veil of the American Fall, to our left, shot rays of rosy light, which melted into amber, then into emerald. They were illuminating the great waters with coloured calcium lights! In whose benighted mind rose the first thought of dressing Niagara up like a transformation scene in a pantomime? It was like putting a tinsel crown and tarlatan skirts on the Venus of Milo. But these brilliant rays which fell across the American Falls, and which were turned on and off like a dissolving view, did not reach to the Horseshoe Fall away to our right. Vast, solemn, shadowy, we could just distinguish its form in the darkness, could hear the deep murmur of its awful voice. And there, between it and us, what was *that* we saw? Was it some huge pale ghost standing sentinel before Niagara? White, spectral, motionless, it rose up and reached towards the stars—shapeless, dim, vague as a veiled ghost. There was something almost supernatural about it, it was like a colossal spectre, wrapped in a robe of strange dim light.

"'How fine and upright the column of spray is to-night,' said a strange voice beside us. This broke the illusion. But yet it seemed impossible that our ghost should be only a pillar of rising and falling spray! We saw it again, daily and nightly, but seldom again like that. We saw it blown along in clouds; we saw it like a great veil hiding the whole face of the Fall; we saw it one evening at sunset leaping and sparkling like a fountain of liquid gold,—but only once again did we see it rise up in that shape, the dim and ghostly guardian of the night. No mortal eye has ever beheld the base of the great Horseshoe Falls; it is for ever veiled and lost in a wild white chaos of foam, tossed up in the fury of its headlong plunge, and hiding its depths in mystery.

"The Indians hold that Niagara claims its yearly meed of victims. It may be so. Or does Niagara thus avenge itself on the civilization that has trimmed and tamed its forests and dressed it up in tinsel-coloured lights? But the thunder of water thunders on eternally, and before its terrible sublimity we are dumb, as in the mighty diapason our feeble voices are lost." We remain eight days at Niagara; its fascination increases; but we must tear ourselves away, and say good-bye to it, at last; we are bound for the "Golden Gate," and great cities, lakes, mountains and prairie lands are lying between it and us.

CHAPTER VI.

THE EMPIRE CITY.

New York—Fifth Avenue—Madison Square—The Elevated Railway—The Cars—The Shops—The People—West Point.

E leave Niagara in the early morning, and start on our tedious journey on the long, comfortless cars (we learned afterwards that we might have taken seats in the parlor car). How we long for a lounge in one of our own easy, well-cushioned, first-class compartments! Here, there are no lounging possibilities, we are forced to sit bolt upright, the back of the seats scarcely rising to our shoulder blades; and the constant passing to and fro of the peddling fraternity, and the slamming and banging of doors as they come and go, is most irritating even to non-delicate nerves. We feel the lack of privacy in these American cars, but in this, as in most other cases, there is some compensation—we are safe from the attacks of lunatics, thieves, or ruffianism of any kind whatever, and we can obtain any quantity of rich ripe fruit, luscious strawberries, bananas and melons, figs, etc.; while there is a tank of iced water in the car for the refreshment, gratis, of thirsty souls. The train rushes through the high streets of busy towns, crossing

crowded thoroughfares and public highways, keeping up full speed always, merely ringing the engine bell, to warn people to get out of the way: they have to take care of themselves, and they know it; no precautions are taken for the public safety; the rails are merely laid down in the middle of the streets, and when the trains are not in sight other vehicles use the road. We stop to dine at Syracuse, sup at Utica, and reach New York a little before midnight. A familiar face greets us on the platform, but not until we have engaged a carriage to take us to the Windsor Hotel, which proves to be just two blocks from the station! Our luggage is in the hands of the expressman, and we could have walked to the hotel had we been aware of its nearness, in less than five minutes! The rapacious Jehu charged four dollars for our brief occupancy of his dingy vehicle; it was the first and last time we were so beguiled.

It is a starlight night, and we catch a glimpse of the tall dark houses, which seem to be reaching up to the moon. The names of the streets, we notice, are painted on the glass gas lamps at every corner, so that in the darkest weather you may always tell your whereabouts. The carriage stops at the monster hotel—a very mountain of cherry-red bricks and mortar, a huge, square building it is, occupying one entire block, built up so many storeys that our eyes can scarcely reach the top; its windows are all shaded by outside linen blinds, which flap and flutter like flags in the dim night. The wide door opens, and swallows us up. We rather dreaded facing the clerk of this magnificent establishment; we had heard so much of the species and the generally cavalier, supercilious manner with which they treated strangers, that we preferred our modest request for a double-bedded room in fear and trembling; but our request could not have been more courteously received and answered if we had been engaging the most gorgeous suite in the whole hotel: I believe the supercilious hotel clerk must be classed with extinct animals. We are politely conducted to the elevator, which carries us up higher—higher, till we fancy we must be approaching the seventh heaven, and at last are deposited in a large handsome apartment on one of the upper storeys.

The next morning we take our first stroll through the "Empire city;" an enthusiastic and patriotic American friend is with us early, anxious to see the effect the first sight of his beloved city produces on our British constitution. We step out from the grand entrance of the Windsor Hotel, and with a majestic wave of his arm he introduces us to "Fifth Avenue!" and watches for the electrifying effect. Our faces fall, our ideas of the "Glories of the Avenue," which we had often heard sung, fade away. We look up, we look down; instead of the wide shady avenue, and brilliant busy scene our fancy had painted, we see only a long, and by no means wide, street, bristling with churches, lifting their lofty spires from amid the rows of tall brown stone houses, which are closely packed on either side, each being approached by a flight of brown stone steps, with ornamental rails, handsome and dreary in their monotonous regularity; but we catch no glimpse of a green tree anywhere! The whole street is stamped with aristocratic dulness; a score or so of well-dressed people are sauntering along the sidewalk, and clean-looking white "stages," which run from one end of the city to the other, are jolting along over the rough cobble stones which pave the roadway; the avenue is several miles long, but is grows less aristocratic, and leaves the even tenor of its way, when it passes through Madison Square, which is pretty and quite Parisian in its appearance, with a splendid growth of fine old trees and shady nooks and corners, quite an oasis in a desert of bricks and mortar; streets of stone houses radiate from all sides of it; and every day, through summer heat and winter snows, George Francis Train, with his ruined intellect and shaggy white beard, haunts the scene; he is generally found seated under one particular tree, cutting out paper boats and figures for the troops of children who swarm round him; and here stands Fifth Avenue Hotel, a stately building gleaming white in the sunshine. Here the stir of life begins, and flows in a restless magnetic current the live-long day. After leaving Madison Square, the avenue winds and wiggles its way to the lower part of the city, and mingles with the everyday working world. Leaving this aristocratic quarter we pass through one of the cross streets, between lines of the same brown stone houses, miniature copies of Fifth Avenue grandeur, and find ourselves in democratic Sixth Avenue, which is full of the bustle and roar of life; shops to the right of us, shops to the left of us, shops everywhere and of every possible kind,—crabs, eels and oysters, Chinese laundries, fancy toys, barbers, whisky bars, and fashionable milliners, elbow each other in true republican fashion.

The side walks are thronged with hurrying crowds of men and women; along the centre of the road, but raised about forty feet above it, runs the elevated railway; it looks like a skeleton gridiron laid on a rack and stretched from one end of the city to the other, its long arms branching off and running through the intricate labyrinths of the lower part of the town, rounding curves, and turning sharp corners, and, at times, so near to the houses you might shake hands with the inhabitants and see what they have for dinner. This airy mode of locomotion is startling at first, especially at night when the shops are closed, and the streets deserted; you hear the rumbling of the train far off, and it thunders over your head, seeming to swing in mid-air between you and the sky, its green and red fiery eyes staring ahead and plunging into the darkness. Beneath this elevated road, which forms a kind of arcade, run lines of red and yellow cars jingling their bells merrily as they roll rapidly along the iron rails in an almost unbroken line, one following the other in quick succession.

Public conveyances are cheap, and there are plenty of them: cars run from everywhere to everywhere. There are, of course, numerous livery stables, and a limited number of public cabs for hire, but they are a very expensive as well as a doubtful luxury, and the drivers are most accomplished extorsionists. It is impossible that a drive through the streets of New York could ever be taken for pleasure, in consequence of the rough cobble-stoned roadway; it is a jolting process, you take your drive at the risk of dislocating your neck. The cars are roomy and easy; both driver and conductor are protected from the weather; they stand on a kind of balcony, with an umbrella-like projection sloping over them, effectually shielding them from sun or rain. Everybody rides in the cars, from the lady in costly furs and velvets to the costermonger. You may find yourself sandwiched between a fat negro and lean washerwoman, and facing your jewelled hostess of the night before.

There are some few trifling drawbacks in this land of liberty: the every-man's-as-good-as-his-neighbour feeling, is sometimes unpleasantly obtruded on your notice; especially when you embark on a shopping expedition, there is an absence of that respectful ready attention we are accustomed to meet with in Europe. You enter, say, a draper's shop: the young ladies are engaged in a gossiping match, or a game at flirtation; *you* wait their pleasure, not they *yours;* when they do deign to attend you, it is with a sort of condescending indifference, and even while they are measuring a yard of ribbon, they keep up a fusillade of chatter with their companions. I speak of the rule, of course there are exceptions. Central Park is the only place where you can enjoy a drive—there driving is a delight, the roads are simply perfect, and scores of splendid equipages and beautiful women are on view daily in the grand drives from three till six o'clock; while the bridle paths, winding through sylvan shades beneath full-foliaged trees, are crowded with fair equestrians and their attendant cavaliers: it is a pleasure to watch them at a trot, a canter, or a gallop, for the American women ride well and gracefully. New York is very proud of Central Park; and well it may be so, for it is one of the finest in the world, there is nothing like it this side of the Atlantic. Twenty years ago it was a mere swampy rocky waste, now it is a triumph of engineering skill and a splendid illustration of the genius of landscape gardening: there are smooth green lawns, shady groves, lakes, beautifully wooded dells and vine-covered arbours; whichever way you turn you come upon delicious bits of picturesque scenery blossoming in unexpected nooks and corners. Here and there huge gray rocks stand in their original rugged majesty, their broken lichen-covered boulders tumbling at their base. From the terrace, which is the highest point, you enjoy a view of the entire park with its numerous lakes, fountains, bridges, and statues, spreading like a beautiful panorama round you. Here, too, you fully realize the cosmopolitan character of the city, for here great men of all nations are immortalized or libelled in stone, and their statues stud the park, side by side with the national heroes. Some idea of the extent of these grounds may be gathered from the fact, that there are ten miles of carriage drives, all as a rule wide enough for six to go abreast, about six miles of bridle paths for riding, and twenty-eight for pedestrian exercise; a wide stretch of lawn is set apart for cricket or croquet playing, and a special quarter for children with merry-go-rounds, swings, etc.; there is also a menagerie containing numerous and varied specimens of animals, the nucleus of what is to be, when completed, a fine zoological collection.

The Park is situated in the centre of the upper town. The avenues run lengthwise from one end of the city to another, which are crossed by straight streets in a direct line from the East River, on the one side, to the Hudson on the other; the famous Broadway running diagonally from the upper town, slanting across streets, squares and avenues till it buries itself in the intricate wilds of the lower town, where the streets are closely massed together and densely populated with wanderers from all nations, Polish Jews, Russians, Italians, Germans, Irish, creating a wild confusion of tongues, all packed in tall tenement houses, in close narrow streets, scores of families living where there is scarcely health-breathing room for one. Castle Garden, where admirable arrangements are made for the reception of emigrants, and the "Battery," once a fashionable promenade, point the lower end of this island city, girdled by the green waters of the Hudson and East River, which meet and mingle here. Wall Street, one of the great financial centres of the world, is situate in the busiest business quarter of the lower town, and runs in a somewhat broken line from Broadway to the East River. The traffic here is enormous, this part of the city is like a human cauldron, with a restless multitude seething and bubbling from morning till night. There must be something in the air which excites the brain and allows to human nature no rest; every man seems to be rushing for dear life's sake, while life itself is rushing after something else, sometimes hurling itself out of this world into the next to find it. All above Central Park is like a ragged fringe of the great city—long half-finished avenues, straggling sparsely inhabited streets, and skeleton houses; much of the original swampy ground lies still unclaimed. The Irish squatters in their rickety tumble-down hovels still cling to the land; the malarial air may wrap them like a shroud, the swamp with its foul unwholesomeness threaten to swallow them up—they will not stir. By slow, very slow degrees, as the Government reclaims the land, they are driven towards the edge, but wherever they can find a footing they squat again.

Although New York is one of the great commercial centres of the world, it is not a beautiful city; there is nothing picturesque or attractive about it; take away Central Park and you have a mere wilderness of bricks and mortar; streets and houses so closely packed as scarce to leave breathing room for its inhabitants. Every one wants to live near the centre, and as its watery girdle prevents the city spreading, it grows upwards, piling one story above another till it threatens to shut out the sky. It is not a clean city either: street cleaning is carried on in a slovenly fluctuating fashion; there are no dust-bins in the backyards, but ash-barrels stand on the curbstone in front of every dwelling, and are the receptacles for all household refuse; dust, ashes, cabbage stumps, fish bones, broken china, are all poured into the ash-barrel till it overflows and becomes an unsightly and unsavoury nuisance. These should be emptied every morning—by order of the municipal authorities—but the order is not strictly enforced and is more frequently neglected than obeyed. The street cleaning process, though excellent in theory, is carried on in a slovenly intermittent fashion.

There are several fine libraries, art galleries, and museums (to give an idea of their valuable and interesting contents would fill a volume), and churches so numerous that if the piety of the people kept pace with their churches there would be a scarcity of sinners. There are places of worship for all denominations of sinners, from the highest to the lowest degree. Those who like to revel in the lurid light of eternal condemnation, and to hear thunder and lightning roll from the preacher's lips, can luxuriate in the prospect to their heart's content; those who enjoy the gentler doctrines of Christianity can be cheered with hope, and consoled by promises of tender grace. Those who like their religion pure and unadulterated, can take it in its pristine simplicity, sans flowers, sans music, sans all outward show, while those who prefer it adorned with candlesticks, embroidered altar cloths and other ritualistic embellishments can be equally well accommodated. There is an abundance of spiritual food for all classes, no fear of famine in that direction. There being no state church, every place of worship is supported, and well supported too, by its own congregation. There seems to be a kind of family feeling—a bond of sympathy between the several peoples and their pastors, which does not exist where the church is a state institution, and the incumbent a state instrument. The churches are all handsome buildings, and are always comfortably, sometimes luxuriously, furnished—no coarse matting or hard wooden benches; but soft luxurious carpets and footstools, and even palm leaf and Japanese fans are liberally supplied. In the few churches I have visited, the services have been most impressive—no mere preaching filled with dry-as-dust platitudes—but eloquent orations, brilliantly delivered. I call to mind one

THE EMPIRE CITY.

special church, whose minister is a Welsh gentleman, from whom I heard one of the most impressive addresses, full of the highest morality, which is the pure religion of humanity, illustrated with brilliant imagery, and interspersed with poetical quotations—such as might have been heard with profit, by people of all creeds, whether Jews, Freethinkers, or Christians, with equal profit. The choirs are admirably trained, the solo singers excellent. Some of the hymns have very beautiful words set to old tunes such as "Auld Lang Syne," or "Home, Sweet Home." Their schools are abundant, and their educational system the most perfect I have seen—every child may have the advantage of a splendid education gratis; and the mode of teaching is such that the veriest dunce must find pleasure in learning. The superintendents and teachers are well chosen; with tact and kindness they lead their pupils, not only to learn from books, but to think out their own thoughts, and by suggestive and pertinent questions, cause them to reflect and comprehend what the lesson teaches, so making the path of knowledge a path of roses; what is pleasantly learnt is well learnt and long remembered, while the learning that is beaten in at one ear often flies out the other. In the matter of hospitals, and charitable institutions of all descriptions, the city of New York is second to none; and all its arrangements are carried out with the large-hearted liberality which characterizes the American people.

Though strongly republican in principle, they do not carry their republican notions into private life. Society is more exclusive than in the old country; perhaps, not being sure of its own footing, it is afraid of tripping, and watches warily lest any stray free lance should penetrate its interior ; each circle revolves within itself, rarely running one into another. Wholesale and retail mix freely in all commercial matters, are "Hail, fellow ! well met ! " on the cars or in the streets, but on the threshold of home they part. The merchant, who sells a thousand gallons of oil, will not fraternize at home, or be weighed in the social scale with the vendor of a farthing dip. It is always difficult for a stranger to gain admission into the best New York society, but if you are once well introduced, it opens its arms and its heart to you with an hospitality that is genial and thorough. After revolving round its magic circle for a time, you will carry away with you such reminiscences of its brilliant coteries and delightful home gatherings as you will not easily forget.

We are able to take but a casual survey of the Empire City, and enjoy for a brief space the hospitality so freely extended to us. We are on our way to the West, and are anxious to cross the Rocky Mountains before the severe weather set in. Before we start on our long journey, we run up the Hudson, and spend a few days at West Point, celebrated for the great military college ; it is a delightful excursion of about three hours, the river winding through a panorama of lovely scenery, the banks on either side wearing their variegated autumn dress of crimson and gold and green ; but it is at West Point itself we realize the full glory and effect of the gorgeous autumn colouring. Wonderfully indeed has nature painted the land ; the maples are clothed in glowing crimson, and the chestnut and the ash wear their warm-tinted robes beside them, while covering the hundred hills around and over-spreading the undulating land are bold patches of purple, orange, browns, gold and greens of many shades, such as an artist would love to dream of. It is one gigantic God-painted mosaic (for such colours could not be manufactured by earthly hands), with a background of cool November sky.

West Point itself is like a bit of an earthly paradise ; it stands high above the river, and is surrounded by scenery that is both picturesque and grand. You may lose yourself in its delightful solitudes within sound of the College bells ; the river winds in and out about the skirts of West Point like a huge silver serpent ; from the terrace of the hotel there is a magnificent view of hill and dale, wood and water, which reminds one strongly of the loveliest, loneliest part of the lake of Lucerne.

There is plenty of gaiety for those who like it : daily parades, military bands, balls, picnics and kettledrums ; and during the summer season the hotels—there are but two—are crowded with the rank and fashion of the State.

CHAPTER VII.

TO THE PHŒNIX CITY.

We Start—Our Car—Our Dressing-room—Chicago—Its Park—The Palmer House.

OF the many routes to San Francisco we chose the Pennsylvania line of railway, which takes us as far as Chicago, having been informed by some old tourists that we should find it by far the most picturesque and agreeable, besides being the smoothest to run over, the rails being steel and laid with special care, and the new carriages being built with all consideration for the comfort and convenience of their passengers. We had rather a dread of American railways, having heard so much of their reckless speed and wilful disregard of all rules and regulations, that we started on our journey in some trepidation of spirit, with a nervous feeling that something *must* happen before the end of it. But we gained confidence as we discovered the surprising fact that life is equally dear to its owners here as at home, and that drivers, engineers, and other employés are as attentive to their duties here as in any other quarter of the globe. We settled ourselves comfortably in the seats of our luxurious Pullman car, and prepared to enjoy the scenery.

We fly swiftly through the highly cultivated State of Pennsylvania; for three or four hundred miles, we are surrounded by a panorama of picturesque beauty—sparkling rivers, winding through undulating hills and verdant plains, with here and there pretty villages creeping up the green hill-sides or nestling at their feet. Presently something that looks like a dark wriggling worm, with a fierce fiery eye, comes wickedly towards us. We are rounding the wonderful horseshoe curve; it is our own engine, which seems to be coming in one direction while we are going in another; but it is all right; it drags us round, and speeds along on level ground once more. We pass the Alleghany Mountains, which on this occasion wear a crown of jewelled flames leaping in lurid fury upon the dusky night, as though they were trying to regain the heaven whence they had first descended. We pass Pittsburg, with its thousand furnaces glowing in their own murky atmosphere, flashing their flames, like threatening fires, in the face of the fair white moon.

As the night closes in, the excitement and novelty of our day's travel calms down, and we turn our attention to the internal arrangements of our temporary home, and are interested in watching our comfortable, velvet-cushioned section turned into a cosy sleeping-place; soft mattresses, snowy sheets, and warm, gaily striped blankets are extracted from behind the ornamental panels overhead; the curtains are let down; and lo! we may go to our rest as soon as we please. But we do not please until we have consulted our conductor, whose sole occupation during the day has been walking to and fro the cars, punching our tickets till they resemble a piece of perforated cardboard. If this process is to be carried on during the night we think we shall have small chance of rest. But the matter is satisfactorily settled; we may sleep in peace. That punching process is our bugbear throughout the entire journey. Some are so careful of their tickets that they never can find them when they are wanted; and the appearance of the conductor is the signal for a general hunt. Pockets are ransacked, portmanteaus are turned out, people nervously feel themselves all over, plunge under the seats, crawl over the floor. "It *must* be somewhere." It is found at last, perhaps wedged in a crack of the window, or it has dropped into the luncheon-basket and is extracted from a jelly-jar, strongly impregnated with an odour of pepper and cheese. I pin mine, as they impale blue-bottles and butterflies, on the side of the car. Gentlemen, as a rule, dispose of theirs easily enough, and wear them, like a dustman's badge, stuck in their hat-bands, or like a cavalier's order, pinned upon their breasts.

This harmless piece of cardboard was the white elephant of our lives. We never knew what to do with it. It looked so little and meant so much. We kept early hours in this our travelling home, and towards nine o'clock the lights were lowered, and, soothed by the monotonous movement and rhythmical rumble of the train, we were soon sleeping as calmly and pleasantly as in our own beds at home.

Our trial came in the morning, when we marched to the dressing-room to perform our toilette and found a whole army of dishevelled females, armed with toothbrushes, sponges, etc., besieging the four-foot space yclept "the ladies' dressing-room," each waiting for the first sign of surrender to march in and take possession. This was the miserable epoch in our daily lives through all the overland journey; in everything else our car life was delightfully luxurious and pleasant. Perhaps there were a dozen ladies who every day had to grapple with the same difficulty and stand shivering, all more or less *en déshabille* (rather more than less), biding their time to take temporary possession of the solitary soap-dish and basin provided for their ablutions. The public are already deeply indebted to Messrs. Pullman and Co. for an easy and luxurious mode of travelling, but the debt might be increased a thousandfold by a small sacrifice on their part. By devoting a single section to the purpose of a second dressing-room, they would add considerably to the accommodation of the ladies, and might fairly issue a placard of "Travelling made Perfect."

No hotel or dining-cars accompany the morning train from New York, but eating-stations are erected at certain portions of the road, where you may get rid of the most wolfish appetite at an admirably spread table, and plenty of time allowed for the knife and fork engagement.

On the second day we found ourselves rushing along the wide plains of Indiana, a sea of tall, sweet Indian corn on either side, its beaded cob, like shining ivory, gleaming from its leaf of tender green. We reached Chicago that evening, and were most kindly received at the Palmer House, a palatial hotel built by Mr. Potter Palmer for the luxurious entertainment of the travelling public. It is more like an elegantly appointed home than a mere resting-place for such birds of passage as ourselves. Each suite of apartments is perfect in itself, with a bath-room and every convenience attached, richly curtained and carpeted, with luxurious lounges and the easiest of easy-chairs; once settled in their soft embrace it is difficult to tear one's self from their downy arms. Being cosily installed beneath this hospitable roof, one feels, like "poor *Joe*," disinclined to "move on." The spacious halls and corridors are furnished in accord with other portions of the house. The walls are lined with *fauteuils*, sofas, and all the appointments of a handsome drawing-room.

As soon as we had enjoyed the luxury of a bath (and after two days' dusty travel, what a luxury that is!), we went to the dining saloon in search of our dinner, and found an unusually good one, excellently served and abundantly supplied. If we had staid for a month and eaten *pro rata* as at our first meal, we should have ruined our digestive organs and rejoiced in internal discords for ever afterward. Our *ménu* was illustrated. On one side was depicted a pigstye and a hovel—"Chicago forty years ago." On the other was a wonderful city—"The Chicago of to-day!"

Knowing of the fiery scourge which a few years ago had marred and scarred the beauty of that fair city, we expected to find traces of ugliness and deformity everywhere, crippled buildings, and lame, limping streets running along in a forlorn crooked condition, waiting for time to restore their old vigour and build up their beauty anew. But,

Phœnixlike, the city has risen up out of its own ashes, grander and statelier than ever. On the outskirts the line of fire can still be traced; gaunt skeletons of houses still remain to point the way it took, and more than one ruined church, stripped of its altar and regal signs of grace, stands blind and helpless in the sunshine; while in the suburbs picturesque shells of once beautiful homes greet us here and there. But once within the boundaries of the city we lose all traces of the conflagration. The business streets are lined with handsome massive houses, some six or seven stories high, substantially built, sometimes of red brick with stone copings and elaborate carving, while others are built of that creamy stone which reminds one of the Paris boulevards. No wooden buildings are allowed to be erected within a certain distance of the city. The fashionable trading localities are State and Clark streets, though there are several others which are well patronized by a less fashionable multitude. On either side are large handsome drygoods, millinery, and other stores of all possible descriptions, the windows being arranged with a tasteful elaboration that might stand side by side with our fashionable establishments at home, and lose nothing by the comparison. The different banks, churches, and municipal buildings which had been destroyed by the great fire-fiend are all re-erected in a substantial style, though with varying degrees of eccentric architecture. The new water-works, situated at the northern end of the city, are the most beautiful illustrations of the vagaries of the architectural brain. It must have wandered into dreamland and caught up its prevailing idea, for never were so many cupolas and buttresses, pinnacles and towers, grouped together on one spot; none but a true artist could have arranged them into so harmonious a whole, and produced from a combination of such opposite forms so imposing an effect.

A painter may indulge in all the eccentricities of his genius, may derive his inspiration from what source he will, there is no restriction to the realms of his art. He may choose his subject, and illustrate it according to his own fancy; he may wander far from the realms of art, and give to the wood a "harmony in blue and gold," or a "study in brass and impudence," and his productions are called "original." But if an architect outruns the bounds prescribed by the five orders of architecture, and dares to give play to his fancy, his work is stigmatized as "bastard art," and he is considered a fit subject for a lunatic asylum. On our drives through and about the city we were struck by the dearth of trees. There were no signs of pleasant green shade anywhere; they had all been destroyed by the great fire. Streets and avenues had been rebuilt, and they were replanting as fast as they could; but nature will not be hurried in her work, her children must have time to grow, and though her fairest fruits are sometimes forced into an unnatural growth, she revenges herself by robbing them of their sweetest flavour.

Along the shore road we drove to the park at the northern end of the city, which gives promise of being a delightful promenade and recreation ground; but it is at present only a park in embryo, though it is growing rapidly. Flowers and shrubs are being planted, grassy knolls built up, and paths and winding ways cut and gravelled. In the course of a few years it will have outgrown its present ragged state, and have bloomed into a delightful pleasure-ground, with the whispering waves of that inland sea, Lake Michigan, kissing with soft foam lips its grassy slopes, while great ships go sailing and steamers ride royally on the breast of the wide waters on one side, and the great city, with its hubbub, bustle and roar, lies upon the other. Chicago is indeed a great city, full of energy and enterprise. Signs of its hidden strength and powers of progress greet us everywhere ; but at present it appears to be wholly devoted to money-making. Art, science (except such science as serves its purpose), and literature are in a languishing state. But it is young yet. Perhaps when it is fully developed, and grown strong in muscle, and bone, and brain, the soul may be born to glorify the commonplace, and stir the latent genius of this city into life and beauty.

With some regret we sit down to our last dinner in this bright, bustling city, and go to bed to dream of to-morrow, for in the morning we begin our journey west, and the magnet which has drawn us across the sea lies at the Golden Gate.

CHAPTER VIII.

WESTWARD HO!

Our Travelling Hotel—The Prairies—The Emigrant Train—Bret Harte's Heroes—Reception of General Grant in the Wild West—"See, the Conquering Hero Comes"—The Procession.

HE next morning we started, *via* the Chicago and Northwestern Railway, for Omaha. This is a most desirable route, over even, well-laid rails, the carriages easy and luxurious, and we are whirled along over the illimitable prairie lands with a pleasant, gliding, almost noiseless motion, which recalled to our minds the gondola movement on the Grand Canal at Venice; this we are told is owing to some new invention of india-rubber or paper wheels which the company have applied to their carriages, which greatly adds to the comfort of their travellers. It was here, for the first time, we enjoyed the luxury of the hotel car. We were getting hungry, and curious to know what good things the gods would provide for us. Presently a good-humoured negro, "God's image carved in ebony," clothed all in white, brought us a bill of fare from which to select our meal. It was an *embarras de richesses*. There were so many good things that we held a consultation as to what would form the most desirable meal. We decided on mulliga-

tawny soup, broiled oysters, lamb cutlets, and peas, and handed the *ménu* back to our swarthy attendant. A narrow passage, every inch of which is utilized, separates the kitchen from the rest of the car. How is it that in so many private houses the odour of roast and broil travels from the kitchen and insinuates itself into the remotest corner of the house? It greets you on the doorstep and follows you everywhere. Here the occupants of the car, but a few feet off, have no suggestion of dinner till it is placed before them.

We were curious as to the working of the culinary department, and animated by a noble desire to obtain knowledge we penetrated the sacred precincts of the cook. He gazed sternly at us on our entrance, but we insinuated ourselves into his good graces, and he showed us every nook and corner of his domain. The kitchen was a perfect gem of a place, about eight feet square. A range ran along one side, its dark, shining face breaking out into an eruption of knobs, handles, and hinges of polished brass or steel. Curious little doors were studded all over it. One opened here and there to give us a sniff of its savory secrets, then shut with a laughing clang, so playing "bo-peep" with our appetites. Presently we should enjoy the full revelation of its culinary secrets. Pots, steamers, and "bain Marie" pans were simmering on the top. Every requisite for carrying on the gastronomical operations was there in that tiny space, in the neatest and most compact form. Scrupulous cleanliness reigned supreme over all. There was the pantry, with its polished silver, glass, and china in shining array. The refrigerator, with a plentiful supply of ice, and the larder were side by side. The wine and beer cellar was artfully arranged beneath the car; none but he who possessed the secret of "open sesame" could get access to it. Thus every inch of space was realized to its utmost extent. It was like a dominion in Toyland, inhabited by an ebony giant, who by a species of culinary conjuring produced an epicure's feast from a handful of wood and charcoal. Towards six o'clock every table was spread with dainty linen, and the dinner was exquisitely served according to the previous orders of each traveller. The simplest dish, as well as the most elaborate, was cooked to perfection, and everybody fell to with a will. Early hours were kept here as in our other travelling home, and the same routine was pursued in the morning. Breakfast was served about eight o'clock. The flat prairie land rolled away rapidly beneath our iron tread, and lay in long dusky lines behind us. Imperceptibly the scenery around us changed. We passed a succession of wild, low-lying hills, brown and bare; then more hills growing higher and greener, rising out of the swampy lands, where herds of cattle and wild shaggy ponies were standing knee deep and grazing among the red willows and long green grass. The skies were leaden, the wind began to blow, and the rain to fall. We passed a quiet little lake, dotted all over with wild ducks, and prairie birds flying restlessly over them. Signs of life became stronger. We flew past wooden shanties, and now and then caught sight of a lonely settler's hut high up in the hills. Presently we rolled into a low, flat, straggling village, or rather town, for every group of a dozen houses is so dignified here. This was Council Bluffs. Here we left our cosy car, and crossed the bleak windy space which yawned between us and the car yclept "the Dummy!" which was to carry us to Omaha.

We were crammed into a long, comfortless, wagon-like car with a host of nondescript folk, some bearing babies, bundles, or baskets of fish or vegetables, some tattered and torn, some unshaven, unshorn, all mixed up *higglety pigglety*. It was stuffy and by no means savory, for the windows were all closed to keep out the wind and the rain, which was now pouring in torrents. For a few moments we looked out shivering on the most desolate prospect. The skies were heavy with huge, black clouds, whose growling thunders went reverberating like a cannonade among the surrounding hills. The wind howled like a shrieking demon, and came creeping in at every crevice, till we shivered in its icy grasp. Dreary without and dreary within!

But we look forward hopefully. In half an hour we shall reach Omaha, where we expect to be well housed and fed. Slowly we begin to move. Our "dummy" finds voice enough to groan and pant painfully with its brazen lungs as it carries us across the bridge which spans the Missouri River and connects Omaha with Council Bluffs. The bridge is a mile long, and we go very slowly over it. The river, which at this point is the colour and consistency of thick pea soup, or a liquefied London fog, winds with a sluggish motion below us, wriggling its way between the iron piers with a sullen, rebellious gurgle, as though it was ashamed of its defiled condition, and hated to be driven from its own bright waters, which were sparkling clear as crystal not so many miles away. But once set floating in a muddy stream in the world of waters, as in the world of men, it is difficult to mingle with the pure living waters again.

At last we creak and rumble into the station at Omaha. Our poor dummy's joints are rusty and want oiling. It seems glad to stop, and so are we. We glance round us, and feel we are on the threshold of a new world. The platform is crowded with a motley assemblage of people, from which the "genteel" element seems to be wholly eliminated. There is a hurrying to and fro of many feet, a general bustle and confusion reigning everywhere. A very babel of voices is ringing round us. The harsh guttural German, the liquid Italian, and the mellifluous Spanish mingles with the Yankee twang and Irish brogue. The emigrant train has just arrived and disgorged its living freight. The platform overflows with them, they are everywhere, all with a more or less travel-stained look. Having been penned up so long in such close quarters they are glad to get out and stretch their legs and rinse the dirt from their grimy faces. Swarthy men, with bare arms, are splashing about in buckets; some are performing their ablutions under the pump, or in anything that comes handy. One sad-eyed German woman, with a child in her arms, is sitting entrenched amongst an army of bags and bundles, and dipping an old handkerchief into a pint cup of water is wiping her child's face and her own, refreshing themselves as they best could therewith. I stop and put a packet of candy into the little one's hand. The mother stares vacantly, and slowly extracting a copper coin from a poor, little, ragged purse, which she drew from her bosom, offers it in payment.

The women as a rule look faded, wan, and anxious; the men energetic and strong, confident and assured, with a bright, never-say-die look upon their faces.

They look as if they meant "work," and were able to do it. There seem to be only a few loafers and loungers scattered among them, weak, indolent creatures, who had not pluck enough to fight their way in their own land, and are journeying in search of a general El Dorado, a sort of "Tom Tidler's ground," where they could go "picking up gold and silver."

They are to wait three hours at the station before they resume their journey west. It is a strange gathering, that flock of varying nationalities, all bound on one adventurous errand—a wave of the Old World breaking on the shores of the New.

The Grand Pacific Hotel having been destroyed by fire, we get into an omnibus which conveys us to the Cosmopolitan, which is a striking contrast to the magnificent hotels which have hitherto lined our route. It is second-rate in style, but also second-rate in price. No lounges; no easy-chairs; no velvet carpets under foot. The floors are sanded; the chairs uncompromisingly hard and upright: but the beds are comfortable enough; meals excellently cooked, though roughly served. We enjoy all the necessities, but none of the luxuries of life. As we only intend to remain in Omaha for a day we walk out to take a view of the town. It is a most dreary, desolate-looking city, with wide, straggling, dusty streets, and next to nobody in them. The shops are numerous enough, such as they are, but seedy-looking and scantily supplied. Nobody is doing anything; there seems to be nothing to do. The shopkeepers lounge in their doorways; they don't appear to have energy enough even to gossip with their neighbours. The very children seem to have no heart for childish roistering! their spirits droop under the atmospheric depression; they come trooping out of school and wend their way homeward in a stolid, orderly fashion. The side-streets are overgrown with dank grass and weeds; in the outskirts of the city little wooden houses, looking exactly as if they had come out of a Noah's Ark, are scattered irregularly about, each standing in its little barren patch of ground. We spend the morning wandering through these dusty, windblown streets. We return to the hotel, take a hasty lunch, an hour's rest, then sally forth again. By this time something has happened to stir the dead city into life. For the hour it is roused from its normal condition. The shops are closed, the population has turned out into the streets, and people come flocking in from all parts of the country—some on foot, some in ramshackle old vehicles which look as though they had never worn a coat of paint, and so dilapidated we wonder how they manage to keep together; the wheels seem to be struggling to run different ways, but the big, bony steed draws them through dust and mire, till the vantage-point is gained in the streets of Omaha. A few fluttering flags are now flying. The Stars and Stripes are everywhere, and on turning a sharp corner we stand face to face with a triumphal arch built up of egg boxes and old beer barrels, which are partially covered with evergreens and paper flowers, and in big, blazing, though somewhat tumbledown letters across the top is written "Welcome Grant."

So the gallant General is expected to-day, and that is the cause of the commotion. He is to make a royal progress through the streets of Omaha, and all the city turns out to do him honour, though the female part of the population is sparcely represented. Indeed there is scarcely a woman to be seen out of doors. It is here we gain our first view of the Western man precisely as he lives in the pages of Bret Harte & Co., where we have so often seen him in our mind's eye; but here he is a personality before us—dark, hollow-cheeked, stern-visaged, slouch-hatted, top-booted; there are scores of him, hundreds of him; he tramps along the side-walk, he overflows into the stony roadway. The aspect of this swarm of rough, unkempt men is rather alarming to us unprotected females. But "he roars him soft," and respectfully makes way for us to pass. It seems strange to find a silent, well-ordered crowd formed of such rough elements. There is no horse-play, no vulgar "chaff," or foul language, such as would characterize a similar crowd in most of our civilized cities. But, alas! the romance that might cling to this Western hero is spoiled by his personal habits. He has small acquaintance with soap and water, and he chews tobacco. The result which marks his track wherever he wanders is visible and revolting. However, he is stout of limb and true of heart. We feel instinctively that a rude word or discourteous act in our presence is simply impossible, so we lift our unprotected heads and march on triumphant. We feel we must keep moving, though we are disposed to lag and see what is to be seen of the show. We have not sauntered many steps when the engine bell rings. "Lo! the conquering hero comes!" There is a buzz, a general stir, and all eyes are turned in one direction. We fall back, and are promoted to a position in the front rank on the curbstone.

There was a coal-black negress on one side of us, dressed in a pale-blue dress with white trimmings, a scarlet shawl, a pink bonnet with red and yellow roses, and a pea-green parasol. She was evidently happy, and her white teeth gleamed through a wreath of smiles. The procession came in sight headed by a band of music, a huge drum being the chief instrument; fifes and flutes squeaking their loudest, each trying to get ahead of the other, running a race with time rather than trying to keep it. The poor "Star Spangled Banner" was torn with discords, tattered in tune, its own creator would not have known it. Next came the General in an old-fashioned coach drawn by six horses, evidently promoted from the ploughshare for this special occasion. Mrs. Grant followed, with her son and some lady friends, all looking smiling, good-tempered, and happy, as though the dreary boredom of a reception awaited them not. Then came a curious procession of wagons, representing the different trades of the town. There was the blacksmith, hammer in hand, labouring at the anvil, bellows blowing, sparks flying round him as though he were in his native smithy; the cutler, the nailmaker, the carpenter, the cooper, etc., all surrounded by the implements of their trade, and plying them, too, with a will. Last of this novel procession came a wagon filled with pretty young girls, all busily engaged hemming, sewing, and frilling at their different sewing-machines. This closed the procession, and "The Magnificent Reception of General Grant by the Citizens of Omaha" was duly chronicled. It flashed along the telegraph wires and flamed in the face of the world before the sun had set.

The multitude melted away as quietly as it had collected, and we went on our way to the Pullman car office to secure our section for the morning. The clerk was with the Reception Committee, and we had to wait for his return. We were entertained meanwhile by the rhapsodies of one of the General's wildest admirers, who turned on the tap of conversation and filled us to the brim with voluntary information.

"I fought under the General fourteen years ago. Ah! he's a man, the General is! Talk of him being President! He ought to be emperor. There'd be no disunited States while *he* was around, I warrant. I haven't seen him for years, but he knew me. They stopped at the corner of Tenth; I jumped on the carriage steps: 'Hurrah, General,' says I, 'I fought under you at ——'

"'All right!' says he, and shook hands. Ah! he's a smart fellow. 'No other General could have done what he did.'"

A tall aristocratic looking man, who was standing by waiting his turn, moved coolly away from the group.

The face of the General's friend knotted itself into an expression of deep disgust. He evidently deemed that cold water was thrown on his enthusiasm.

"There goes a copperhead," he snarled. "I can smell 'em a mile off. We haven't done with 'em yet: we've only scotched the snake, not killed it; we shall have to thrash 'em again, and I'll be the first to shoulder a musket."

In this strain he continued. We transacted our business and descended the stairs. His voice followed us, growing more fiercely eloquent, till we were out of hearing. I fancy he had been drinking the General's health too freely.

We were not very sorry to leave Omaha next morning, for we had rested little during the night, having made a bad selection of rooms. Our door opened on to the general parlour (all sitting-rooms are called parlours), and a gruff, growling wave of conversation swept over our ears from time to time till long past midnight. Indeed, we were kept lively in more ways than one. Meanwhile a violent rain began to fall, and beat frantically against our window panes, and I dreamt that the whole sky was turned into a dome of whalebone and calico, and this globe of ours was whirling around beneath a gigantic umbrella. I was not sorry when our twenty-four hours at Omaha were over.

CHAPTER IX.

ACROSS THE ROCKY MOUNTAINS.

Our Fellow-passengers—Unprotected Females—Prairie Dog Land—A Cosy Interior—Cheyenne—The Rocky Mountains—" Castles not Made by Hands "—Ogden.

E start once more on our pleasant Pullman car; we arrange our tiny packages and make ourselves as much as possible "at home" in our cosy section. The car is crowded, as the different lines of railway end here, and all who are westward bound must come on this one daily train from Omaha. We look round on our fellow-passengers. As a rule, they are simply commonplace, such as nature manufactures by millions and turns out merely labelled men and women, with no special characteristics except their sex. There are, however, some exceptions. In the opposite section is a big, burly fellow in jackboots, a huge sombrero, a frieze coat, which looks as though it ought to be stuck full of bowie-knives and pistols, and such a growth of crisp dark hair, he seems smothered under it; a pair of bright eyes gleam out from its bushy surroundings, full of enterprise, energy, and spirit; he is a miner, we learn, going on by stage two hundred miles from Cheyenne to

the Black Hills. The companion of his section is a tall, delicate-looking young man, so thin and fragile it seems as though a gust of wind would blow him out of this world into the next. He rarely speaks, but sits leaning his head upon his hand, coughing the terrible, hacking cough which tells a sad story. He is travelling in search of health, he tells us; the more eagerly he pursues, the faster it seems to fly from him. In our mind's eye we see the phantom Death chasing him from land to land; it will too surely run him down and lay him to rest beneath the bright Californian skies, and hide him from the world's eyes where even his own mother will never be able to find him. We are sorry to see this forlorn stranger solitary and alone; we are anxious to show him some sympathy, but there is nothing to be done; it hurts him to talk, and he has all he wants within reach of his own hands. His rough companion, bound for the Black Hills, seems to take a tender interest in him, and shows his sympathy in a silent, unobtrusive way difficult to specify. In the next section to ours there is a pretty young girl; she is travelling quite alone from Boston to Arizona, a journey of twelve days and nights, in perfect comfort and safety. A lady can do that in this country without running the slightest risk of annoyance or inconvenience in any way. The conductors and all the train officials devote themselves most loyally to her service, and are always at hand to give her any advice or information she may require. They pass her on from train to train or from stage to stage till she arrives at the end of her journey, having received the same courteous attention throughout. Indeed, to thoroughly enjoy travelling in perfect comfort and freedom from anxiety, one must be an unprotected female. To her the manly heart yields his interest in car or stage; gives her the best seat, that she may be screened and curtained, while he broils in the sun; for her he fights a way to the front ranks of refreshment rooms, skirmishes with the coffee-pot, and bears triumphant ices aloft; for her he battles with baggage-masters, baffles the hungry-hearted loafer, scares the barefooted beggar, and, not being her legitimate owner, he carries her bandbox, and, should she be burdened with that doubtful blessing, he even carries her baby! I have seen him do it. There was a general demand upon his chivalry on board this car, but there was plenty of him and only four of *us*. Besides ourselves and the pretty girl before referred to, there was a snuff-coloured young lady with snuff-coloured hair, snuff-coloured eyes, and dress to match, a grayish complexion, and rather grave, sad expression of countenance. She was not good-looking, but one felt an interest in watching her. Her face had a story in it.

Having so far taken note of our fellow-passengers, we lean back in our seats and look out upon the vast prairie-lands, which roll before and around us like a gray-green, motionless sea. The prospect is wild and dreary. Occasionally we see a trapper's dug-out or watch a solitary hunter galloping towards his hut somewhere up in the distant mountains. The scene grows monotonous; nay, wearisome. Nothing but the gray-green prairie-land and bright blue sky; the novelty of it has worn off. Presently we come upon the prairie dogs' wild domain, and see scores of these funny little animals scampering along till they reach each his particular hole, where he sits on his hind legs a moment, glancing curiously round and listening, then, turning a somersault, disappears, head first, down his burrow. They are plump little creatures, like guinea pigs, only much larger, and something the colour of the prairie-grass; they are sociable little animals, and live not only in the companionship of their own kind, for the burrowing owl and even the rattlesnake seem to form part of the family. The owl may often be seen solemnly sitting at the mouth of the hole, and the bones of the rattlesnake have not unfrequently been found therein. Once we catch a glimpse of a herd of antelopes flying, like the wind, across the plain. They have come and gone like a flash; nothing more breaks the monotony of that day's journey.

The blinding sunlight dazzles our eyes; we withdraw them from the scene without and glance round upon the cheerful prospect within. Some are indulging in reminiscences of old times, when it had taken them six weary months of toil, privation, and danger to cross these plains, which they are now doing luxuriously in seven days. In one section a rubber of whist is in progress in sociable but solemn silence; in another a pair of travellers bound for the Black Hills are engaged in the game of poker, and cut, deal, shuffle, and play with such rapidity that we can catch no idea of the game; some lounge over the whist-table watching the players; the snuff-coloured girl leans back in her seat with folded hands lying idly in her lap, gazing with vacant eyes, not on the desolation round her, but possibly on her own invisible life, which may be a more dismal prospect still; the pretty girl gets out her tatting, and we have a pleasant chat and exchange small confidences together: her parents are dead, she tells me, and she has not a relation in the world except her brother, who is settled in Arizona, and she is now going to make her home with him.

"I haven't seen him since I was three years old," she added, showing his portrait; "he is sixteen years older than I am."

"You are quite sure of a welcome?"

"Oh, yes; I know he'll be glad to see me. He wanted me to come, and he is such a good brother," she added, confidently. "He'll come to meet me in San Francisco, if he can."

So time passes till we reach Cheyenne. There we all turn out in anticipation of having a thoroughly good meal, and are not disappointed. We enjoy a capital dinner, a very necessary thing in these mountain regions. The hot soup is excellent; then we have broiled trout and a roast of black-tailed deer, the most delicious-flavored, tender meat conceivable; fresh vegetables and fruits are plentifully supplied; and, as a crowning bliss, we enjoy the luxury of black coffee; and, in a perfectly happy, contented frame of mind, we re-enter our Pullman home.

Everybody is content, and everybody has a good word for Cheyenne. Why is it that things are not equally well managed throughout this well-travelled route? As a rule the eating-stations are wretchedly supplied. We have thrown away many a noble appetite on a tough, tasteless steak and watery soup, that had scarcely strength to run down our throats. Indeed, Cheyenne, Humboldt, and Laramie are the only stations where a thoroughly good, comfortable meal may be relied on. A well-filled luncheon-basket is a necessity, a comfort, as well as an economy, for the charges at these places are a dollar for anything, unless you crowd to the emigrants' refreshment bar, where cooking is by no means studied as a high art.

Leaving Cheyenne we charge gallantly forward, climbing higher and higher, till we are in the regions of snow and ice, and at last reach Sherman, the highest point of these Rocky Mountains, eight thousand two hundred feet above the level of the sea. The rarefied air affects the breathing of some of our party, and one gallant officer, who has gone through the smoke and fire of many battles unharmed, is seized with an ignominious bleeding at the nose. For us, we suffer not the slightest inconvenience. We have left the rolling prairies behind us, and now, by imperceptible grades, begin to descend this wide range of Rocky Mountains. Vast, rugged, and bare in their stony strength they lie before us; a bright blue sky bends bell-like over us, bathes us in a kind of spiritual sunshine, and shuts us in from the troublous world beyond. We feel we are intruders in this wondrous solitude; it seems as though Nature should have it all to herself here, and hurl us poor pigmies out of it. But in these days Nature is allowed to hold nothing sacredly her own; as she retreats we follow her even to her farthest fastnesses,—in time we shall reach her even there. Our living street dashes on through this world of the olden gods. We fancy that in some far-distant ages this must have been a wide overwhelming sea, lashed to fury and then turned to stone. As we descend the scene changes; the rocks assume strange, fantastic forms, weird, solemn, or grotesque. On every side we are surrounded by some new wonder. There is something in the grandeur of this silent world which makes us feel small and sad; we cease talking, and are borne through this sublime region in awe-struck silence.

Ruined castles, not made by hands, with buttress and battlements falling to decay, frown darkly over us. The remains of some ancient cathedrals, where we can fancy the olden gods held solemn service, cling to the gray rock beside us. But tower and buttress, castled crag and battlemented ruins fade from our sight, and we come upon new scenes of equal wonder. We pass through serried swords of rock, which look as though they had been lifted there by some dead Hercules at war with the mightier gods. We whistle and shriek as we rush past the giant's jaws, whose jagged teeth seem set ready to grind us to powder, but they are fixed immovable till the judgment day. We pass the Pulpit Rock, where the stony preacher has stood silent looking southward since the world began. There is a tradition that the Prophet of the Lord, the leader of the Latter Day Saints, whose province we are fast approaching, once preached there to his people during their early perilous journey, while they were ignorant of the marvellous Salt Lake and valleys beyond, where they have since made their home. There are numerous small towns and villages hidden away among those mountainous regions, which are intersected by fertile valleys, and where beautiful rivers are eternally flowing; but we see nothing of them, we are only told that they are there. We are now entering the famous Echo and Weber Cañons, of which we had heard so much. Here the grandeur of the whole rugged range seems to have reached its highest point. We are in a narrow gorge between rocks of colossal and majestic dimensions, rising perpendicularly on either side of us, so high and so near that our eyes have to climb steadily till they reach the topmost peak. We, with our petty passions and frail human life, the last, and, as we are told, the best of all God's works, feel dwarfed and insignificant beside these gigantic memorials, which stand through all ages the insignia of His immortal honour and glory. We steam for miles through this rocky world of wonders, amid a stillness so profound that the whistle of our engine echoes, re-echoes, and is flung back upon our ears multiplied and sounding like the shrieks of invisible demons giving us a mocking welcome to their silent land. We are nearing the narrows, where the cañon is drawing its rocky sides together, closing us in as it were. There seems to be no escape for us; we feel as though we must be dashed down the precipice which yawns below. But we round a sharp curve, and the scene widens. On our right is a wide ledge of rugged, gray rocks, where, we are told, the Mormons made a stand in 1857, and erected a fort close by, the ruins of which are still visible. There they piled up masses of rock and stones to hurl down upon the United States Army, which it was found expedient to send against them. The Nauvoo regiments, we are told, encamped here close beneath the prow of the "Great Eastern," a huge red rock, so called from the resemblance it bears to that portion of gigantic vessel; a small cedar-tree waves like a green flag over it, and the deck and other parts of the stony vessel slope away and are swallowed up and lost in the shapeless mass of gray rocks surrounding. A little farther on, sombre and weird, stand The Three Witches, as though whispering together, plotting mischief, manufacturing and sending forth storms, hurricanes, and cyclones to devastate the world of man below. Now we are fast approaching what is perhaps the most marvellous of all these strange formations, "The Devil's Slide," whither his Satanic Majesty is supposed to retire for gymnastic exercises when he has nothing else to do, which is not often, though the "City of the Saints" is so near at hand. It is formed of two slanting walls about a foot thick, which stand out with their ragged, jagged edges about fifty feet, and slope down the face of the huge body of rock nearly close together, but leaving room for a whole company of fiends to amuse themselves by sliding down between them. We flash past The Thousand Mile Tree, the solitary green thing which flourishes in the precipitous wilds, and which tells us we are a thousand miles from Omaha, and within an hour's ride of Ogden. The night closes in very suddenly in these regions, and even as we are looking on the wonders round us they grow indistinct, and are soon lost in the gloomy shadow which comes stealing stealthily down as soon as the sun has set.

It is quite dark when we steam into the station; the gong is sounding (with that whirring, muffled, deafening sound which only a Chinese gong can make) an invitation to dinner, of which we are glad enough to avail ourselves. Porters are dashing about with lighted lanterns, luggage is lifted, and stacked, and wheeled across the platform to the other train, for there is a general change at this point, and all passengers are shifted from the Union, which ends here, to the Central Pacific, which takes up the journey and progresses westward. An hour is allowed for dinner, and amid the clatter of knives and forks, a hurrying to and fro of many feet, the sound of genial voices, chatter and laughter, we dine. Soon, too soon, it seems, the now familiar cry "All aboard! all aboard!" greets our ears. A few hurried good-byes and the westward bound speed on their way. We watch the red fiery eye of the engine light fade from our sight, as it winks and blinks away in the darkness. We re-enter the house, where we have decided to remain for the night. All is silent and deserted now that the guests of an hour have departed; the lights are out, and the few dusky servants flit to and fro in a noiseless way. We have got the place all to ourselves, and have plenty of time to look about us. It is a most comfortable resting-place, more like a cosy English inn than the more pretentious-sounding hotel. There are no houses near it, the town of Ogden proper being some little distance off, though still within sight of the depôt. Our resting-place is sandwiched between the two lines of railway, the Union and Central Pacific. It is a long, narrow, wooden building, only one story high, the lower part being devoted to railway business purposes, Pullman-car office, etc., and a large dining-room where, as the train steams in with its freight of hungry travellers, an excellent, well-cooked meal awaits them. The upper part consists of about ten or twelve cosy white-curtained sleeping-rooms. We should advise every one to rest here for a night on their way westward; it forms a delightful break in their journey. Except for the passing trains this is a most lonely, isolated spot, weird and still, lying in the heart of the mountains. In the evening a blinding snow-storm came on, and the wind, howling fearfully with a rushing mighty sound, shook the doors and rattled at the windows as though it wanted to come in and warm itself at our blazing wood fire. As I said before, we were the only guests in the house, and the landlady came in, bringing her work. The shaded lamps were lighted, the wood crackled and blazed, and cast a pleasant glow to our very hearts as we drew our chairs round the fire.

Our landlady had lived in this locality five and twenty years, and her mind was well stocked with anecdotes, and filled with the legendary lore of these wild regions. She opened her stores to us, and, as she sat sewing, kept our interest alive till nearly midnight, telling us of stormy times, interspersed with many romantic incidents during the early days when the Mormons first crossed the plains, previous to making their home among the mountains, when the railway was unplanned, unthought of, and wagon trains of adventurous men and women made their slow and hazardous pilgrimage to the Western World.

The next morning we took the train to Salt Lake City, and found ourselves plunged at once in the world of Mormonland.

CHAPTER X.

THE CITY OF THE SAINTS.

Salt Lake — Our Mormon Conductor — Mormon Wives — Their Daughters — Their Recruits — Their Agricultural Population.

HERE are few passengers on board the train as we steam through the suburban districts of Mormonland. The magnificent chain of the Wahsatch Mountains rising in the east, and the great Salt Lake stretching away toward the west, the rest of the scene made up of fertile lands, green meadows, fields of yellow corn, and purple clover, form an enchanting panorama as we fly past them; we are full of an undefined curiosity and anxious to see this City of the Saints of which we have heard so much. We soon discover that none but the "Saints" are employed on board this train, none but Mormon faces gather round us, they check our baggage, punch our tickets, and render us every necessary courtesy, which would do credit to the gentlest of Gentiles. Our conductor seems disposed to make himself quite at home; he takes a seat beside us, and commences a pleasant conversation; he knows we are from England, and proceeds to give us all kinds of miscellaneous and useful informa-

tion. He points out the different features in the landscape, and tells us of thrifty villages and thriving farms which are scattered among the mountains. He talks freely of the flourishing condition of the City of the Saints; but he avoids any special allusion to the peculiarities of the saints themselves. During our two hours' run from Ogden to Salt Lake City he grows more and more sociably disposed. We try to guide the conversation into the channel where we desire it should go. We wonder whether he is a Mormon or one of the Gentile sect, which is now numerously represented in that once exclusive land. We ask the question pointblank.

"Yes, ma'am, I'm proud to say I am," he answers, swelling with invisible glory; it is now he informs us that the whole line of railway was built by the Mormon people, and is exclusively run by them, no other labour being employed.

"I came here," he adds, "when I was six years old, when our people were forced to leave Nauvoo. I remember trotting along by my mother's side as we were driven out of the city at the point of the bayonet, the soldiers pricking and goading us like cattle. I shall never forget that time,—never, if I live to be a hundred years old; but we pulled through, and here we are in the most beautiful and flourishing valley in the whole wide world."

"And—I am afraid my question may seem impertinent—but may I ask how many wives you have?" I ask, growing bolder. He laughs, pulls off his cap, and exhibits a remarkably fine mass of bright brown curls.

"See my head of hair!" he exclaims. "Well, I have

only got one wife; if I took home another, this head of mine would be sand-papered! There are scores of us," he added, "who never dream of taking more than one wife."

"Then polygamy is not imposed on you as a part of your religion?" I inquire.

"Certainly not; but it is our right if we choose to adopt it. It is different now from the early days, when it was necessary, for our good God's sake, that his people of Zion should increase and multiply, so as to fill the kingdom of heaven." I felt disposed to suggest that the kingdom of heaven might perhaps be able to get along without the aid of Brigham Young's progeny, but as that observation might appear irreverent I withheld it, and he continued: "For my part I've found that one wife is quite as much as I can manage. I've never felt inclined to increase my family that way, and I don't believe there is a happier man in all Salt Lake than I am."

We reach the City of the Saints at last, and find it as fair and beautiful as we had expected. It is in truth an oasis in a desert, a blooming garden in a wilderness of green. We can scarcely conceive how this flowery world has lifted itself from the heart of desolation; it is only one more proof that the intellect and industry of man can master the mysteries of nature, and force her in her most harsh uncompromising moods to bring forth fair fruits. It lies in a deep wide valley, bounded on the east by the mighty range of the Wahsatch Mountains, which lift their lonely ice-crowned heads far into the skies, their rugged stony feet stretching away and reaching towards the west, where the great Salt Lake unrolls its dark waters, and widens and wanders away until it is lost in the distance. The streets are wide, the houses of all sorts and sizes, some one storey high, some two or even three, all built in different styles, or no style of architecture; each man having built his dwelling in accordance with his own taste or convenience. The streets are all arranged in long straight rows, and stretch away till they seem to crawl up the mountain-sides and then are lost. On either side of the roadways are magnificent forest-trees, which in summer-time must form a most delightful shade, though now it is autumn and the leaves are falling fast. Streams of water with their pleasant gurgling music flow on either side, through a deep cutting (which we should irreverently call the gutter), rushing along as though they were in a hurry to reach some everlasting sea. The women come out with their buckets and help themselves, while the children sail their toy boats, clapping their hands gleefully as the tiny craft is tossed, and tumbled, and borne along on the face of the bubbling water. Street-cars come crawling along the straight streets, crossing and recrossing each other at different points; but a private cab or carriage is rarely to be seen. Every house, be it only composed of a single room, is surrounded by a plot of garden ground, where fruits, flowers, and vegetables all grow together in loving companionship. Everything seems flourishing, and everybody seems well-to-do; there are no signs of poverty anywhere; no bare-footed whining beggars fill the streets; tramps there may be, passing from one part of the State to another, but these are all decently dressed and well fed, for at whatever door they knock they are sure to find food and shelter, charity to those in need being a part of the reigning religion.

The children who swarm on all sides are the healthiest, rosiest, happiest looking urchins conceivable; some perfectly beautiful specimens of young humanity. One felt sorry to think they must develop into the bewhiskered man or befrizzled woman; there was not a pale or sickly face in all the multitude. There are no signs of rank or fashion anywhere; there are no drones lounging about in this community, they are all busy bees; every man and every woman, too, does his or her share in the labour market, all according to their special abilities; and here is the only true republic in all America, elsewhere it is the name and not the thing. Here republicanism exists in its genuine form; it is not a commune, and encourages no communistic principles. Here every one must work, uniting therein for the common good of all. Wealth, represented by gold or other possessions, is unequally distributed as in other large cities. Some live in large houses, some in small, some wear broadcloth, some wear frieze; but the man who labours with his hands and the man who works with his brain, those who plan and those who execute, live together in a common brotherhood—for they are equally well educated, and have grown up in or helped to make the world they live in. The idle or the dissolute are speedily hunted out of the community. There is an equality in tone and manner among all conditions of people which strikes rather discordantly upon our ideas of the harmony of things, but we soon get used to it. We meet with a general pleasant courtesy, which is never vulgar, never over-free; there is a sense of equality, a sort of "one man as good as another," which is always felt though never obstrusively asserted. The woman who washes your linen, and the man who wheels your baggage, do it with a sort of courteous friendliness, considering that you are as much obliged to them as they to you; no kind of manual labour is looked upon as discreditable or below the dignity of any man. I have seen a Mormon bishop, in his shirt sleeves and corduroys, working hard in a timber-yard or carpentering at a bench. Schools and churches of all denominations and creeds abound; every child has a right to an equal education at the expense of the State of Utah. The Mormon city is now by no means held sacred to the Mormons, for people of all nations come flocking thither, erecting their own places of worship, and following their own faith. A plot of land has been lately set apart for a Jewish *synagogue;* but woe upon any one of them who shall attempt to interfere or win a single proselyte from the Mormon fold. While liberal (with a forced liberality, perhaps) towards other religions, they are devoted to their own; and in all social and domestic matters, they keep as much apart from the opposing forces as though they lived in different kingdoms. In all business relations they mix freely enough, and have extensive trading transactions with all nations, and carry on their operations with a shrewdness and tact which is popularly supposed to be the reigning characteristic of the "Jewish persuasion." There is no exclusion where the "almighty dollar" is concerned. They allow no chance of money-making to flow past them. Signs of prosperity and plenty are everywhere; to the mere passer-by or transient traveller, who can judge from outward appearances only, the State of Utah is the most flourishing in the Union. With its mines, its metals, its marvellous agricultural productions, its wealth of fruits and flowers, it seems as though the horn of plenty emptied itself in the lap of this favoured land. Out of doors in the streets the brisk, bustling population are crowding to and fro, all is gay and bright; the sun shines, the genial air stirs and invigorates the spirit, the pulse beats to healthful music, while the surrounding scene of swelling hills and glorious mountains is beautiful to behold. It is only on the threshold of *home* that the shadow falls; indeed, there is no such thing as home, regarding it from our point of view, as the centre of domestic happiness, of affectionate intercourse, and mutual confidence; it simply does not and cannot exist. When the interests and the affections are subdivided into so many different channels, they flow in a weak, sluggish spirit through all. I have had the good fortune to get an insight into the inner lives of the Mormon women, and have seen the skeleton grinning on their hearthstones. They are well cared for so far as creature comforts are concerned. The wives of the wealthier classes have handsome, well-furnished houses, and devote themselves to the care and education of their children; but there is a gloom and emptiness at their firesides, a vacant place, which is filled only with a mockery, an unreal shadow. He who is the head of one household to-day hangs up his hat in another home to-morrow. The ladies of refined, cultivated minds, and there are many of them, have a patient-waiting look upon their faces painful to behold; it seems as though the cross they carry is sometimes heavier than they can bear, and they long to lay it down and be at rest. My remarks do not apply indiscriminately to all, for there are many wives who are perfectly happy in the polygamic state; women to whom the children are more than the husband, whose maternal instincts are much stronger than their conjugal affections. This type of womanhood is not specially restricted to Mormonland; but to women of a more delicate spiritual organization, who feel the necessity of loving and being loved in the divinest, purest sense, this life of divided affections is torture. They live a life of daily crucifixion of spirit. They suffer doubly, as they are imbued with a strong sense of religion and believe that polygamy is right; indeed, one of God's holy ordinances. They are constantly engaged in a spiritual warfare, struggling with and against themselves. The voice of nature rebelling against her enforced bondage is regarded as the voice of the evil one, to be stilled only by prayers and self-mortification. The Mormon ladies are not the light-minded, sensuous race they are popularly supposed to be; on the contrary, they are grave, earnest women, strong in the faith they have been brought up in; their minds are completely under the control of their bishops and elders, whose words are to them as the written law of the Lord. It is impossible for any legislation from the outer world to remedy this evil; it lies in the spirit of the people beyond the reach of human hands. It is easy enough to strike the chains from the body, but it is impossible to free the mind from the bondage of a superstitious faith. Polygamy is an ulcer at the root of their religion; it may be dispersed by time and careful treatment, but can never be torn out.

The greater number of the present generation of Mormon women were born there, or from their infancy have drank in with their mothers' milk the teaching of their elders, until it has grown into the essence of their lives; how could it be otherwise? Until late years there had been no communication between Salt Lake City and the outer world. They knew nothing but what they were taught by those whose interest it was to keep them in a state of spiritual bondage. Their parents, in a frenzy of religious fervour, had traversed the wilderness, struggled through famine, and fire, and sword, had gone through the valley of the shadow of death in search of this modern Zion shut in by inaccessible mountains; their children were bred and born in a whirl of enthusiasm, and naturally inherited the spirit as well as the life of their parents. So much for the present generation of matrons; but they are passing away, and things are looking brighter for the rising population, since the railway has brought civilization with its train of worldly vanities into their midst, and the voice of their sister women has reached their ears, to say nothing of the Gentiles who swarm around them, and whose very presence must have a subtle influence over them. A change has come over the irreverent spirit of youth. The girls are rather shy of entering into polygamous marriages; they have seen enough, and seem to have no desire to enact their mothers' lives over again. Their suitors sigh in vain. The Mormon girls, as a rule, are very beautiful, with fine eyes, and soft, rich complexions like a peach-blossom, and seem disposed to join the general march onwards. In one of our saunters through the city we met two bright, blooming young girls, about seventeen, two of the many granddaughters of Brigham Young, gay, happy-looking creatures. It would be terrible to think they would ever sink into the faded, woe-worn Mormon wife.

I admired their city, and inquired if they would be content to live always at Salt Lake?

"Oh dear, no!" said the youngest and prettiest. "I want to go to Paris to study music; then, if I like, I can come back here and teach, you know," she added with a roguish laugh.

"And I should like to go to Europe to study medicine. I shall never rest here," said her cousin; "and I think I am going next spring."

This is a tolerable sample of the spirit which now animates the young people. The Church has to send its elders across the sea in search of recruits for the matrimonial market, and they rarely fail to return with a good supply as regards quantity; for the quality I would not vouch. During our stay at Salt Lake some half-dozen elders returned from one of these foraging expeditions, and brought back a few score of emigrants, both men and women, some with large families, but all of a most unpromising appearance. It seemed as though they had raked the social gutter, and brought thither the scum of all nations; for a more stolid, stupid-looking set of people I never saw. Well, insomuch as they rescue these poor creatures from stifling courts and alleys, the regions of poverty, ignorance, and dirt, where they have scarcely air to breathe or food to eat, they are doing a good work. Immediately on their arrival at Salt Lake these people are sent off to the agricultural districts, where so many acres of fertile land is awarded to each family, together with wood and all necessary materials for running up a house, and they commence to farm on a small scale, raising stock or grain as may be most expedient. If a man be intelligent and industrious he may speedily become a thriving farmer and landowner in one of the most beautiful valleys in the world. So far, if the Mormons let them alone, all would be well, but they don't; they teach them their religion, and the men are apt scholars. The seeds of polygamy once sown in the agricultural mind, it grows and flourishes like the rank weeds among their golden grain, and it is universally adopted. If a man wants a dairymaid, a cook, or even a scarecrow—he marries one. A large amount of field labour is done by women, and they, in most cases, are the wives of their employers. Polygamy seems to work well enough in the rural districts; quite different from its manifestations in the large cities, where the women have more time to brood and to feel; besides, the people are of a different calibre, and are drawn from a lower rank in life. I once drank tea at a farmhouse, far removed from the noisy city; there were four or five of the farmer's wives, all busily engaged in their several duties; one was looking after the washing and ironing, another was making up and packing butter and eggs for market, others were passing to and fro, while the children swarmed like bees on all sides of us, their chattering voices and merry laughter making the only music that is ever heard in that solitary homestead. The farmer took us round the farmyard to show us his pigs, poultry, and cattle; we seized an opportunity to remark upon his feminine household, and expressed a wonder that so many wives managed to get along without jarring.

"They've got too much work to do to think of quarrelling; besides, they're all in one boat, you know—no one has got a pull over the other; and so long as folks don't come spying around, putting rubbish into their heads, they will be content to live—for the glory of God."

CHAPTER XI.

AMONG THE MORMONS.

Society—A Mormon Wife's View—The Shops—Amelia Palace—The Tabernacle—The Organ—Endowment House—A Mormon Widow—Currency in the Old Days—The Elders Hold Forth.

URING our stay in Salt Lake City we found the Mormons most friendly and genial in their disposition towards us; but they do not like to talk of their religion; to the ladies especially the subject is distasteful; neither do they care to receive into their houses visitors from the Gentile world. They have been so vexed and annoyed by the indiscreet questions of curious tourists that they are disposed to shut their doors upon the whole race. Through the influence of some friends in England I made the acquaintance of a Mormon wife, who admitted me within her family circle, where I received advantages which are accorded to few strangers. She has travelled a great deal in Europe, but is now permanently settled in a beautiful house in the centre of the city; her mind has been enlarged and enlightened during her sojourn abroad, and, though still a good Mormon, she has withdrawn from polygamy and left her husband

in the full possession of three other wives; perhaps they suffice to absorb his conjugal affections. At her house I met some pleasant Mormon families. Gentlemen do not escort a battalion of wives to these social gatherings, but each accompanies the particular wife to whom he is for the time devoted. No favour must be shown; his affections must be weighed to a fraction, and divided equally between the several claimants thereto. The ladies were refined and pleasant enough; I cannot say much for the gentlemen. The Mormon men are genial and good-natured, but as a rule are coarse and sensual-looking, full of the physical strength and energies of healthy life; one cannot imagine a bad digestion or ill-regulated liver among them.

Everybody asked us "how we liked Salt Lake." That question being satisfactorily answered at least fifty times in the course of an hour, we talked and chatted in much the same fashion as the rest of the world would have done under similar circumstances. Knowing that the typical state of society here was utterly different to that in any other part of the world, we were in a vague state of expectation and excitement, and watched for some indication of it to come to the surface; we watched in vain. It was the same here as elsewhere. In general society all the world over, there is a frothy bubble of conversation carried on; little is said that is worth repeating, indeed that is worth saying. I received a good deal of local information, and was both amused and interested in the gossip that gradually grew into circulation. Late in the evening, while chatting more confidentially to a coterie of ladies, I tried to seize the helm, and without any actual breach of good breeding to steer the conversation towards matrimonial matters, but on that subject they were scrupulously silent. They were delighted to talk of their children; some, and they were young-looking matrons too, told me they had "fourteen blessings;" others who had not had time to produce such a growth of humanity seemed, however, to be doing their best to increase the population as fast as they could.

A woman is appreciated and respected according to the number of her children; those who have no family are merely tolerated or set aside as "no account." As a rule the childless wives live together under one roof, while those "more highly favoured of the Lord" have separate houses, and are more honourably regarded.

I visited one lady, the wife of a wealthy merchant, an English gentleman who had outraged his family connections and nailed his colours to the Mormon mast, though he had at no time indulged in the luxury of more than two wives, and at present has only one. Their residence is extremely beautiful; it is built in the fashion of an old-fashioned country house, with gabled roof and pointed windows, and stands in a large garden, beautifully laid out with rare shrubs and luxuriant flowers, a lovely home; the mistress thereof is a stately, noble-looking woman, with a grave earnest face, and eyes that seemed to be looking far away from this world into the next. There were two or three young children playing with their toys on the hearth-rug; some others were having a game at hide and seek, " whooping " in the garden. It seemed to me that a whole school had been let loose to enjoy a holiday.

"Surely," I exclaimed, "these children cannot *all* be yours?"

"They are, and they are not," she answered, "I have fourteen children; some are still in the nursery, some are out in the world. Those," she added, indicating a pair of toddlers on the hearthrug, "belong to my sister wife, who died about a year ago; but they are the same as mine; they know no difference. Our children were all born under one roof, and we have mothered them in turn."

"This must be an unusual state of affairs," I ventured to remark, "even in Salt Lake. I should hardly have thought it possible that two ladies could have lived happily together under such circumstances."

"Nevertheless it is true," she answered.

"But do you mean to say," I urged, "that you *never* feel any petty jealousies?"

"I do not say that," she said somewhat sharply. "We are none of us perfect, and are all liable to the evil influence of earthly passions; but when we feel weak and failing we pray to God to help us, and He does."

"You are a strange people," I could not help observing. "In no other place in the world could such a state of things exist."

"Because nowhere else would you have the same faith to support you."

"But would you desire your daughters to enter into a polygamous marriage?" I persisted.

"If I could choose," she answered gravely, "they should each be the one wife to a good husband; but that must be as God pleases. Whatever their destiny may be their religion will help them to bear it."

Evidently desiring to end the conversation, she invited us into the garden, showed us her greenhouse, and gathered us some flowers, and we took our leave, having spent a delightful afternoon.

"I am afraid I have been more inquisitorial than good breeding sanctions," I said apologetically; "but how can I gain any information unless I ask for it?"

"I am very glad to have seen you," she replied, with a cordial hand-shake, "though as a rule I do not care to receive strangers—so many come with no introductions and intrude upon our privacy, and ask us questions, and then circulate false reports about us. They seem to regard us as zoological curiosities; quite forgetting that our homes are as sacred to us as theirs are to them. We used to be very hospitable," she added, "but now we receive no one unless they are introduced to us as you have been."

The Mormons are very fond of theatricals and are great patrons of the drama. A good company there is sure to draw a good audience. The patriarchal days, when Brigham's large family formed the greater part of audience and actors too, are past; they have a commodious theatre, so far as size is concerned, but it is a square brick barn-like building to look at. The business streets are lined with shops, which are amply stocked with all necessary and some superfluous articles, but the windows are not what we call "dressed" to attract the passer-by, but are exhibited in a higgledy-piggledy sort of fashion; the owners sit behind their counters or lounge in the doorways reading the news, and think nothing of keeping you waiting while they finish reading a paragraph, and seem supremely indifferent whether you buy or not. A spirit of piety inspires their business transactions, a godly text being placed over the doorway, and sometimes being woven into the mat at your feet. They have a large co-operative store in the main street, with an inscription in large gold letters running along the top: "Holiness to the Lord." There is very little in the city that is architecturally worth looking at, with the exception, perhaps, of the Amelia Palace, which is a large and very elegant mansion, built in the modern villa style, with a great deal of ornamentation. It is reported that Brigham Young erected and presented this beautiful residence to his youngest and prettiest wife, favouring her so much above the rest; but this is indignantly denied by the Saints generally.

"Brigham" (whose name is held in great reverence among them) "had no favourite," they say. "The Amelia Palace, so called because she once stayed in it for a few days, was built expressly for the reception and entertainment of strangers and visitors of distinction, and for no other purpose." Unfortunately its promoter died a short time after its completion, and it seems to be a bone of contention among the Mormons, and looks as lonely and deserted as though it had been thrown into chancery. They are also building a new tabernacle for winter use, which has been some years in the course of erection, but will be finished now within a few months. It is built of white granite hewn from quarries in the State of Utah, and is being constructed in a highly ornamental and imposing style; it is to be used for all general services during the cold weather, owing to the great difficulty in warming the larger tabernacle, which stands a few hundred feet off. This far-famed structure strikes one as a huge monstrosity, a tumour of bricks and mortar rising on the face of the earth. It is a perfectly plain egg-shaped building, studded with heavy entrance doors all around; there is not the slighest attempt at ornamentation of any kind; it is a mass of ugliness; the inside is vast, dreary, and strikes one with a chill, as though entering a vault; it is 250 feet long and 80 feet high; its acoustic properties are wonderful—the voice of him who occupies the rostrum can be distinctly heard in the remotest corner of the building. If you whisper at one end your words are repeated aloud at the other, without being caught up and hunted through every crevice by ghostly mocking echoes. A gallery runs all around, supported by rows of thin, helpless-looking pillars. The seats in the body of the building are raised on sloping ground, like the pit of a theatre,—a wide expanse of empty benches, dreary and depressing to the wandering eye, which finds no pleasant spot to dwell upon. In the centre stands a fountain with four plaster-of-Paris lions *couchant*, poor, mangy-looking beasts at best. From the white plastered ceiling or dome, being concave perhaps it may be called so, hangs a gigantic star, hung round with artificial flowers and evergreen pendants, something like a monstrous jack-in-the-green turned upside down. The whole interior is gloomy and dark; I doubt if people could ever see to read their prayers. At one end of this huge barnlike building hangs an immense blue banner emblazoned with a golden beehive, which flaunts over the heads of the faithful. At the other end stands an organ, the largest in the world they say, and it may be so, for it is certainly immense. They are justly proud of it, for it is of home manufacture entirely, and was built precisely where it stands, under the supervision of an English convert named Ridges, and contains upwards of a thousand pipes, some of such a circumference you feel as though you could wander up and down them, and be lost in a world of music. Notwithstanding its immense size, it has not a single harsh or metallic sound; on the contrary, it is marvellously soft-toned; from the low flutelike wailing voice of the *vox humana* to the deep bass roll which stirs the air like a wave of melodious thunder, it has all the delicacy of the Æolian harp, with the strength and power of its thousand brazen voices. The case is of polished pine of elegant and simple design. All the wood, metal, and other material used was brought from the forests or mines of Utah. Sloping down from the organ towards the auditorium are semicircular rows of seats, for the elders and dignitaries of the Church. In the centre is a desk with a shabby blue sofa behind it; this was used by Brigham Young and his two chief councillors. Below this are the seats for the twelve apostles and for the choir, and benches where the elders may congregate to consult together. In front of all this combination stands a long narrow table, an altar perhaps it may be called, covered with a red cloth, whereon is arranged a gorgeous array of silver cups, of all shapes and sizes, as though prepared for an unlimited christening party or an everlasting service libation to some heathen deity rather than to a Christian God. Passing out from the tabernacle we glanced at the Endowment House, where many of their religious ceremonies are performed, and where, if rumour speaks truly, gross licentiousness is carried on under the sanction of the Church—where some ugly secrets and mysteries lie hidden, of which no one can speak and live. Across the road stands the president's office, and next to that the "Beehive House" of Brigham Young notoriety. It is a long, low-roofed, adobe building, railed in, a desolate-looking place where, in old days, some dozen of his wives were domiciled; it is now occupied by his widows—some of them. A high stone wall filled in with adobe incloses the president's residence and many other buildings, with arched gateways and heavy wooden gates; there is a double archway leading to some factories and stables, surmounted by a beehive in the grip of a monstrous eagle—an illustration of the Mormon faith in the cruel clutch of the Stars and Stripes. Close by is the school-house, first erected for the sole education of Brigham Young's family, which was large enough to fill it; it is now devoted to the benefit of the masses. The whole of these buildings are crowded together, and are generally surrounded by a high wall, which gives them a gloomy appearance, suggestive of an Eastern harem. There is, however, a wide difference between the Mohammedan and the Mormon—the two polygamic nations. Whereas the former keep their women in a state of slavery, idleness, and ignorance, the Mormons give their women every possible advantage of education, and permit, nay encourage, them to take their part in the world's work and in the management of affairs generally.

The Mormon marriage-vow reads "for time and eternity!" There are, however, forms of matrimony "for time" and "for eternity" alone, and the one may be contracted independently of the other. Thus, a man may, and frequently does, marry a widow "for time," under the obligation to hand her back to her deceased lord "for eternity." A woman may, by gracious permission of the head of the Church, seal herself in "celestial marriage" to any deceased saint she may elect to honour with her preference. Also, a marriage may be arranged by the living for the dead. I heard of a case wherein a widow, anxious lest her lord should feel lonely in the celestial spheres, shortly after her bereavement hastened to the Endowment House to seal to the beloved lost, not *one*, but *two* dear friends of hers. I inquired whether the two brides would not consider it a wasteful proceeding to bestow themselves on the dead? "Oh no," answered my informant gravely, "of course they were dead too."

This presented rather a ludicrous picture to my mind's eye; there is evidently no escape for the Mormon from the evils of this world, even though he flies into the next, where good Christians hope to find peace. I imagined the seraph's surprise, perhaps dismay, at finding two cherubs in full chase accredited claimants to his eternal affections, whether he would or not.

We paid a visit to President Taylor at his office, with an *arrière pensée* that he might present us to his wives, but he did not. He received us most courteously, and we spent a pleasant half-hour in the exchange of polite nothings; he pointed out to us the portraits of the brothers Smith, the founders of their faith, which hung upon the walls, but when we tried to bring about a discussion upon the Mormon faith, or the working of that faith upon the Mormon people, we ignominiously failed. He is a remarkably fine-looking man, about seventy, with a rather large loose mouth and cunning gray eyes, which look as though they would never let you see what was going on behind them.

In the old days before the railway reached them, when the city was first settled, indeed for long afterwards, there was no money in circulation, and the Mormons lived on a general exchange system. A facetious record of the time says: "A farmer wishes for a pair of shoes, gives a load of wood in exchange, and is straightway shod; he gives a calf for a pair of pantaloons; seven water-melons are paid for admission to the theatre. One man paid seventy-five cabbage per quarter for the teaching of his children. The dressmaker received for her services four squashes per day. The Church dues were settled in molasses. Two loads of pumpkins paid a subscription to the newspaper. A treatise on *Celestial Marriage* was bought for a load of gravel. And the cost of a bottle of soothing syrup for the baby was a bushel of string beans."

All this is changed now: there is plenty of gold and

silver in circulation, and the general exchange system, once universal, is now dead.

The matter of marriage is very simply conducted; if a man desires to make an addition to his family in the shape of a wife, he makes such desire known to the president of his Church with whose permission he proposes to her, she of course, as in all Christian countries, having the right to refuse or accept him. On the other hand, if a lady has any predilection for a certain gentleman, she is encouraged to make her preference known to him, her tender feeling being considered as a prompting of nature which ought to be obeyed.

We were anxious to hear the holding forth at the Tabernacle on Sunday morning, and went early to secure good seats. Slowly the auditorium, galleries and all, filled to overflowing, with a motley set of people who seemed to set worldly fashion at defiance. There were some elderly heads in corkscrew curls and poke bonnets, trimmed with sad-coloured ribbons or faded flowers; some of the coal-scuttle celebrity projecting till you only got a telescopic view of the faded face within it. As a rule they wore short scanty skirts and old-fashioned kerchiefs or shawls pinned across their breasts. Such a collection of antiquated millinery and quaint combination of colours it would have been difficult to find elsewhere. Here and there a pretty young face bloomed from an artistic arrangement of lace and flowers, as though the hand of a French milliner had dropped it from the skies. An occasional parody on the famous Devonshire hat loomed upon our sight. One or two were got up like fashion plates direct from press. It was a strange combination of the Old World and the New. Manhood was represented in a similar fashion. Some in top-boots, frieze jackets, and stubble head of hair, with gay-coloured bandannas round their throats. Others in misfitting suits hanging loosely on their ungainly limbs. There was a sprinkling of dandyism among them in frockcoats with flowers in their button-holes; but broadcloth and fine linen generally occupied seats near the organ, and were grouped around where the elders and priesthood were seated in great solemnity.

I was sorry to learn there was to be no general service on this Sabbath morning; four of the elders had just returned from Europe, and were to stand forth and give an account of themselves to the community. The service (for so I must call it for want of a better word) commenced with prayer, which seemed rather to carry an assurance of their own worthiness to the throne of grace than a supplication for its mercy; then the organ poured forth its volume of rich sounds, and the voices of the thousands present united in a grand old hymn, glorious to hear. That ended, a young elder, clean shaven and in funereal black, stood up in the rostrum, in front of the table, and held forth: "He had travelled under the guidance of a special providence" (he spoke as though it were a special train), "and claimed the thanks of the multitude for his safe return." Then commenced a tirade of self-glorification; not a word of supplication, of prayer, or praise fell from his lips; his moral attitude was one of exultant vanity, as though he and they had absorbed all piety, all virtue, and left not a grain for the hungry world outside. He talked a mass of irreverent twaddle, as though he were in the secrets of the Almighty Ruler of men; he communicated to those present the private information which he had received direct from heaven, "that that modern Babylon, that most foul and evil city of Great Britain, whence he had just returned, should be destroyed by the fire of God's wrath! Not one would be saved, not one, except those few brands which *he* had plucked from the burning" (those brands being represented by an awkward squad of ignorant humanity, who looked as if they had marched in the rear of civilization, and been covered with the dust from its trampling feet; indeed, they seem to have gathered together the scum of all nations to be cleansed and purified by the process of their patent piety!). He wound up his edifying discourse with the assurance "that *they*, and they *only*, the saints of the modern Zion, who were gathered in that sacred valley, could be saved! While flames of fury were licking up the rest of the world, *they* would be in glory singing with harps of gold in their hands;" indeed, he dealt out death and damnation to all the rest of the world, but grasped salvation as their special right. This assurance seemed to give general satisfaction, for the poor withered faces round me lighted up with a frenzied faith and rejoiced in their own election.

There was little more to be done in Salt Lake, only the springs to be visited, and they are neither of them a great distance from the city. The sulphur springs are about a mile from our hotel, the Walker House, and can be reached by horse cars by those who dislike walking. At these springs there are baths of all description, Turkish, Russian, hot-air, etc., beside the natural baths, which are lukewarm, and being of a sulphurous nature are very penetrating and delightfully refreshing, providing you do not stay in too long. The hot springs are the greatest wonder in the city; there is a small alcove in the limestone rocks, even with the surface of the ground; the water steams and bubbles up boiling hot, with a temperature of 200°! Eggs can be cooked therein ready for table in three minutes. Close by beyond the green meadows, is a beautiful sheet of water called "Hot Springs Lake," which is supposed to be fed by other hot springs beneath the surface; and strange to say, in spite of the temperature of the water, some excellent fish are to be found there.

Having conscientiously done our duty, so far as sightseeing was concerned, we bid adieu to Salt Lake City, the great social problem of to-day.

CHAPTER XII.

ACROSS THE SIERRAS.

Ogden Station—Bustling Bedtime—Boots—An Invasion—A Wedding Aboard—The American Desert—The Glorious Sierras—Cape Horn—Dutch Flats—"Here they are"—A Phantom City.

HE sun is setting. The skies, so beautifully blue an hour ago, are changed by some celestial alchemy to realms of gold. Pale sea-green banners float faintly hither and thither. For a moment we seem to get a glimpse of heaven "through its gates of gold." Slowly the pale yellow changes to a rich red hue, with a rapid mingling of amethyst and royal purple, like the jewelled mantle of some invisible king, with feathery plumes flying, and trains of brilliant cloudlets hurrying across the face of the heavens, as though some gorgeous festival was being held on high. Then the gray sombre clouds come gathering together, like heavy household troops at the close of a grand procession, and the brilliant scene is over. There is no long dreamy twilight in these regions. The sun does not "slowly sink to rest." It drops down in a blinking, lazy sort of way, as though it was tired of

shining so long in one place. Its fleecy flock of clouds surround it. We have scarcely time to behold its glory; even as we exclaim, "What a gorgeous sunset!" the gates of heaven are closed, and it is night, though a scattered colony of soft gray shadows still linger among the mountains.

We are at Ogden Station, waiting to resume our journey westward. The engine snorts, and spits, and whistles, and clanks its iron harness, in a hurry to be off. Lights are flashing hither and thither. The nervous man, hot, dusty, and with an agonized face, rushes after his baggage. He *will* keep an eye on it; he cannot be persuaded that the baggage-master's certificate is surety for its safety. He watches it swallowed up in the van, then with a sigh of relief returns, to begin a fresh hurry and worry about something else. We feel ourselves quite old, experienced travellers by this time, and have learned to take things easily. Our nervous friend cannot even eat his supper in peace ; he rushes out between every mouthful to make sure he is not left behind. Presently the conductor's well-known call, "All aboard, all aboard," greets our ears, and we leisurely walk out upon the platform. There stands the long line of "silver palace cars." (Query: Why "silver," when they are painted bright yellow?) We have left the rich, brown, sombre-hued Pullman cars of the Union Pacific, and are now about to resume our journey on the "Central Pacific," in cars of gold. An obliging official stands at the entrance of every carriage, and shows you to your special section, as courteously as you would be shown into the reception-room of a friend. The engine bell, which sounds to us like the voice of a friend, sends forth its monotonous "cling clang, cling clang," its brazen clangour grows faint and fainter, and is still. With a final rattle and a shriek we plunge into the night, the sparks, like fiery comets, flying from its smoky throat. We strain our eyes for a parting glance at the Wahsatch Mountains, glorious in their grand loveliness, and at the marvellous cañons and gorges which we know are yawning and opening their mysterious depths on either side of us. But they are wrapped in a weird shadowy twilight; we can only see their dim outline, and are left to imagine their darker depths as we fly past them. The thin crescent crown of the baby moon was visible a while ago, but it has gone now, and the stars come out—celestial shepherds keeping watch over their fleecy flocks on high. We know we are rushing along by the fishless waters of the green salt lake, but we look out upon a world of darkness; we shall see nothing till the morning, so turn our thoughts bedward.

Our car is still in a state of commotion, some people are so long settling down. There is a wiry-looking elderly lady in corkscrew curls, who seems as restless and lively as a summer flea. She bounces from one side of her section to the other, rummaging her satchel, then her valise, for something she can't find, fishes a vinaigrette from her lunch-basket, and with a grunt of satisfaction sits sniffing at it for a while; then hops up as though she had been suddenly pierced with needles, and begins setting things tidy. Her section overflows with tiny packages of all shapes and sizes. They will fall off the seat and roll into somebody else's section; she scrambles and dives after them, shaking and patting her property as though she had just rescued a rat from drowning. She is always losing something, and shaking herself to find it. Then came a general stir, the letting down of berths and making of beds. The gentlemen retired to the smoking room during the preparations for retiring. One by one the ladies disappear behind their curtains. Our restless friend vanishes into her berth with a bounce; her curtains bulge and flutter; at last, with a series of moans and mutterings she is still, but not silent, even in her sleep.

The gentlemen return with a creaking of boots and banging of doors. One by one they too disappear. One who is "fat and scant of breath" laboriously climbs into his berth and rolls into it like a worn-out hippopotamus; another climbs up with the agility of a cat; a third swings himself up as though he were performing an acrobatic exercise, then a pair of pantaloons dangle for a moment in the air and are suddenly drawn up by their owner, and all is peace. There is nothing left of mankind but his boots, standing in solemn array along the floor. Any one with an eye for character might have gained some knowledge from a study of these "boots." The spirit of their numerous owners seemed to cling to the uppers or linger about the soles. Here was a pair of spick and span patent leathers, suggestive of spotless linen and irreproachable character, with not a thought beyond etiquette and broadcloth. Others had a careless philosophical look, with uncompromising soles, tough uppers, with little or no attempt at shining, slightly worn down at the heels, and turned up at the toes. Some bulged out in suspicious places. Some looked as if they had tramped the world through; others as though they had trod on velvet.

We slept soundly, lulled by the monotonous swing of the cars, till about three o'clock in the morning, when there was a slight stir in our car, a gruff rumbling of masculine voices. The young lady in the opposite section was roused from her slumbers.

"Get up, miss, please," said the conductor; "a gentleman has just boarded the train and wants to speak to you."

"It is I, Agnes," said a manly voice; "make haste and dress yourself." There was a rustle and flutter behind the curtains.

"What is the matter? Is there anything wrong?" said the girl's voice in some alarm.

"Oh no; I rather think everything is pretty considerably right," was the assuring answer. "Be quick, there's a dear girl."

She made a hasty toilette, and the pair went out upon the platform to discuss their plans. A whisper flew round with the daylight that there was to be a wedding at the place where we were to stop for breakfast. This startling intelligence created a general interest. There was a whispering and a wondering of the why and the wherefore of this strange proceeding. The lovers were too much occupied with one another to make any communication even had they been disposed to do so. The lady was coy; she hesitated. The idea of a wedding without orange blossoms, bridesmaids, or even a slice of wedding cake! But the bridegroom elect sternly whispered:

"Now or never." From the brief scraps of conversation which fell to our ears we gathered the simple fact that the engagement was a clandestine one, and was disapproved of by their mutual friends, who were awaiting the arrival of the lady at "Sacramento." Once under their influence they would contrive to break it off, and put an end to it. The gentleman got an inkling of this, and prepared to frustrate their diabolical purpose. He had travelled with all speed to ——, secured the services of the judge, and left him waiting there while he came on to meet and prepare the lady. While we were quietly taking our coffee and eggs those two were made one. A great deal of handshaking and good wishes passed round.

"All aboard, all aboard," came the familiar cry. The newly married couple were driven off in an old ramshackle chaise, the best the place afforded, in the direction of the Black Hills. We had no old shoes to throw after them "for luck," but somebody routed out a baby's worsted sock and flung it straight into the bride's lap, and they drove off amid chatter and laughter and a world of good wishes.

We wake up in the morning and find ourselves speeding along the great American desert, a wide expanse of desolation covered with tiny gray-green buffalo grass, only there are no buffaloes now to eat it. It is devoured by meaner animals. Looking through our glasses, we see what looks like an army of animated ant-hills. We are told they are immense herds of cattle, thousands strong, who are sent up there to get their own living some months of the year, and then descend to the valleys as fat as butter, a mine of wealth to their owners. The earth is slightly covered with snow, and looks as though it had been sprinkled with salt and put in pickle. All is blank and bare; there are no more architectural wonders of the great unknown, no more ruined castles and towers standing solemnly in the silent air. Hour after hour the earth flies beneath the hoofs of our iron horse. We are not sorry when the night comes and shuts this desolation from our sight, for the day has been a long and a dreary one, and we retire early to rest.

We go to sleep in the dismal, snow-covered heights of Nevada, and wake in the glorious, pine-clad forests among the foot-hills of the grand Sierras, having passed their summit during the night. There is no more glorious sight in the whole wide world than this which now opens upon our view. We hold our breath, awe-struck and wondering, as we swing round the shoulder of the mountain and plunge down its rugged sides. We feel as though we were rushing through the air. There is nothing but this narrow trestle between us and the boiling caldron a hundred feet below. We lift our heads and look up at the wonderfully wooded heights, where the pointed pines seem to prick the skies, and down to the deep valleys below, winding through sunless gorges till they are lost in narrow cañons where the foot of man has never ventured yet, and where the grizzly still finds his home undisturbed. All the picturesque beauty and solemn grandeur of the wide world seems to be gathered together here in this noble range of the Sierra Nevadas, covered with all the luxuriance of summer's divinest bloom—a kind of spiritual sunshine, falling straight from heaven on lake and river, gorge and cañon, covering and glorifying all. A beautiful purple mist lies in a dreamy softness everywhere. We dash round sudden curves and up grade and down grade, new and picturesque beauties opening on all sides of us. There is a general stir. "We are nearing Cape Horn," cries somebody, and in another moment we are speeding round a sharp curve, rushing along the face of the mountain, clinging to the narrow ledge of rock. Our engine itself seems dizzy as it swings us round with a shriek and a rattle, looking down two thousand feet upon the boiling river below. Soon the scene grows more magnificent still, the views more vast and extensive; the wonderful chasms are frightful to behold; the mountains open into wide galleries of rocks and boulders, stretching out and upward till they are lost in a world of pines and peaks of ice and snow. All the Kohinoors that were ever dug out of the bosom of the earth are poor and pale before these diamond peaks now flashing in the sunlight. We would like to stop the train, and get out and wander up into these forest mountains and down into the glens, and dabble in the sparkling waters, so pure and bright they might be flowing direct from the throne of the Almighty God, but we are, perforce, carried on. We pass the mining districts of Dutch Flats, where hydraulic operations were once extensively carried on, and have broken up and ravaged the country round, damaged its fair face in the greed for gold, and left but bare and ragged mountain-sides, whose gaping wounds are slowly healing and are being gradually covered by nature's tender green. We can still trace where the immense body of water has been hurled against the mountain and torn down hundreds of tons of earth and stone, and sand and gold, which were all flung down and caught in a series of iron sieves or gratings, some charged with quicksilver to attract the smaller grains of gold which escaped the sifting process.

This part of the scenery is interesting from its association with the old, dead days, when the solitude rang with the rush and din of thousands, all hurrying and jostling one another in their search for gold. The tumble-down ruins of the miners' huts are still clinging to the edge of the water or at the foot of the broken mountain, like a weird memory lingering in the haunts of old.

We sat silent now, enjoying the genial air. On our first view of these glorious Sierras we had run the gamut of our unbounded and rapturous delight; we had pointed out our phrases with big notes of mental admiration; we wanted a new coinage of words before we could express ourselves. We had grown tired of the old phrases,—for the time, at least,—so we sat in silence, letting our eyes rest and our thoughts revel on the scenes we were passing through.

Presently our engine-bell began its monotonous "cling clang," and we steamed into the station of Sacramento; and there, on a table running along the whole length of the platform, an excellent lunch was served. Tea and coffee, chicken-salad, ham and eggs, and no end of fruits and flowers, were most temptingly laid out; and here we gained our first glimpse of the moon-faced, almond-eyed Chinese officiating as waiters—clean, quick, and obliging.

Having supplied ourselves with all we required, we asked of our attentive Celestial—

"How much to pay?"

"Two bittee," he answered, smiling.

I inquired again, emphasizing my words. The same answer, with an additional grin. Then, speaking slowly, severely, in a louder tone, looking sternly in his face, I repeated, pausing between each word—

"I—want—to—pay."

"Two bittee," he answered, grinning from ear to ear, and looking so pleased with himself that I felt inclined to laugh too.

"Twenty-five cents," explained a gentleman at my elbow. "They count in bits here, and two bits is twenty-five cents."

By this time I had noticed two gentlemen and a lady searching eagerly among the passengers, evidently for somebody they could not find. Having scanned all the faces assembled on the platform, they wandered from one end of the empty cars to the other. Then held a brief consultation together.

"So very strange," I heard one say. "She certainly started from Chicago. We'd better telegraph."

I fancy they are searching for the bride. They will search long before they find her. She is far away, up in the Black Hills by this time. But nobody attempts to put the clue in the hands of her seekers.

After a stop of twenty minutes we resumed our way in very jubilant spirits. We knew we were nearing our journey's end. We passed through the beautiful Valley of

Sacramento, all abloom with fruits and flowers and aglow with the glorious sunshine. We took in every feature of the landscape, though we were watching eagerly the while, and looking forward to the first glimpse of the Golden City. We gathered our things together, then commenced to smarten ourselves up to make a decent appearance in the face of the New World. In another hour we shall be there. We make a few minutes' halt at San Pablo, and are just putting a few finishing touches to our toilette, when "Here they are!" cries a familiar voice. We look up, and there is the well-known face of an old friend, come out from the strange world to greet us. And how glad we are to be so greeted! There is a good deal of laughter, an exchange of gossip from the Old World to the New. We speed through the streets of Oakland, our bell "ding-donging" to warn the people out of our way. There are shops and houses on either side; people are flocking to and fro on the sidewalks, buying and selling, some lounging lazily gossiping over the garden gates among the tall hollyhocks and big tuberose trees. They glance indifferently at us as we rush along, as though it was quite a common thing for people to come three thousand miles over desert and mountain to visit their wonderland. We pull up at Oakland Ferry, having been for the last ten minutes skimming over the face of the water on an invisible trestlework. Here again, familiar faces, with their hands full of flowers and their hearts with welcome, were there to meet us and escort us across the bay in loyal numbers. It is eight miles across the bay to San Francisco, and the ferry-boats are like floating palaces, with velvet lounges, gorgeous in carving and gilding, with a painted ceiling, giving views of the surrounding neighbourhood, and mirrors on all sides, reflecting and multiplying you in such numbers that you cannot get away from yourself. You come face to face with your own ghost whichever way you turn. The sea-breeze coming to us, salt laden, through the Golden Gate, is delicious, and stirs our blood, and sends it leaping madly through our veins. Sister boats pass and repass us on the way, and more important vessels, with the Stars and Stripes or flags of many nations fluttering from their mastheads, are gathered in crowds in the beautiful bay, and, as they are riding at anchor, dip and courtesy as we pass. Thousands of shrieking seagulls swoop down, throw up their heads, and, dipping their white breasts in the water, float upon its surface as proudly and almost as gracefully as baby swans. We all crowd up to the bow of the vessel. In vain our friends point out the different rocks and islands which stud the bay, and the long, curving line of the distant shore. We have no eyes, no thought for anything but San Francisco. That is our Mecca—the shrine whereon we are prepared to lay our heart's devotion.

The sun is setting, and the whole of the Western hemisphere is draped with crimson clouds slashed with flames of purple light, and, slowly looming from their midst, the Golden City breaks upon our sight. We cannot distinctly distinguish a single feature. The palace-houses which crown the hill-top, church steeples and spires, are all hidden and shrouded in purple mist, which rolls down the steep streets, spreads everywhere, and covers everything with a soft, sweet mystery, and we only see, or seem to see, a wide, extensive range of buttressed, battlemented castles—a ruined castellated world. And so we catch our first view of San Francisco, like a phantom city lying in the arms of the sunset.

CHAPTER XIII.

THE GOLDEN CITY.

The Streets—Kaleidoscopic Scenes—The Stock Boards—Wild Cat—Bulls and Bears—The Markets—The "Dummy"—Lone Mountain.

E pass through a deafening crowd of hackmen, who are ranged on either side of the landing-stage, and a posse of hotel porters, each in a monotonous sing-song calling the name of his hotel. To all insinuating invitations we sternly answer "Occidental," and are allowed to pass without further let or hindrance. We find our comfortable hotel coach waiting, and jolt and rumble through the stony Market Street. We see nothing but throngs of people, flaring gas-jets, and lighted shop-windows, and in a few minutes are deposited at the door of the Occidental, a strange sound to us then, but soon to become familiar as a household word.

A cosy suite of rooms had been prepared for us, and here again friendly hands had filled our room with flowers, giving us a most sweet floral welcome to California.

On this, our very first evening in San Francisco, friends we have not seen for years come rallying round us; their bright, familiar faces and pleasant voices ringing out a kindly welcome, bring back a glimpse of the old land and the old scenes wherein we had all played our part in the dear long ago. For a moment I only see their faces through a mist, but the mist is in my own eyes. Everybody is anxious to come to the fore and escort us on our first tour round their Golden City.

The next morning early we sallied forth to get our first general view of San Francisco, as we like to familiarize ourselves with the face of a friend before we criticise his features or attempt to discuss his character. Our hotel is situated in—or, as we may say here, *on*—Montgomery Street, one of the busiest portions of the city. There are some notably handsome jeweller's and other shops; but by far the greater number, both there and on the lower part of California Street, are public notaries, bill-brokers, stock-brokers, attorneys, and mining agents; in fact, every facility for financial ruin yawns on all sides of you. There is a tempting restaurant sandwiched in here and there, or you may descend into a kind of cellar and take your refreshments comfortably underground. There are, besides, numerous barbers' shops, as no American, East or West, will shave an inch of his own chin; and open spaces where gentlemen lounge on velvet chairs and read the news while their boots are having "a shine for five cents," for here, as in other parts of America, you must clean your own boots and shoes or go out and have a public "shine for five cents." The shoeblack's being a strictly outdoor industry forms no part of anybody's domestic duty.

There is a general rush and flow of mankind through this busy street, the Exchange being situated hereon. The moment its doors are open everybody seems to be flocking up or hurrying down the steps. There is an endless stir and passing to and fro. They gather in crowds upon the sidewalks, swarm at the street corners, and surge into the roadways. Curbstone brokers, the ragged fringe of the stockboards, lie in wait everywhere, like spiders, waiting to catch some silly, inexperienced fly in their financial web of fine promises. There are men of all kinds and all nations, a kaleidoscopic company of Jews and Christians, Orientals of divers degrees, even South Sea Islanders washed up from the shores of the Pacific, the grim-visaged Tartar chief, and foreigners from all parts of the civilized world make up the incongruous gathering, all babbling together, creating a very Babel and confusion of tongues. You may hear men grumble in guttural German; swear in high Dutch; insinuate in soft, mellifluous Italian or musical Greek; and, indeed, bargain, wrangle, and chat in every language under the sun. The spirit of speculation is in the air; its subtle influence stirs the very centre of life; everybody speculates; everybody has "something in stocks;" the poorest servant girl, the hard-working mechanic, with the rest of the labouring population, invest their little all in stocks. You may see their eager faces crowding round the windows where the rise and fall in stocks is exhibited every hour. Millions of dollars are floating about in investments in worthless mines, which will never yield an ounce of gold. Well, the stocks are up to-day, down to-morrow; the fever is in the blood of the people; they will drain their pockets, sell their clothes off their back, the home that shelters them, the very land they live by, all in the race for wealth. So long as they have a cent or "wild cat" is to be got in the market, they'll have it. Well, somebody grows rich. Somebody rides on the great third wave, though thousands sink beneath it and are lost.

I, like the rest of the world, fell into the gilded snare, and with one of my too confiding friends, was induced to take a hand at this game of speculation. Silently and secretely we matrons laid our plans, letting not our right hand know what our left was doing. We had reason to believe that a certain mine would disgorge heaps of gold within the next two weeks; shares were low at the present time, but as soon as gold came to the surface, they would double, treble, nay quadruple, in a single day—perhaps rise from five to a hundred dollars per share! In a frenzy of gold 'fever we rushed off to a stockbroker's office, and invested all our ready cash, even to our last dollar, in that promising stock. We turned our faces homeward, beggars in the present, millionaires in the future. We seemed to tread on air, and sent our thoughts flying through the realms of imagination, building castles in the air, and making glorious plans for the future; we felt as though we already held that El Dorado in our pockets, and disposed of it, each in our own fashion. My friend chose a lovely spot, overlooking the bay and the green hills beyond, and announced her intention of building a house there, and presenting it to her liege lord on the next anniversary of their wedding day; she decided on the kind of wall-paper, the particular dado, and even on the style of furniture, which was to be selected on purely Art principles. My ideas were equally magnificent, though my plans were more indefinite, and certainly did not run in the house-building line. For two weeks the one golden idea possessed our minds; every morning we watched eagerly for news. At last it came. The miners had reached the expected spot, and struck—not gold, but water! Our hopes were washed away, our expectations drowned in a sea of repentance.

But this is a digression. To return to our first day's experience. While we were jostling our way through the bustling streets of San Francisco's business quarter, staring on all sides with all our eyes, and, like *Chowder* seeming "to want another pair," some one of our party proposed a visit to the Stock Boards, it being just about the time when the financial hounds would be in full cry, and the "bulls" and "bears" tossing and tumbling among the stocks, sending them up or pulling them down in the wildest fashion. To "bull" is to send up the stocks; to "bear" is to pull them down.

We were ushered into a gallery overlooking the scene of operations; directly in front of us was a platform; two or three men were writing at different tables, and, at one in the centre of the platform, stood a stout, stolid-looking individual with a small bell beside him; below, seated in circular rows rising from the floor of the building, were the shareholders in the different mines, watching, with anxious faces, the financial fight. In the railed-in centre, which was something like the old gladiatorial arena, the stockbrokers themselves held the floor. There was a momentary lull as we entered; it was the close of the first session. Every face was turned towards the platform, waiting till the sphinx should speak. A few hurriedly uttered words from the stolid individual above alluded to —and such a commotion! A deafening roar of voices, pitched in a hundred different keys, clattering and clanging one against the other! A sea of excited faces, eyes flashing, arms tossing wildly, fingers flung out and snapping in each other's faces, a struggle, a rush, a swaying to and fro of the crowd, which seemed wedged into a solid mass! It seemed as though a sudden, go-as-you-please free fight was going on. We fancied they never could emerge whole from the conflict; their clothes must be torn from their backs, their limbs from their sockets. One stroke on the bell, and, as though by a magic touch, all is still—all silent. In that few minutes' commotion fortunes have been lost and won.

The clerk, in a monotonous, sing-song tone and rapid utterance, goes over the amount of business transacted. Strange it seemed to us, that out of that "confusion worse confounded," that tangled skein of words and babel of sounds, he extracted the clear argument, drew out each particular thread, and reiterated the quotations of stocks and by whom they had been bought or sold, never in a single instance making a mistake. Through all that din and confusion of tongues it had been plain sailing to him. The "bulls" had it to-day, the "bears" would have their turn to-morrow. So the world goes round.

Next we strolled up Kearney, the Bond or Regent Street of San Francisco. It is a very handsome street in the most fashionable quarter of the town, with elegant, tastefully arranged shops on either side. It is quite the fashionable promenade on Saturday afternoons. All the *élite* of the city, elegantly dressed women (the San Francisco ladies do dress elegantly, though sometimes with a daring combination of colours that are somewhat disconcerting to the æsthetic taste), and men in broadcloth and beaver, turn out like soldiers on parade, and lounge up and down. Friends and acquaintances congregate together and hold their receptions on Kearney Street. It is quite a kaleidoscopic scene of bright dresses and pretty, smiling faces. The dusty business men, in their cutaway coats and slouch hats, keep to their own quarters in Montgomery Street, hard by, and seldom venture to intrude on dainty Kearney Street. But, alas! there is a blot on this bright picture. There are sundry open alcoves, cigar and tobacco stores, pretty and pleasant enough to look at, for they are gay with gilding and mirrors and bright with flowers, but there is generally a crowd of the tobacco-chewing population congregated here, and the sidewalk is in such a disgusting condition from this chewing and smoking that it is impossible for a lady to pass without gathering up her skirts, and even then she runs the risk of having a quid squirted over her as she passes along. All over America, more or less, this evil habit obtains, and everywhere with the same revolting effect. It is, however, much worse in the Western cities than in the Eastern States. In New York, especially, they seem to be awakening to the error of their way, and expectorate less frequently in the presence of ladies. It is even possible to ride for an hour in a car without being disgusted once. But here in the West the vice rides rampant. It is impossible to escape from it. In the streets, in the cars, on the railway trains—it follows you everywhere, wherever men (I was going to say gentlemen, and some are so far as the tailor can make them) are travelling to and fro. This state of things would not be allowed in any other city in the civilized world, and it might be easily remedied if the authorities would take the matter in hand as they do in the case of other nuisances, which may be more serious, but are far less disgusting. On all the ferryboats there is a placard: "Gentlemen are requested not to spit about the deck; it is used by ladies." And they don't. The floor of the deck is as clean as a drawing-room. Why should not the same rule hold elsewhere?

We stroll through the markets, and wonder where the mountains of fruit and beautiful flowers have come from, and where they are going to. Such heaps of luscious peaches, plums, and nectarines, bushels of rich, ripe strawberries, raspberries, blue and green grapes, melons and oranges, and red and gold bananas, and vegetables of every possible description in tons and scores of tons piled on all sides. Nothing wilted or stale; all fresh, and crisp, and green. Everything is in such royal profusion it seems as though nature had opened her heart and showered her best and fairest flowers throughout this Golden State. Provisions of every kind are to be found in these markets, of which there are several, and all in populous places, easy of access. Dairy farmers send their golden butter, plump chickens, and boxes of white, fresh eggs; and long-legged fowls, prairie hens, and a whole tribe of feathered favourites hang like malefactors suspended overhead; and dainty white pigs, with lemons in their mouths, tails curled up and tied with pink ribbons, and pigs that had outgrown the lemon period, and were waiting to be turned to bacon, and silver trout and salmon,—such rich, luscious-looking salmon,—with their scaly armour glittering in the light, and big-whiskered lobsters, prawns, and crawling crabs, all opening their formidable mouths and stirring their hundred feelers in protest against their unnatural usage. Every crustaceous delicacy the sea affords is there, all ready to tempt the appetite of omnivorous man. Everything was refreshing and pleasant to the eye, and so artistically arranged that we looked round on a perfect mosaic of beauty, a kind of poem, not made up of similes, rhymes, and rhythms, but of fruits and flowers.

The streets of San Francisco are a wonder and a marvel. On every side there is an ever-changing, animated scene, unenlivened by organ-grinders, dancing dogs, or Punch and Judys. The industrious fleas or the intelligent canaries are all equally unknown here. The attraction of the streets is entirely due to the polygot gatherings of people from all lands, and the variegated tide is eternally flowing to and fro. Strange vehicles of all indescribable descriptions are dashing about the up-and-down stony streets at a breakneck pace. Clattering milk carts, travelling soda fountains, brewers' drays, sociable rockaways, and solitary "sulkies," their owners perched up between the spidery wheels, seemingly seated on nothing, are all rushing along pell-mell, helter-skelter. The streets are a perfect network of rails, and huge red cars, blue cars, and yellow cars, with their jingling bells, cross and recross at every turn. We look out for a collision, but none comes, and we elbow our way on. We are jostled on one side by a Polish Israelite, in whom there "is no guile," with a long beard and high peaked hat. A moon-faced Mexican, with long hair, golden earrings, and red serape, walks in his shadow. A slipshod woman, in a grimy Oriental dress, flits past and disappears in a dark alley. A South Sea islander, a New Zealand chief, and a Mongolian merchant catch our eyes among the surging mass of European faces, and the blue-bloused, pig-tailed Chinaman, with his gliding, silent tread, swarms everywhere. He is always busy, always at work, carrying such weights as would set a donkey staggering. He has a long, hickory pole across one shoulder, and balancing at either end are huge round baskets filled with goods of all descriptions, enough to fill a waggon, but John carriest he weight easily enough. At the corner of California Street we come to a dead stop. There stands a kind of double vehicle, the foremost part being open, with a canopied top, seats running all round, and a man in the middle keeping solemn guard over a huge lever or crank. On the benches on either side were seated some half-dozen people, facing outwards, their feet dangling or resting on a narrow plank at their pleasure. We took our places on the front seat, faces set forward ; a pretty balcony or wire lace-work ran in front of us breast high. The hind part was a common omnibus car, such as we are used to see all the world over. What magic would set the whole in motion ? Of course we were going somewhere. There were no horses, no engine, no visible means of propelling us forward. A newly arrived Mongolian, seeing this strange vehicle for the first time, eyed it curiously, "No pushee, no pullee, no horsee, no steamee; Melican man heap smart." At the sound of a bell the man turns the crank and off we go, flying in the face of the wind at the rate of ten miles an hour. We charge up one steep hill, then dash down, and up another, and so on for about four miles. Never was such a delicious breeze, such a flow of fresh, invigorating air. Long lines of elegant houses, some of distinguished architectural grandeur, with stately palms lifting their grand, green heads like sentinels on either side of the entrance doors, or rising from the smooth-shaven lawns embroidered with flowers of brilliant hues, fly past us on either side, their peaks and gables silhouetted against the bright blue skies. Streets and alleys, some wide, some narrow, diverge and radiate from either side of us. And through this vista of quaint habitations, of all sorts and sizes, we get such delicious bits of harbour and river scenery as would have delighted an artist's soul. On we go, till we lose sight of sea and river, and the whole city unrolls itself beneath our feet, sliding down from its hundred hills, spreading in picturesque and panoramic beauty on all sides of us, till it is lost in the amethyst haze beyond. Whirled through the air by our invisible steeds, we look down upon church spires and steeples, massive towers and palace houses, on miles of streets, green squares, and blooming gardens, which Eve herself might have revelled in and dreamed of her paradise regained. With cheeks aglow, and spirits buoyant with the delight of our magic journey, we reached the foot of

Lone Mountain. Before we left our strange vehicle, called by the natives "the dummy," we ascertained something of its mysterious engineering. It is of similar construction to that in use for a time on the old Blackwall railway at home, being propelled by an underground cable, which runs along the centre of the road between the regular track rails, and the hidden underground force is controlled by the crank, deftly handled by the official who stands in the middle of our "dummy."

We are at the foot of Lone Mountain, towering high among the surrounding hills, with the holy cross planted on the top. It is the loveliest grave-garden in the world; not an echo reaches it from the busy, bustling city below. Surrounded by wild, widespreading uplands and undulating sandhills, barren, and soft, and gray, with the boom of the Pacific waves thundering among the low foothills, it stands in isolated solitude, this beautiful city of the dead. There are no grim head and footstones, no tons of monumental marble crushing down upon the helpless dead, enough to give a ghost the nightmare to think of its poor body being buried under it. Here the dead are really laid to rest in a veritable flower-garden. The ground is arranged in plots, varying from twelve to thirty feet square, and each plot is owned by one family, who decorate it according to their own fancy. Every family grave-garden is surrounded by a low, light fence, and is entered through a rustic gate, and is laid out with narrow, neatly gravelled paths, a foot wide, and borders and flower-beds, some filled with beautiful roses, some a mass of purple and white violets, others with different kinds of sweet-smelling flowers of bright and variegated hues. Everything is kept in perfect order; not a weed is to be seen. Opposite the entrance-gate is a small slab chronicling the name of the dead below. It is sometimes so hidden by the luxuriant growth of evergreens and flowers that you have to search to find it.

Here, in the fragrant and peaceful shade of this fair garden, the old pioneers, the heroes of the strange days of '49, the storm of their turbulent lives over, the battle fought, the victory won—or lost! lie at rest.

CHAPTER XIV.

THE OLD MISSION.

The Windmills—The Golden Gate Park—The Seal Rock—The Cliff House—The Mission Dolores.

ALEXANDER wanted more worlds to conquer. If Don Quixote had sought for more windmills on a general tilting-ground, he would have found them here. They are everywhere. We wonder what they are all doing. It is so unusual to see such a world of windmills in a large city. Looking round from California Street hills we see scores of them; they come upon us, one after the other, till we forget to count them. They are of all sorts and all sizes; some short and stumpy, with fat arms, wheezing laboriously as the wind sends them around, as though they were working against their will; others are tall and lanky, their long, gaunt arms whizzing and whirring through the air, always hard at work except when the wind is still, and that is not often; they are painted all the colours of the rainbow, and look quite gay flashing round in the sunshine. Every house of the slightest pretensions has a well and waterworks on its own premises; the windmill stands sentinel above them, and sends the fresh cool stream through the leaden arteries of the household, and irrigates and refreshes the land when no rain is falling and the summer sun tries to burn the green verdure to tinder, for this is a rainless land for six months of the year. During summer not a drop falls to moisten the parched face of the earth. Everything is done by artificial irrigation.

We soon leave the city and its windmills behind us, and enter the Golden Gate Park, where, a few years ago, the Pacific waves were rolling; but these hundreds of acres have been reclaimed from the sea, and are planted with rare shrubs, young trees, evergreens, and blooming flowers. It is tastefully laid out, a landscape garden and park in one; there are picturesque winding paths and shady nooks and corners where you can hide from the sun's searching rays, and, while you listen to the singing birds overhead, hear the boom of the breakers on the shore below. We pass through this paradise of green and reach a silent sea of yellow sandhills, smooth and soft as velvet, billowing round in graceful, undulating waves as far as the eye can reach; there is a sudden curve, and the wide Pacific Sea, in all its glory, lies before us clothed in the sunshine, its white foam lips kissing the golden shore; its long, level line stretched against the distant skies. We drove down to it; nay, drove into it, and watched its tiny waves dimpling into a thousand welcomes beneath our wheels. The sun and the sea conspired together to fill the air with bright beams and balmy breezes. We felt the soft spray blowing in our faces, stirring our blood, and setting our cheeks aglow, and, as we breathed the crisp, soft air, laden with three thousand miles of iodine, we seemed to be taking a draught of the elixir of life. The full fascination of the sea seized our senses; we could not tear ourselves away. Presently, mingling with the monotonous moaning of the waves, we heard a sound like the barking of a kennel of dogs. Before us, rising out of the sea about a hundred yards from the shore, was a picturesque mass of broken crags known as the famous Seal Rocks, whereon thousands of those sensible creatures, from the soft seal baby to the barnacled old patriarch, lay basking in the sunshine, barking their satisfaction aloud, floundering about, rollicking and rolling one over the other, and splashing into the sea, while some stood solemnly on end watching the fun. Standing just above, on a steep, rocky eminence which rises abruptly from the shore, stands the Cliff House, where an excellent table is always spread for those who choose to partake of the good things thereon. It is a favourite resort of the good folk of San Francisco; they turn their backs upon the noise and bustle of the city and enjoy here perfect solitude; they can descend from the piazza some fifty rugged steps, and stroll along the wild seashore, undisturbed except by the shriek of the sea-gull and the barking of the seal colony mingling with the soughing of the wind, and the low, sullen roar of the waves; or saunter up and down the piazza, sipping their coffee or smoking the beloved weed, and watch the great, red sun sink like a ball of fire, and drown itself in the Pacific Sea.

On our way home we passed the old Mission; at least, all that is left of it, which is not much—the mere remnants of some redwood houses and the ancient church, a quaint-looking, low-roofed home of desolation, with its adobe walls of sunbaked clay about four feet thick, which promise to withstand the encroaches of time a century longer. A chime of three bells still hangs in three square portholes; their long tongues, red with rust, droop dumb and motionless from their silent mouths. Only a hundred years ago they were brought from Castile, blessed by the holy fathers, and brought here to the edge of the wild Western world to ring out and summon the heathen and the wanderer to worship the one true God. You enter the ruined church through a low, arched doorway. The broken font is still there, but the last drop of holy water was spilled from it long ago. The mullioned windows are of a quaint, fanlike shape, and the genial sun tries to pierce through the grime and dust and send its beams dancing over the crumbled ruin within. The painted wooden shrines of St. Joseph and St. Francis (who gave the settlement of Yerba Buena the name of San Francisco) are still there. Near by are the Madonna and Child, but the paint has worn off, and they are all discoloured and stained with the damp wind and the rain which drips, in the rainy season, from the dilapidated roof. The crumbling decorations, though they are of a rough, rude workmanship, still bear the stamp of artistic design, though crudely executed by unaccustomed hands, who laboured for the love of God. It is about a hundred feet from the threshold to the altar. Give reins to your imagination, set it galloping back a hundred years, and see the priests, the white nuns, and hooded friars clustered round the empty altar busy in the service of the Lord; the aisles filled with kneeling Indians, who know little of the faith they have adopted except that there is an unknown God somewhere who makes their corn grow, watches over their lives here, with a promise of a life hereafter; men from Mexico, Peru, and Spain, and wanderers from all along the wild Pacific coast are standing reverently round; censers are swinging, lights are burning, and a choir of voices chant the Ave Marias. A Christian host gathered in that wilderness by the sea. Where are they all now? Vanished like the children of a dream.

A mouldy, funereal odour clings about the ruined walls, and we are glad to step out into the little graveyard outside, where the English hawthorn and white winter roses are blooming and the grass growing rich and luxuriant above the moss-grown graves. Whole tribes of Indians lie buried in the dust beneath our feet. There is no more desolate spot in the world than a disused graveyard. We read strange unfamiliar names upon the broken, half-buried stones, and crumbling urns, dilapidated angels, and crippled cherubs are tottering round us. Here and there we decipher an English name, and, beneath, the information: "Died by the hands of the V. C.;" "In mercy we slay the enemies of the Lord." The V. C. means the Vigilance Committee, who, in the early, lawless days, executed justice swift and sure upon proven criminals. The strict justice of their decisions was never called in question. A certain number of men of known integrity were invested with supreme power of life or death, and the guilt of a man being once fully assured he had a brief trial and swift execution. There was no legal quibbling, which often lets loose some atrocious criminal to prey upon the world again until, at the end, he is launched out of it. Near the low, arched gateway stands the dilapidated figure of a woman, her sightless eyes and lifted hands pointing upwards—mute significance of one hope for all the miscellaneous dead.

A fresh breeze was blowing outside, but here it seemed to hang heavy and still, laden with the damp odour of mouldering graves, which mingled with and destroyed the sweet scent of the flowers that are flourishing so luxuriantly above the dead. This was the first we had seen of the many remnants of the old mission days, when the Spanish fathers first came to the wilderness to sow the good seed and reap the harvest in their Lord's name. About the year 1820 the missions began to decay, the soldiers were recalled from the Presidio, where they had been stationed for the protection of the friars and their property, and from that time the missions dwindled, till the fathers were recalled to Spain. They carried with them all their cattle and movable goods, and left their buildings to decay. These are scattered throughout the State of California, wherever the fathers held temporary sway. Still, though they and their labours have passed away, and are well-nigh forgotten, they have left their traces behind them : throughout the country we find the old Spanish names still clinging to the soil, such as Santa Clara, Santa Rosa, Santa Barbara, San Rafael, San Jose, Los Angeles, Monterey, Carmelo, etc. Mr. John S. Hittell, in his " History of California," has given a most interesting and graphic account of these missions, their people, their work, and their effect upon the country from their first establishment to their decline.

The city has grown out of the wilderness, and crowded so close to the crumbling walls of the ruined mission that as we leave the gloomy precincts we step out into the populous streets, which are full of hurry, bustle, and vigorous young life. It is like stepping from the old century into the new. Gaily painted cars and omnibuses are dashing up and down the wide Mission Street, each following the other so quickly that before you can step into one another is on its heels.

As we rattle up one street and down another we cannot help noticing the scarcity of shady trees in all parts of San Francisco. People take great pride in their beautiful flowers, their smooth velvet lawns, and stately palms, which lift their crowned heads on high, their broad leaves drooping like blessing hands over the household; but never a shady tree is planted anywhere.

Although the blissful shade, so highly prized and so eagerly sought for in other lands, may not be desirable here, where people literally live in the sunshine, yet we feel that the planting of rows of leafy, green trees on either side of the streets would turn them at once into magnificent boulevards. They could still walk in the sunshine, but the luxuriant green would be refreshing to the eye. The long range of California street hills so planted would be a paradise for the gods to stroll in.

CHAPTER XV.

SOME SAN FRANCISCO WAYS AND CUSTOMS.

Street Architecture—Curiosities of Climate—Brummagem Baronets—The Sand Lot—The Forty-niners—"Society Ladies."

OME stands on her seven hills; San Francisco sits enthroned upon a hundred. The one is enjoying her centuries of rest after her triumphant onward march of a thousand years; the other is just awakening, like a royal babe in swaddling-clothes, her infant hands outstretched to seize the sceptre she will one day wield as Empress of the West. She looks down upon scenes of surpassing beauty—wide-spreading hills and valleys, wooded dells, and dark pine forests reaching away till they are lost in the purple hills beyond. She is more than half surrounded by water. Along the east runs the beautiful blue bay, sixty miles long, studded by green or rocky islets, and honeycombed by smaller bays, wherein lay shady villages and thriving towns. To the north lies the Golden Gate, opening out to the glorious Pacific Sea, whose white-crested waves break and boom like muffled thunder along the sandy shore, rushing onward and bounding with its bright waters the western part of the city, which has scarcely a level square in the whole

of it. It is built in an up-and-down, zigzag fashion, some of the streets creeping up the hill sideways like a crab; some, such as California, Clay, and Sutter, dashing straight up, as though they were in a hurry to get out of the city and be lost in the great beyond; while one end of Montgomery Street rushes up the steep slope of Telegraph Hill so precipitately and abruptly that the basement windows of one house have an excellent view of the chimney-pots of the next.

The houses are all built of wood, to which the cunning builder gives all the massive appearance of substantial stone buildings. They are generally painted white, sometimes picked out with drab or gray. The fronts are always elaborately carved, and sometimes bordered round the windows with the natural red wood left unpainted. This mass of dazzling white houses gives the city a wonderfully brilliant appearance, especially when seen from the street hills. On California Street hill are some really palatial residences, the homes of the railway and bonanza kings. Some are built in the most ornamental style of a kind of mongrel Gothic, with as many peaks, spires, and gables as could be crowded into one spot, oddly shaped windows—oval, oblong, diamond-shaped, or square—breaking out in unexpected places, variety of form being in every way more considered than the strict adherence to any special form of architecture. If we could make a twelfth cake as large as an island, and stick one of these special mansions on the top, its airy elegance would be the admiration of the world. General Colton has here a really splendid residence. A "villa" he modestly calls it; we style it a mansion. It is built in the pure Italian style of architecture, elegant and graceful, yet stately and imposing in its grand simplicity. It stands out in striking contrast to the decorated dwellings on the other side. Every man who builds a house lays "a trap to catch a sunbeam" in the form of a bay window. They are everywhere, in every street, and on both sides of it. The Palace Hotel seems built entirely of bay windows from its base to the height of its seven floors. This immense caravansera is honeycombed with them, and it has the appearance of a straight square mountain covered with bird-cages. The sun in other cities is a luxury of life, here it is a necessity. "Sunny suites" are advertised and sought for everywhere. In other places people usually avoid the sun, and seek the shady side of the road. Here they bask like lizards in the sunshine; it is only dire necessity that drives them into the shade. There is no scarcity of sunshine either; the land is flooded with it. Nowhere is the sun so bright, so genial, and strong, always looking down with warm friendly eyes, never sending its fierce, fiery lances down to smite and slay with their cruel stroke. The heat is tempered by a cool, invigorating breeze, and while the sun inclines you to throw off your sealskin, the wind warns you to cling to it. Some never leave off their furs, others never put them on. The variations of temperature during summer and winter are so slight that one style of clothing serves for the whole year. Your wardrobe never suffers from an irruption. You may meet a lady promenading in lace and muslin in December, and in velvet and furs in June; or in a single walk through the city you may meet one lady in the airiest of costumes, another cloaked and muffled up to the chin; one gentleman in a linen duster, another in a top-coat. Nobody is ever too warm, nobody is ever too cold. It seems like a riddle, but you must come here to read it. Everything seems *bouleversé*, even to the climate. There is no settled rule anywhere or in anything; it is a sort of "go-as-you-please" city. There is a general rush and hurry everywhere, a kind of picturesque lawlessness, which is most refreshing to those who come from the other side of the world, where propriety always wears her best bib and tucker, and etiquette in her regulation dress, tied with the reddest of red tape, reigns supreme, and natural impulse is bound down in the straitest of strait-waistcoats. Fashion is the only tyrant, the spoilt pet and ruler among the ladies, for if a San Francisco lady is not in the fashion she is nowhere. In their desire to attain to the utmost height of that fickle goddess they sometimes "o'erleap the selle, and fall on the other side;" but as a rule they are well and tastefully dressed. The gentlemen are supremely indifferent on the subject; each dresses to please himself, and consults only his own individual comfort and convenience, whereas in most large cities, where the sacred "chimney-pot" prevails, one man is as like another as two peas, faultlessly attired in the same fashion, from the crown of his head to the sole of his feet. Here it is altogether different; here are hats with high crowns, low crowns, or no crowns, straw, felt, willow, or wide Panama; gray suits, white suits, and blue suits.

But the Californian proper is very particular in his choice of a necktie, which is always of the most brilliant hue. Even in Eastern or Continental cities, where black ties are the rule, he will burst out in gorgeous colours. In the evening, however, when he presents himself before the ladies, the swallow-tail coat is strictly *de rigueur*.

Social life flows on in an easy, pleasant, *sans souci* fashion, for the San Franciscans are a most hospitable people, and are disposed to open their hearts as well as their doors to their visitors from the outside world, and do all in their power to make their beautiful city a home to the passing stranger. This open-hearted hospitality is sometimes imposed upon by an influx of British baronets, whose names are unknown in their native land, and pseudo lords, made up by their tailors, whose names have never figured in the peerage. Occasionally these Brummagem gentry dip their fingers into the purse of the open-handed Californian, and sometimes make themselves too fatally agreeable to the ladies; but as a rule their false pretensions are discovered, and they are quietly driven from the city, before the damage done is irreparable. The inhabitants are apt to give too easy credence to a self-asserting class, who swagger about the hotels as true gentlefolk never do, and whose brassy impudence for a time passes as pure gold. But perhaps it is better to be sometimes deceived than always distrustful.

There is no settled "society" here, regarding the subject from our point of view. It is impossible there should be in a country which is in a constant state of fermentation, fluctuating from one extreme to the other, where the game of speculation is being played on all sides, and everybody takes a hand. The cauldron is for ever bubbling and boiling over, and somebody goes to the bad. Men and women who have held their place in brilliant circles one year drop out of it the next, and sink down and are lost, no one knows how or where. The circle closes, and the dance of life goes on.

Of course there are many people of wealth and position who have played a winning game, and are satisfied now to settle down and watch the growth of the beloved city they have helped to make. Most of the families of culture, intellect, and refinement are those who came there thirty years ago, when the gold fever first broke out and drew some of the best blood from every land towards itself. And those men and women, too, who came out in the old, rough days, have grown purer, stronger, and better from mingling with the new life in a new land. There has been no effete civilization here. Every man has depended on his own brains, his own hand for his well-doing. It may truly be said, in this land above all others, that every man is the architect of his own fortunes. Of course much of the coarse, vulgar element of mankind has swarmed and is still swarming into this Golden State. Some regard it as a sort of Tom Tiddler's ground, where they can run about picking up gold and silver. When they find their mistake, and learn that here, as elsewhere, men must bring labour of hand or brain to the market and pay in full for every crust they eat, they enrol themselves in the noble army of the unemployed, parade the streets in lazy battalions, hold mass meetings, and howl over their misfortunes, shake their fists in the face of calamity: "Why can't they drink the wine of life and revel in champagne and roses?" They will do anything, everything, but work for it. These people, who are not native born, but are the mere refuse of other nations, which has rolled across the sea and been flung upon the shores of the Western World, have won for themselves the title of Sand-lotters. They have their meetings on a vacant sand-heap on the edge of the town, which is held entirely sacred to them, and here they bluster, and storm, and loudly assert their "rights." They decide who is fit to live and who is fit to die. Figuratively, they hang the capitalist on his own threshold and divide his wealth among their worthier selves. If the general atmosphere were more combustible their incendiary speeches would set the land in flames. These people, though contemptible in themselves, create a general agitation and confusion, drive capital away from the city, and have given rise to a general sense of insecurity. As a grain of sand will set all the delicate working of a watch awry, so they have disturbed the peace for a while; but it is a storm in a tea-cup, that will soon be over. The party of law and order is firmly knit together, and dignified in its silent strength. So long as the dronish population confines itself to buzzing and burring around, carrying on a boisterous war of words only, they keep a dignified silence; but at the first attempt to sting, it will be crushed like a wasp. In no other country would a foreign element be allowed to create so much disorder. The native population are a peaceful, law-abiding race.

"This is a land of liberty," they say; but when liberty becomes license to the vicious, alas for poor liberty!

America is willing to stretch a welcoming hand to all comers without regard to creed or nationality, to give land to such as desire to make a home among them, and a free liberal education to their children, to throw open its offices of State and General Government to all candidates who are fit to fill them. It is large in generosity as mighty in strength, and it is a small thing to ask that its laws be kept and its institutions respected by the stranger who benefits by the national hospitality.

Young children must go through certain physical disturbances before they arrive at a state of healthy maturity, and I suppose young States must go through similar mental distractions before they settle down into a dignified calm. The adolescent State of California is no exception to the rule, but it is cutting its wisdom teeth and learning to comport itself with a dignity befitting the great Union of which it is a part.

Men no longer carry their lives in their hands, as in the old days of lawless, romantic adventure, but I am afraid a few still secretly carry arms in their pockets, and use them, perhaps, upon small provocation. But things are improving and changing rapidly; the people are prospering, and, the essentials of life being secured, their thoughts and ambitions are soaring into higher regions. Civilization, which for years past, has been marching westward, subduing prairies, cutting down forests, piercing mountains, and spanning rivers, seems to have ended her grand progress and, for a time, sat down to rest here; resting, though working still, establishing rule and order. There are no stagnant ideas, no stereotyped monotony here; everything is full of electrical life; people think, move, and act quickly; they are not content with what *is*, but look forward to what *shall be*. This beautiful California—land of the sun, of the palm and pine—has only one chapter in its past, but it is creating for itself a glorious future.

Things happen here that we cannot conceive happening in any other city in the world. Walking through the streets one day, we met a strange figure carrying a particoloured umbrella—red, white, and blue. He was a gray-haired, elderly man, dressed in a faded military uniform, with tarnished epaulets, and a scarlet feather in his cap. He may be seen wandering through the streets of the city in all weathers. He has been so wandering for the last twenty years or more. He labours under the delusion that he is "Emperor of all the Americas." The people humour him, and allow him to indulge in that delusion. He issues proclamations, which are printed in the newspapers, and posted at street corners. Sometimes, being in want of twenty dollars, he levies a tax upon his "loyal subjects." Some wealthy citizen answers the demand at once; he is never denied. He dines where he pleases, free; patronizes such places of entertainment as he chooses, free; rides on the cars or on the trams, free; indeed, he has the freedom of the city in the truest sense of the word. On inquiry we learn the reason of this general indulgence. He was a mason and a forty-niner, they say, and was ruined by the great fire, when his wits were shaken, and this royal delusion rose on the wreck of his

SOME SAN FRANCISCO WAYS AND CUSTOMS. 171

reason, and the kindly people, in the spirit of true *camaraderie*, will never let the old man want.

Here is another anecdote characteristic of San Francisco kindliness, being the history in brief of Bummer and Lazarus (the names being descriptive of the habits of one dog, and the appearance of the other, on his first entrance into public life). "Bummer" was a big dog, a vagabond much beloved of the town, who could not be coaxed into civilized ways. He disdained to live in a house, or to serve one master. He was a kind of canine tramp, who lived by his wits. Like the Emperor, he too enjoyed the hospitality of the city. Lazarus was a little mangy cur, thin, sickly, and half-starved. One day some other dogs attacked poor, miserable little Lazarus. Bummer, perhaps moved by kindred feelings—the assailants being household property, and Lazarus a tramp like himself—plunged into the fray to the rescue of Lazarus.

From that day the two wanderers were a canine Damon and Pythias. They became well known in the city. Lazarus looked starved and sickly no longer. Bummer introduced him to his own chosen haunts. They went together to such restaurants as they chose to honour, and dined gratis. Messrs. Bummer and Lazarus were always welcome, and never sent hungry away. It was observed that the big dog always gave his small companion a full share of the delicacies of the season. When an Act was passed commanding all dogs in the city of San Francisco to be muzzled, a clause was made exempting "Bummer and Lazarus." However, their time came. Bummer died one day; Lazarus was found dead by his side on the next. An old resident of the city who knew the dogs well, and had fed them many a time, told me this story. They are stuffed now, and have their place among the many mementoes of "old days"—old in the space of thirty years.

Only the healthy and the strong keep their grip on the land, and these, the early pioneers of the State, form the most delightful society in San Francisco. Their homes are the abode of elegance and refinement. We are sometimes disposed to wonder how all this culture has reached this far-away land,—the "Wild West" we call it,—wild now in nothing but its natural attractions; in no country in the world are there more luxurious, happy homes than here in San Francisco. Those who are in a position and have the power to entertain their friends, do so with genial cordiality. Some have one evening in the week, some another; there is no set formality; but we meet with the gracious courtesy of the Old World warmed by the hearty whole-souled welcome of the New. Those who have the power to indulge their æsthetic fancies gather about them all that is beautiful in the way of art that can attract and satisfy the most artistic taste.

The home of one lady is at this moment present to my mind's eye. She has travelled over the world, and brought back with her some perfect gems in the way of bric-à-brac, paintings, and sculpture. There are among them two exquisite marble statues, both unique in conception and excellent in execution. The one is "Delilah," a grand, grim piece of workmanship; the other, the more poetical and sympathetic "Lost Pleiad;" the yearning, searching look upon her face reaches the heart, and we

SOME SAN FRANCISCO WAYS AND CUSTOMS. 173

wish we could help her find her way home. Here it has been our good fortune to fall in with some of the "Forty-niners," as all who came over in that year are called. Many may have come over adventuring earlier or later; no matter, they have no distinguishing title to chronicle their advent. Only the "Forty-niners" are regarded as the original pioneers. Their numbers are lessening day by day; but a few are now remaining, and they are all a fine, stalwart race of men, with no signs of age or decay, some with delicate poetical faces, which it is difficult to associate with the rude times we know they have passed through; they have grown gray with the passing years, but not old; they look as though they could brace themselves together and do their work over again. In this electric air age seems chary of advancing; youth blooms long after it would have perished elsewhere. The perennial springtime in earth and air seems to have communicated itself to the lives of men. They are full of anecdote, and brimming over with the romance and stirring adventure of bygone days, and proud of their beautiful city, too; as well they may be. They have watched it grow stone by stone, street by street, and have helped to make it what it is. They found it a heap of hovels and sandhills, and when they are carried to their graves in Lone Mountain, they will leave it the fairest and loveliest city in the world.

In addition to these pleasant gatherings, San Francisco frequently breaks out into grander gaieties, and entertains her hundreds in the most magnificent fashion. Society sounds her trumpet, and her armies gather round her in gorgeous array, when frivolity and fashion hold high revels for a season. There is no genial sociability then; it is all gaslight, music, roses, and champagne. Gentlefolk are divided into two classes, "society ladies," and ladies pure and simple. The "society lady" has her dresses chronicled in all the public papers; whole columns are devoted to the description of dresses. To all the Pacific coast is made known the important fact that the young and beautiful Miss So-and-so wore pink silk trimmed with point-lace, while the lovely Miss Such-a-one wore pea-green and apple blossoms, her stately mamma, appearing in imperial velvet and rubies. And so on. Woe be to the audacious damsel who dares to appear in the same dress twice running! Everybody knows all about it, and the cost of every yard of satin or inch of lace is catalogued in the feminine mind. And woe be to the simple toilet which will not do credit to the reporter's pen! The girls all wonder how their dresses will look in print, and to that end select them. Here a noble course of ruin begins—so far, at least, as an extravagant woman can ruin a man, and we all know how much she can do towards it. There are sometimes more dollars on a woman's back than remain in her husband's pocket.

It is a pernicious habit, this advertising business, and brings to the surface the smaller, meaner passions of the female nature. There are numbers who would gladly break from this iron rule of custom, but they either have not the courage to strike the first blow or are borne down by the great majority on the other side. But things here, as elsewhere, will right themselves in time.

CHAPTER XVI.

THE FLOWERY KINGDOM.

A Visit to Chinatown—Its General Aspect—A Tempting Display—Barbers' Shops—A Chinese Restaurant—Their Joss House—Their Gods.

IT is nine o'clock in the evening when we start for an investigating ramble through Chinatown. Time was when men went over "the sea in ships" when they desired to visit the celestial land; now they can go there and back in an hour, and not travel on telegraph wires either. The mountain has come to Mahomet, and deposited its load in the very heart of the "Golden City."

Kearney Street is brilliantly lighted, the shops are temptingly arrayed in their best wares, and a well-dressed world of men and women are strolling up and down, chatting, laughing, bargaining, and buying. We watch the California Street dummy charge up the hill with its last load of passengers, its red fiery eye blazing boldly on us as it drops down the other side of the hill, and is lost to sight. We feel quite at home here, though we are eight thousand miles away from our native shores. A sudden turn out of the bustling thoroughfare, a few steps forward, and we know we are in a foreign land. We are escorted by a private friend and a police detective, without whose protective presence it would not be safe to venture into these dingy courts and alleys which lie festering in the very heart of the "Flowery Kingdom." We keep close to our escorts; we feel that we have stepped beyond the bounds of civilization, and are surrounded by a subtle element utterly foreign and inimical to our own. We are in the city of the idolatrous heathen, in whose sight our Christian civilization is an abomination and a snare. Pig-tailed, blue-bloused Celestials swarm in the roadway and on the sidewalks. They surge round us with their silent, stealthy tread. At the sight of our escort's face, or the sound of his voice, they slink away and are gone like shadows. The streets are dimly lighted; the gas does not blaze, it blinks behind its glasses, but the big white moon gives light enough for us to see the cheap gaudy magnificence around us. We are passing the Joss house. It flaunts its scarlet streamers overhead, and flanks its doors with legends in saffron and gold. Within is a glitter of tinsel, a subdued light, and the flicker of a tiny lamp before some figure of barbaric ugliness. The air floats out loaded with the fumes of smoking sandal-wood and strange odours from the East. The doors are open, but we do not enter yet. We stroll up the street, taking an exterior view before we penetrate to the interior. Coloured lanterns are strung along some of the balconies, or hang from the windows. Red and black signs in crooked characters are everywhere, and from all sides resounds the echo, it seems, of a hundred unknown tongues. The slant-eyed pagans leer at us curiously as they pass to and fro. They bear us "white devils" no good will, if we read their looks aright. Lights stream from cellar flaps, creep through open doors and window chinks, but the shops are only lighted by a succession of dingy oil lamps. Discordant noises of rasping fiddles, gongs and sundry unknown tuneless instruments mingle with the clatter of strange tongues. The very laughter comes to us jangled and out of tune, and the air is filled with odours the reverse of sweet. Mouldy fruits, wilted vegetables, stale fish, too long divorced from its native element, all mingle in one common and most unsavoury scent.

The Chinese shops make no endeavour to attract the eye or tempt the appetite of the Celestial horde. But, perhaps, what seems to us a disgusting display may seem to them a tempting sight. The butcher, who is a general merchant as well, sells Joss sticks, teapots, tobacco, and scores of other things. He flanks his door on either side with the carcass of huge slaughtered hogs. They are not quartered and jointed in Christian fashion, but are hacked, and hewn, and torn assunder just as the meat is wanted, and present a mangled, shapeless mass, sickening to look at. Split chickens and fowls are flattened out like sheets of paper and nailed against the wall. Delicate titbits, steeped in oil and dried, are strung up and hung like cherry bob across the windows, and scores of oily cakes, like lumps of yellow soap, are laid on benches. Lumps of delight they are in Celestial eyes, judging by the lingering glances they cast thereon. The shops are very dingy and dark inside, and those which are not devoted to the sale of eatables have a spicy, pungent odour everywhere, no matter what articles of merchandise they sell. We went into two or three shops in search of some special article which we might carry away as a souvenir of our visit, but could find nothing but cheap, tawdry trash, beryl bracelets, bead necklaces, tiny cups and saucers, etc. There was no brilliant display of gold embroideries, vases, and Oriental magnificence, which characterizes our Chinese shops at home. The Chinese merchant sits in silent state behind his counter, watching our every movement with his stealthy almond eyes. He makes no attempt to force his wares upon us; indeed, he seems sublimely indifferent whether we buy or not. His long, shapely hands are folded before him as he sits on his high stool serene and dignified, while we peer curiously about, examining anything that catches our eye. We see nothing we care to purchase, so we make a smiling apology for our intrusion, and he bows us out with courteous but most majestic silence.

We pass on our way, look down the cellar flaps, and see the barbers at work in their underground shops. Within a radius of half a mile there are no less than fifty of these places, devoted to the cleansing and decoration of the Mongolian head. You may glance down these steps at any hour of the day or night and you will see the operators busy at their tonsorial labour. Never was such clean shaving, such delicate cleansing of eyes, ears, and nostrils, such trimming and pencilling of brows and lashes, such a scraping and polishing of oily faces, such a plaiting of the beloved and sacred pigtail, and the Celestial pagan issues from the hands of the barber a proud and happy man, the perfect ideal of a Chinese beau; every inch above his shoulders is scraped and polished to perfection. This luxurious treatment which he receives at the hands of his barber is a law among the followers of Confucius. The Chinaman feels the necessity of frequent rejuvenation under the razors, probes, and pencils of the barber, who is one of the best employed and most important persons in the community. The almond-eyed pagan is never seen without his pigtail; the loss of it is considered the greatest calamity that can befall him. When he is engaged in his household work he winds his pigtail round his head in the fashion of a Grecian knot.

Our next visit was to a Chinese restaurant, which is patronized by the wealthier as well as the lower order of that peculiar people. The ground-floor is a kind of general utility store for the sale of miscellaneous comestibles. Bright, blue-bloused little China boys, their pigtails just sprouting, are squatting on the floors, cutting and chopping up meat and vegetables. In the kitchen, a few steps above, the cooks are busily at work preparing the unsavoury savoury feast for the hungry horde who are presently expected to supper. Beef or mutton is rarely if ever used in their culinary operations. Pork, rats, rabbits, geese, or fowls form the staple part of their substantial food, but these are never eaten in their natural simplicity; they are disguised and minced, and mixed with spices, vegetables, entrails, oil, and rancid butter, sometimes stewed, and sometimes being rolled in a thin wafery crust of paste. We saw plenty of these arranged for frying, like sausages in disguise. There is a greasy oleaginous look about everything, a smell like rusty bacon everywhere. A culinary war was being carried on in the kitchen, the pots and pans were specially clean and bright, the cooks went clattering round lifting lids and stirring one thing after another, and handing us a long iron spoon hospitably invited us to dip in and taste, assuring us it was " velly good," which invitation I need not say we courteously refused. A few steps higher on the first floor is the dining-room or grand saloon, which is only used by the wealthy merchants. It is furnished with very dark walnut, with quaint ebony carvings of birds, curious beasts, and flowers, all beautifully executed, and worthy of a better place. The tables and chairs were of the same heavy dark material. The room was divided in two by a wide archway. There was an alcove on one side for musicians, and all kinds of queer, quaint musical instruments, some twisted like serpents, some like grotesque, misshapen guitars, were hung against the wall. Lacquered cabinets and tea-trays, with tiny covered cups and saucers, and hideous bronze ornaments, were scattered around. Rich tapestried hangings were draped across the windows, and the wide balcony was filled with flowers, and a string of lighted lanterns were hung over the outside railings. On one side of the room, about two feet from the ground, was a raised platform covered with matting and cushions, a block of wood in the centre to hold a lamp. Thither the luxurious Mongolian retires to smoke the inevitable opium when the feast is over. At the entrance-door of all eating-rooms stands a bowl of chop-sticks; each guest as he enters supplies himself with a pair. The floor above is arranged in a simpler, rougher fashion for an inferior class of visitors. The floor above that is simpler and rougher still. And so the grade goes upward, and so does the tea. The real, fine, aromatic herb, in all perfection, is served on the first floor; water is added to the leaves (for they are an economical race), and served on the second; more water for the third. And so on, till a decoction of damaged water is served to the lowest, albeit the highest class of guests, for the poorer class here mount heavenward so far as this earth is concerned.

Laundries abound, though they are by no means confined to Chinatown. They are found in all quarters of San Francisco. Sometimes the Chinese laundry is a mere wooden shed, wedged in between tall houses, or standing in some out-of-the-way nook, where you would hardly think of pitching a pigsty. We passed some of these rickety places, the white linen drying on the roofs, flapping to and fro in a weird, ghastly fashion in the moonlight. The work is carried on by night as well as by day, for these moon-eyed Mongolians are a most industrious race, and in their economy of time and space a double set of workmen occupy a single room, and labour in relays. When the day-labourer retires to his shelf the night-worker rises from it, and carries on the business till the morning; so the fire is never out, and the starching, ironing, plaiting, and pleating is always going on. Passing through the streets of San Francisco at any hour of the night you see the faint glimmer of the laundry-lamp flickering through the dingy window-panes.

We next turned into one of their many Joss houses, where the worship of their hideous idols was in full swing. We ascended a dingy, dirty staircase and entered a large room on the first floor, which was furnished with gods and altars of all descriptions. Crowds of worshippers were passing to and fro, now in single file, now in battalions; some were smoking, some were conversing in their low, liquid language one with another. One jerked his head with a kind of familiar nod, which was meant for a reverential obeisance to a specially ugly deity. Another threw a stick into the air in front of the altar, and according to the way it pointed as it fell his prayer would be granted or not. I do not know whether Joss was propitious, but his worshipper picked up the stick and retreated downstairs. There was certainly no established set form in this religious business; but I suppose there must on occasions be some special ceremonials when priests are needed, for two or three of them, dressed in the fashion of stage heralds, came out from a little back room, stared at us, and retreated, closing the door behind them. The worshippers passed in and out, and to and fro among their gods with perfect nonchalance. There was neither reverence, nor superstitious awe, nor fanatical devotion visible among them. What seemed to be their favourite, judging from the number of his worshippers, was a huge monster like an immense painted wooden doll, with flaming vermilion cheeks, and round black eyes starting from his head. He was dressed in wooden robes of the gaudiest, strongly contrasted colours, and surrounded by all kinds of tinselled magnificence, in the way of gilt paper, artificial wreaths, and wax roses as large as cabbages, while standing before him on the altar was a bowl of ashes stuck full of Joss sticks, some burnt out, some still smouldering, the offering of later worshippers.

The altar is of ivory, and is exquisitely carved and gilt. It illustrates the history of some great battle which was fought two thousand years ago. It is protected, and so partly hidden, by a wire network. There are sundry other smaller altars and idols in the same room. Some are distorted libels on the human form divine; others are grotesque representations of birds, beasts, or reptiles held sacred by the Chinese; some are of bronze, or of brass, and some of painted wood. There are no seats, and the floor is thickly sprinkled with sawdust. The walls are hung with scarlet and blue paper prayers and gilt thanksgivings. Among these was an advertisement, which our guide translated to us. It was the offer of a reward, not for the discovery of a murderer, but a reward for the committal of a murder. Ah Fooh and Wong Ah had roused the anger of the great Joss, who promises to grant the prayers and take into special favour him who will put the obnoxious Ah Fooh and Wong Ah out of the way; viz. the gods will favour him who commits the crimes, which are no crimes when the gods command their committal. Our guide informed us that the objectionable parties would assuredly "disappear," no one would know how, or when, or where. Such murders are never discovered. The Celestials hold their secrets close, and it rarely happens that one will bear evidence against another in our courts of law. If he does, well, it is likely enough he "disappears" too. They care nothing for our laws and customs, and have a supreme contempt for our legal institutions. They have their exits and their entrances, their lotteries, their imports, exports, diversions, secret tribunals, and punishments of which we know nothing. They are under the surveillance and rule of the Six Companies, who hold supreme authority over them. They have laws within our laws, which are to us as a sealed book. They rarely, if ever, appeal to the United States authorities for the settlement of their difficulties. If they do the judgment is sure to be reversed in their own courts, the prosecutor is tried and punished by the secret tribunal, and the whole affair is shrouded in a mystery that the outside world can never penetrate.

We passed from this large and most important chamber through a nest of dingy, dirty rooms, each presided over by a god or goddess more or less hideously grotesque, and lighted only by a tiny glass lamp, which hangs before every shrine, and is kept burning night and day. Each has a bronze bowl of Joss sticks burning in his or her honour, filling the air with smoky, stifling incense. Lying about on sundry small tables are miniature copies of their ugly idols, and tiny curiosities in the shape of birds, beasts, and fishes, all part and parcel of Chinese mythology. There were some superb china vases (which would make the eye of the collector twinkle), filled with tawdry paper flowers, standing here and there among Joss sticks and split bamboos, sometimes used in the interpretation or divination of the will of the gods. Brummagem decorations and tinselled magnificence abound everywhere. In one room was a curious adobe oven. We wondered whether it was used to bake Christians or purify the heathen, but we learned that it was used at certain seasons of the year when Satan is symbolically burned, he being represented on the occasion by torn strips of red paper, which have been appropriately cursed and sentenced by the priesthood. The smaller gods had fewer worshippers, and it was strange to observe there was not a single woman among them. Perhaps, having no souls to be saved in the next world, they have grown weary of praying for the good things of this. In every room, great and small, there is a rough wooden structure like a very tall stool. Within it hangs a bell, and above it either a gong or a big drum. These are used to rouse the drowsy gods from their slumbers, or to attract their attention when they have been too long forgetful of the desires of their devotees. Wherever we went a crowd of these olive-skinned, pig-tailed figures gathered silently as shadows about us, staring at us with their melancholy, expressionless eyes. The Chinese seem all to be made on one pattern. They have all the same serenity of face, of gait, and manner; their features never stir, their eyes never vary, they never gesticulate, are never excited: only the meaningless smile that is "childlike and bland" occasionally creeps over their faces. The more we see of these strange, passionless people, the stranger they seem to us, and we more fully recognize that they are an utterly alien race, whom we can never comprehend. Looking on their sphinxlike faces we wonder what feelings, what human passions, what emotions, lie hidden beneath them. We might as well try to solve the riddle of the Sphinx's self. But in spite of their impassibility we feel that the barbarous element is there, steady, strong, and cruel. The Chinese are a puzzle, which the subtlest minds have failed to piece together. California has a hard nut to crack, and I fear it will break its teeth before it gets to the kernel.

CHAPTER XVII.

A WORLD UNDERGROUND.

The Pawnbroker's Shop—The Opium Dens—The Smokers—A World within a World—The Women's Quarters.

E were rather tired of our night's wandering, but as we did not desire to encroach upon the kindness of our guide by occupying his time on another evening, we resolved to see all that was to be seen at once; we therefore retired to a restaurant for a temporary rest and refreshed ourselves with tiny cups of tea. Neither milk nor sugar is served with this refreshment; only a grape or raisin is swimming in the liquid amber, which has a delicious flavour, quite different from the finest Chinese tea imported for European consumption. Our escort endeavoured to dissuade us from farther penetration into the mysteries of Chinatown, as he feared we might be shocked at the sights and scenes there; but we had left our nerves at home, so girding on our mental armour, we sallied forth again.

We turned into Sacramento Street, and descended one of those cellar flaps, where the barber was still busy with his tonsorial operations. We passed through his pigtailed congregation of customers, some of whom looked as though they sorely needed combing, and found ourselves in a dingy pawnbroker's shop, lighted by a single oil lamp, and certainly not more than twelve feet square; but every nook and corner, hole and crevice, from floor to ceiling, was crammed with a miscellaneous collection of unredeemed pledges. There were clocks, caps, quaint Chinese ornaments in great variety, which the collector might search the civilized world for in vain; firearms and pistols of all patterns and all ages (most of them, we were informed, were loaded); daggers and knives without end; among them was the curious fan-shaped stiletto, which may be carried in the hand by a lady without rousing a suspicion as to its real use, for when sheathed it represents a closed fan; some of the knives, their favourite weapons in social and street warfare, are short and broad, some long and narrow; the most formidable are about a foot long and six inches wide; these are used in pairs, one in each hand. Our escort informed us that with these implements he had known one belligerent Chinaman slash another into an unrecognizable mass in less than five minutes. Besides these there were beds, bedding, divers articles of clothing, cooking pots and brass pans; in fact, everything except the sacred pigtail, without which a Chinaman can hope for no honour in this world nor any glory in the next.

Through this, we stooped our heads and passed under a low doorway into a black hole—I can describe it in no other way—where there was a bin for ashes or kitchen refuse and a heap of battered pots and pans; a wooden bench or stool, black with grime, a few wooden bowls and chop-sticks, while sundry bits of rags hung on a line over our heads. A coolie was crouching over the fire in one corner, stirring some horrible compound with a long wooden spoon. The fire sputtered and sent forth feeble flame flashes and dense volumes of smoke, through which the swarthy form of the crouching coolie loomed upon our sight like the evil genie of some Arabian tale. This was a kitchen! There was no chimney, no window, no drainage. And in this foul den scores of hungry Celestials would come presently to feed. From this we entered a labyrinth of galleries, running in all directions. On either side were rows of small chambers, honeycombed with an economy of space that outwits the invention of the white man altogether. The majority of these are just long enough to lie down in, and broad enough for a narrow door to open between the two beds of straw, each of which contains two sleepers. On reaching the end of this gallery, we were informed that it was a hundred and twenty feet long. There is no ventilation, and not a breath of air enters, except from the cellar through which we entered, and even that comes filtered through the barber's and pawnbroker's shops before alluded to.

We gladly return to the fresh air, but only for a moment's breathing-space before descending to still deeper depths. The very bowels of the earth, it seems, are riddled and honeycombed by these human moles, who, like the ghost of the murdered Dane, can "work in the dark." We light a candle, which burns but feebly in the subterranean darkness of this double night. We thread our way single file, keeping always within an inch of our escort's coat-tail, and descend into these lower regions. Here in the heart of a city filled with light and beauty, we find ourselves groping our way two storeys underground by the light of a tallow candle! Through dingy courts and alleys, up steps and down steps, round corners, and up or down zigzag stairways, we explore the mysteries of Chinatown. It is as dark as Erebus; only the light of our one solitary dip flickers in our eyes; we feel as though there is something weird and ghastly clinging to ourselves, for our voices have a smothered, hollow sound, even to our own ears. No one really knows how far these human gophers have burrowed underground; they wander, it seems, from one living grave to another; perhaps to avoid taxation, the assassin, or the grip of the law. It is a dismal city of refuge for lost souls.

If Dante could have cast his sorrowful eyes into these dark regions, he would have found here an appalling reality which outstrips the imaginary horrors with which he has illustrated his *Inferno*. We gather up our skirts and pick our way slowly, for the ground is slippery with Heaven knows what, and the walls are reeking with black slime, the odour is horrible, and everywhere there is an accumulation of filth which ought to breed fever and death, but does not. We suddenly turn into another of these narrow galleries; on either side are mangy-looking curtains, some partially closed, some open; the ceiling is so low we can almost touch it standing on tiptoe, yet on either side there are two tiers of hard wooden boards, divided by a slight partition into sections, each being large enough for two occupants, and every bunk is full.

This is one of the numerous opium dens. Some are preparing the enchanting poison—a tedious process, which reminds one of an incantation scene; the two lie face to face, chatting in low voices, a look of delicious anticipation glowing in every feature; they recline at full length, their heads reposing upon blocks of wood or roughly improvised straw pillows; a small lamp flickers between them; their long pipes are of bamboo cane; at the lower end of the stem is an earthen bowl; a jar of opium, a kind of thick, black paste, stands close to the lamp; the smokers dip a wire into this paste and then hold it in the flame till the particles of paste which cling to it fizzes and bubbles; it is then deposited on the rim of the pipe-bowl, and the smoker at once inhales three or four whiffs, which empties the pipe, and the process of refilling is renewed. It is evidently a labour of love with them, for their eyes glisten and gloat upon the bubbling drug. They take no heed of us; we are mere mortals, *they* are far on the road to paradise. Their talk grows gradually less and less, feebler and feebler; their low laughter has a delirious sound; their eyes are filled with a dreamy light, but their lips are glued to that magic tube; they are rapidly floating away to a land we know not of; their fingers relax their hold; they sink back upon their pillows and are suddenly silent; their dusky faces ashen pale, having the look of some plague-stricken corpse: this one pair of opium-smokers represents the many. We drop the curtain and pass on, making our observations as we go. Some have had their delirious dream and are sluggishly stirring, slowly awakening back to life, and with wan, haggard faces stagger out of the dingy den into open day; some flit past us like ghostly shadows, wandering through the shades of Hades; they glide along shrinking against the wall, and stare at us with lack-lustre eyes, mere spectres of humanity, not humanity itself. But when such men as William Blair, Richard Baxter, De Quincey, Coleridge, and others become victims to the habit of opium-eating, what wonder is it that an enslaved and degraded race should rush into a temporary world of dreams and enjoy its delirious delights, little heeding of the thraldom eternal and immutable which will follow their awakening?

This terrible drug (which, for a time, fills the brain with feverish dreams of ecstatic delight, but is the sure forerunner of unimaginable horrors and agonizing death) lies within the reach of all. One of the most celebrated opium-eaters tells us that "happiness may be bought for a penny and carried in the waistcoat pocket, portable ecstasies may be had corked up in a pint bottle, and peace of mind may be sent out in gallons by the mail-coach." In some parts of India opium is taken by the criminal condemned to death. If he can only get his brain filled with opium fumes he may be said to die happy. We grope our way through this Inferno, obscured by the dense smoke of the poisonous drug, and are glad to breathe the fresh air of heaven once more.

Then we pass on to the women's quarters. The Chinese rarely, very rarely bring their wives or families across the water; but they import large numbers of female slaves of the most degraded class, and for the most immoral purposes. These poor creatures have no sense of degradation, no knowledge of morality, they but fulfil the condition they are born to. So loosely, indeed, are social and domestic ties held by these people, that if a wife displeases her husband, or a child her parent, they have the right, and frequently exercise it, too, to sell either one or other to some trafficker in human kind, and take the profits as in any other mercantile transaction. A sense of dignity or family pride prevents the higher class of Chinese from entering into this sale or barter business. They have other ways of disposing of their surplus womankind.

We entered a long and narrow court with tall, dark houses on either side, so tall they seemed to shut out the skies; but in this confined space are domiciled twelve hundred of these female slaves, for slaves they are still, though sojourning in a free land, and by the law free agents, but the law is powerless to reach them. They are held in bondage by their own people and by the laws of their own nation, which no good Celestial, especially a woman, would dare to call in question. They have no thought of any higher state. If, by chance, as sometimes though rarely happens, a creditor appeals to the United States law to settle his affairs, no matter what decision is given it is sure to be set aside by their own tribunal, and the prosecutor has reason to bewail his temerity in daring to appeal to any other. In all cases, whether of murder or lesser criminalities among themselves, they are examined, tried, condemned, and their punishment, be it torture or death, is carried out by their own secret tribunal, whose laws are to us a sealed book, and whose councils here are held in some hidden underground spot that we know not of.

We picked our way through the dingy, deserted court, for though it was the women's quarter, there was not a woman to be seen. Some were evidently indulging in social festivities, for the sound of the gong, rasping fiddles, and screeching voices broke upon the silence of the night. Shadowy forms, like creatures from another world, stole by us with their noiseless tread and disappeared in the doorways on either side. We grope our way along by the light of our one solitary dip, and become suddenly aware of a dim light falling across our pathway. We look round and observe an open grating about a foot square, and framed therein is the face of a Chinese belle. There she is precisely as we see her on our fans and tea-trays, her hair dressed in wings or fancy rolls and pinned with gilt pins, and profusely decorated with paper flowers of various colours, one half of her face being painted a bright vermilion in one blotch, beginning from the chin, covering the eyebrows, and reaching back to the ear. On either side were the same gratings, with the same painted beauties behind them, looking out from the grated windows into the dark night. There sit those unhandsome, unwholesome sirens, like painted spiders, watching for their prey. Our escort struck a single thud upon the door of one of these houses, which acted like an "open sesame." Slowly and silently it swung back upon its hinges, and we stepped at once into a small, dimly-lighted room furnished with bare benches only. Grouped round a tiny lamp upon the floor sat some half dozen women engaged in sewing and embroidery work. Other specimens of this unlovely womanhood in gorgeous celestial costume were lounging in waiting attitude about the room. The head of this establishment, a repulsive-looking old woman with blear almond eyes, jagged, projecting teeth, and a yellow skin dried and wrinkled like a piece of old parchment, welcomed us warmly in the usual pigeon English; the others nudged each other, and giggled and gabbled when we spoke to them, regarding us with curious eyes the while. Once, while we were taking a survey of things round us the door was opened noiselessly, as though on oiled hinges, and a Mongolian man's face appeared for a second in the aperture, but on catching sight of our party it disappeared, and the door swung silently to again. There was one very young girl about fifteen among this degraded sisterhood; she was really pretty, a perfect type of Chinese beauty, with a delicate olive complexion, with a sweet, childlike, innocent expression of countenance — innocent because utterly ignorant and dead to any sense of shame or wrong, blind to the moral ugliness of the life of which she formed a part, because her baby eyes had seen nothing else, she had been reared in it and for it. Knowing no other aim or purpose in life, the mystery of modesty or purity was a thing unknown. We shook hands with this child woman and spoke to her, but she only laughed and shook her head. We wondered how this young thing had fallen into this revolting company. "Had she a mother?" we inquired. "No," the ogress of the den answered, "she all mine, me buy her, her mother sell her for tlee hunnerd dollars. She velly good—she bling plenty money."

Though nominally free, these poor creatures are so utterly the property of their owners that they have no redress for ill-treatment or wrong. However they are ill-used or beaten they dare not complain; for them lives no human sympathy, no mortal regard; they are mere bits of animated clay, and nothing more. They are never allowed in the public streets, but live out their lives in these dingy dens, and when they are no longer useful in their way, are flung out in the gutter to rot and die. We went up stairs and found scores of frowsy men and women, smoking, playing dominoes, or eating rice with chop-sticks, flinging it down their throats with marvellous rapidity as though they were eating for a wager. Once we fancied we had stumbled on a bit of Chinese domesticity. We found social groups of men and women drinking tea together in a homely fashion. Our inquiry as to their matrimonial relations was received with a suppressed chuckle; the idea of any woman being the wife of any man struck them as a novel style of joking. I must not omit to say that these, as a rule, were the cleanest and neatest rooms we had seen in the whole of Chinatown.

We went our way through the silent moonlight with a strange, weird feeling falling over us, as though we had been wandering in dreamland, or living through the misty pages of the "Arabian Nights."

CHAPTER XVIII.

CHINESE AMUSEMENTS.

Gambling Dens—Theatres—An Acrobatic Performance—New Year's Visits—The Bride—The Hoodlum—A Scare—The Matron's Pretty Feet.

AMBLING is another of the favourite vices of the Chinese, and is popularly indulged in by all classes, though it is strictly forbidden by the United States' laws; but the evasion of legal authority is mere child's play to them. These numerous gambling dens are so carefully guarded that only the private police (some of whom, I am told, are in the pay of the Celestial authorities, and when gold dust is thrown in the eyes who can help blinking?) can ferret them out, and only then on rare occasions and with great difficulty.

So great is their passion for games of chance that they will sell or pledge anything to obtain the means to indulge in it. Not only are cards, dice, and dominoes used, but straws, sticks, brass rings, etc., are thrown upon a table, or on a mat upon the ground, while silent, eager faces crowd round, and the fate of the players literally hangs upon a breath. There are a hundred of these establishments under the eyes of the police. Some of them employ private spies to warn them in case of danger; but these places are seldom raided by the police, for they know it is almost impossible to storm the barriers in time to catch delinquents in the act. On the first sign of danger a warning signal is sounded throughout the building, and a sudden change seems to take place in the ground plan; passages are shut off; the pursuer, rushing along the winding ways he thought he knew, finds himself in a blind alley; a mysterious sliding-panel takes the place of a door, or he rushes into the suspected chamber,—he is fooled again! He finds nothing there, only a harmless Celestial, smiling and bland, most innocently employed making a cup of tea! Every sign of guilt is swept away. The arch hypocrite knew the enemy was coming long before he had time to appear.

Dramatic performances, too, are a passion with the Chinese. In a space of half a mile there are no less than four theatres, though there is nothing to distinguish these places of amusement from the general run of houses except the scarlet hieroglyphics which are pasted on the doorposts and a row of paper lanterns over the doorway; sometimes a flag flutters from the balcony. A discordant din of gongs, tin trumpets, and squeaking fiddles wanders out into the street. Celestial economy of space follows us even here. Within a few feet of the entrance door a moon-faced Mongolian sits receiving custom, fifty cents for admission the beginning of the evening, the charge dwindling down to five cents as the hours roll on. A paper curtain was lifted aside, we ascended a flight of dirty stairs, and were at once ushered into our box, which had been previously secured for us; once seated therein, we proceeded to survey the scene at our leisure. The house was crowded from floor to rafter. It is divided into two parts, the pit or parquette, which slopes upward from the footlights to the back of the house; above that is a gallery, which extends over and seems ready to fall on the heads of those below, and rises steadily backwards till the last row of Mongolian heads seems to touch the ceiling. On one side are three private boxes, if they can be called private, for they are simply partitioned off, breast high, from the rest of the gallery; these are reserved for the use of the more distinguished visitors. On the opposite side a similar portion of the gallery is partitioned off for the use of the women, for even in this (the only recreation the poor creatures seem to have) they are not allowed to participate with their lords and masters. The partitions in all cases are so low that every one is in full view of the rest of the house. There is no attempt at ornamentation anywhere; the walls are whitewashed; benches, etc., are all of the roughest description. The stage is merely a raised platform, with a few wooden steps on either side, up and down which actors and audience are constantly passing; there is no scenery, no decoration of any kind. The musicians are seated at the back of the stage, and on either side is a curtained doorway, through which the entrances and exits are made. No drop-scene falls between the acts, and there is no attempt at realization anywhere; no regard is paid to the fitness of things. Say there is a wedding, a battle, and a death; the priestly cortége walks out at one door, the warriors enter at another, each whirling one leg as he leaps from an imaginary horse; there is a tremendous uproar and they dash at once into the fray. The musicians in the background are pounding away at their discordant instruments, each making as much noise as he can with no regard whatever to rule or rhythm, while one invincible hero with a pasteboard sword keeps a whole army at bay. He slays them by scores, but as fast as they are slain they get up, run round to the back, and begin the fight over again. At last the hero is overpowered; a hundred swords pierce him to the heart, he is trampled on, and he goes through all the contortions of a horrible death; then gets up, smiles, nods at the audience, and conquerors and conquered crowd off the stage together.

At the moment we entered a battle royal was going on; the noise was deafening; we had been warned of this, and plugged our ears with cotton-wool, but that was slight protection; the waves of sound struck upon the drums of our ears till our brains seemed to feel the blows, and our heads ached distractedly.

It was a strange sight—that mass of shaven faces, their slant eyes fixed with intense earnestness on the stage, revelling with solemn delight in the ludicrous performance. They never applaud, they never condemn; but sit stolidly smoking. The women, too, indulge in the fragrant weed, and largely patronize the seller of sugar-cane and sweetmeats, who stalks about the house with a basketful of these dainties on his head, but makes no sound, utters no invitation to buy. The battle was succeeded by a domestic disturbance of the most uncelestial character; the wife ran about the stage screeching like a wild cat, her indignant lord pursuing her with furious threats and grimaces, leaping over invisible chairs and tables. At last a window was brought in; she rushed behind it, and so made an imaginary escape from his fury; being so far safe, she leant out, Juliet-fashion, he making frantic attempts to get at her; and they rehearsed their difficulties with an accompaniment of gongs and fiddles, their screeching voices reminding us forcibly of a wrangling duet between two irate tomcats on the back tiles. This was succeeded by a half-military, half-acrobatic performance. First a warrior entered with a wild mustache and gray-green beard, marvellous to behold; his nose and ears were painted white, with black rolling eyes, and altogether a most ferocious aspect. He flung his sword up in the air, whirled round on one leg, shook his fist menacingly, as though defying some one to mortal combat. His challenge was accepted. A score of warriors entered, surrounded him, shook their swords, and rushed about as though in the fury of battle. Soon their arms were flung aside. They had evidently changed their minds, and the warfare resolved itself into an acrobatic display. They twirled round like dancing dervishes, leapt into the air, made two or three somersaults, rolled themselves into balls, fell and rebounded from the floor like india-rubber. They turned like wheels upon the ground, or spun like tops in the air. So rapid were their movements the eye could scarcely follow them. One weird half-naked figure, with his face and body painted in stripes of different colours, went through the most wonderful contortions. He tied his legs round his neck, leaped high in the air and came down upon his elbows, walked on his head without the use of his arms or legs, rolled himself into a knot and flung himself into the air. Having gone through sundry other evolutions too complicated to mention—indeed, having done everything but turn himself inside out—he left off.

These performances are supposed to lighten and vary the dramatic representation, which generally lasts six or eight weeks, giving two or three acts every night.

On the occasion of the Chinese New Year, which fell in early February, we accompanied a friend to pay a ceremonious visit to some wealthy Chinese merchants, with whom he had been in the habit of transacting business. It was a general visiting day, when everybody belonging to the flowery kingdom called on everybody else. All the streets in Chinatown were gaily decorated with flowers, flags, and paper lanterns; gongs were beating, cymbals clashing, and fiddles scraping in every direction; the streets were thronged with moon-faced Celestials in gala dress, all pricked out and polished fresh from the hands of the barber.

Our first visit was to Ki Chow, one of the leading merchants of San Francisco. We descended from the street, as usual, and found ourselves in a large cellar filled with benches and forms; a fire was burning in one corner, where cooking was being carried on. This was where Ki Chow's *employés* fed. Leading out of this was his private apartment, which contained a few rough wooden seats, a worm-eaten desk, and two tables, furnished on this occasion with an elaborately chased silver service, goblets, tankards, etc., and a display of cut glass of rare antique shapes, ornamented with gold and crimson; decanters filled with choice wines, trays and filigree baskets with cakes and sweetmeats. On one table was a hideous figure of a favourite Joss, before whom a light was burning. Sweets, wines, and other good things were placed before him for his godship's special entertainment. The liberal and dainty display on the other non-illuminated table was for our mortal gratification. We were compelled by Chinese etiquette to take a tiny toy glass of wine, which we cautiously sipped, it being a foreign production, and as our host informed us, "velly stlong;" it was rich, luscious, and of a peculiar flavour. "It velly good, it made of lice," said Ki Chow, the loss of the unpronounceable "r" in this case giving the announcement a peculiar character. He next passed round tiny blue willow-patterned plates, containing cake covered with red cabalistic characters, dried fruits, nuts, candied water-melon, and numerous unknown uninviting compounds of a gelatinous nature. The fruits and candies were very good; the oily cakes we could not bring ourselves to touch. Ki Chow invited us into the cellar adjoining, which was his bedroom; it contained a bed with silken hangings, chairs, and a table decorated with a vase of blooming flowers, which seemed sorely out of place in this dingy stifling nook, lighted only, like a prison, from a grating along the top. Ki's wardrobe was strung up on a line overhead. He was evidently proud of his bachelor quarters. He nodded, smiled, and volunteered the information—

"Me have tlee wives, all gone back to China; when they here, me have big house."

On our expressing a desire to see a Chinese lady, he offered to present us to a friend who had lately married and brought his wife to San Francisco. We accepted the invitation and accompanied him to Wong How's forthwith. It was a large roomy house in Sacramento Street; the entrance-door was on the latch as usual, and we ascended a flight of cleanly swept stairs to the first floor; one tap at the door and it was opened by a most majestic-looking Chinese gentleman, very handsomely dressed in blue silk and gold embroidery.

He received us with high-bred courtesy, with a layer of formality on the top of his politeness; he spoke in the purest English we had heard from Mongolian lips. This apartment was very handsomely furnished, with quaintly carved ebony chairs, and lounges and tables beautifully inlaid in the finest style of Chinese art, some with gold filigree, others with ivory or tortoise-shell, and the windows were draped with curtains of gorgeously embroidered silk. Here, too, were tables spread, one for the god, one for the visitors.

We had scarcely seated ourselves when other visitors began to arrive in quick succession, one after the other, and host and guests salaamed and saluted each other in true Oriental fashion, lifting the two hands to their foreheads, and bending lower and lower till their heads almost touched the ground; then followed handshaking, and a babble of soft, liquid tongues, evidently exchanging cordial good wishes. We inquired for the lady.

"Oh! she come plesently; she flightened; me only mallied tlee months, and she never seen no more man but me; to-day she bling coffee and sweets for evelybody; it is our custom fol a wife to wait on her husband's fliends once in evely year; she never see man other times."

In a few minutes the poor little bride entered, bearing a silver tray filled with little cups of the national beverage. She was gorgeously dressed in pink silk, trimmed with silver embroidery, interspersed with pearls, her hair bowed and puffed, and decorated with pins and flowers, according to the fashion of her people. She was leaning on two waiting-maids, who had much ado to support her tottering steps between them. She was painfully shy, and trembled, so that the cups and saucers rattled on the tray, and kept her eyes fixed upon the ground, trying to screen her face with a large feather fan; but we could see her lips quiver, and the deep blushes that dyed her face and neck contrasted with the red paint upon her cheeks. We compassionated her distress too much to keep her long under our gaze, and having received our empty cups upon the tray, she was scurrying off in a great hurry to get out of sight, but was somewhat harshly recalled by her lord, and more dead than alive, blushing and trembling more than before, she dragged herself across the room to serve her master's friends as any other slave would have done.

"She velly pletty," remarked Wong How confidentially to me, as the poor creature shuffled off the scene. Of course we contributed our share of admiration, and her owner coolly said: "Me got two more like that in China."

We were the only Europeans present, and while we were gathering scraps of information from our host, the door opened and some rakish-looking young hoodlums, the special production of San Francisco, being a cross between the French gamin and the English rough, half entered the room, exclaiming with a jaunty, patronizing air—

"How are you, John? We've come to pay you a morning call; hope you're glad to see us." Our host stepped forward with much dignity, saying—

"Excuse me, I have ladies here." The intruders at this moment caught sight of us, snatched off their caps, and with some half-uttered apology beat a hasty retreat. A number of cigars and a quantity of sweets, which they had no doubt purloined from some other "John," rolled out of their hats upon the floor, and they never stopped to pick them up. Wong How secured the door from further intrusion.

We were listening to the chatter and watching the collection of dark expressionless faces, when Ki Chow's countenance suddenly changed; an unearthly pallor overspread his face; he lifted his finger with a rapid motion. "Come!" he exclaimed, as he flew to the door and descended the stairs, we following as fast as our feet could carry us. Arrived in the street, we hurried after Ki Chow and inquired "What was the matter? What had occasioned his sudden flight? He had not even given us time to exchange parting civilities with his friends!" By this time Ki had recovered his usual equanimity; he turned upon us a face smiling and bland; innocent and unconscious as a child he exclaimed—

" Me no understand. Me takee see other lady."

What it was that caused our sudden retreat we shall never know. It must have been something serious, for I shall never forget the horror-struck expression of Ki Chow's face. Until that moment he had most deferentially made way for us to precede him; then, he had flown down the stairs, his blouse and pigtail flying behind him, merely calling to us " Come ! "

The "other lady," to whom he now introduced us, was a matron of five years' standing; a relative of his, I believe. We found her in a similarly handsome apartment to that we had just left, attended by two maids, who stood behind her and only moved to assist her in rising or walking. At her feet was a quaint little bit of living China, a miniature man, pigtail included, frolicking among his toy-gods and tin soldiers. He stared at us with his beady black eyes and retreated behind his mamma, who rose up saying—

" How you do ? Me velly well." She shook hands and invited us to be seated. She spoke a little English, giggled a good deal, seemed pleased with our admiration of her clothes and of herself (for she was as gorgeously apparelled as the other), and appeared ready and willing to gratify our curiosity so far as she was able. We examined the gold ornaments she wore upon her arms and neck, and the huge hoops in her ears. Her outer dress was of light blue, artistically and richly embroidered with silk, the colours beautifully blended together. We picked up her long loose sleeve and counted six dresses which she wore one over the other, all of different-coloured silks; they were so soft that the whole together did not seem much thicker than half a dozen layers of tissue-paper! We examined her complicated head-dress, which was quite an architectural trophy, so greased and waxed and strained, such wings on one side, such plastered puffs on the other. We inquired how much time was daily spent in the arrangement.

"Me no dless evely day. Me takee down in tlee or four days, and doee up again."

"How do you lie down? how do you sleep?" we inquired. She despatched a maid for her pillow—a round block of wood, covered with silk—which she placed at the back of her neck.

"Me sleep so, allee same so." A novel way of taking rest.

We showed her our big feet; she showed us her little feet, *i.e.* a small misshapen hoof. We had always believed that the Chinese ladies really had small baby-feet which had never been allowed to grow; but Ki Chow, informed us that they never meddle with the feet till the child is from *six* to *eight* years old, when they gather the toes together and twist them under the foot, then bind them with strong ligatures, which on no pretence whatever are loosened or taken off for two years, the whole of which time the child is, of course, undergoing great torture.

"Me have two little girls in China," said Ki Chow,

coolly. "My wife lite me word she makee tlem pletty feet now, and they cly, cly, all night, all day, allee same, till two years gone."

It would be curious to inquire how this barbarous custom first obtained, and how long, in these days when enlightenment is creeping into the heart of China, it will be permitted to endure.

CHAPTER XIX.

CHRISTMAS ON A CALIFORNIAN RANCHE.

Old Friends—The Ranche—Christmas Day—Salinas Valley—A Magic City—A California Sunset.

HRISTMAS has come. So the almanac tells us, but we can scarcely accept the fact, Christmas being associated, in our minds, with frost and snow, fogs and rain, which seem so far away now we feel as though the damp, chill atmosphere could never enfold us again. Here we look from our windows on a bright, sunlit scene, where the tall, green palms stand fair and stately in the city gardens, and calla lilies lift their fair faces to be kissed by the sun. The skies are intensely blue, and the breeze clear, cool, and invigorating as the breath of our own spring mornings. Every day we say, "This is the finest we have ever seen," but the morrow comes and brings with it another as lovely as the last. Our thoughts fly homeward, as, indeed, they often do. We know that the sleet is beating against the windows, the bleak wind tearing through the streets, whistling through every crevice, chilling the marrow of those who are shiver-

ing at the fireside, while the world without is lying stiff and rigid in its shroud of winter snow. We think of the friends who have been so long and so dearly associated with this season. The charmed circle was broken "A year and more agone!" Since then link by link has dropped, familiar faces have faded into shadowy memories. One after another, they have followed rapidly "into the silent land," "the land of the great departed," till this world seems to be growing empty and the next filling so fast we feel we shall scarcely be sorry when the order comes for us to "move on" and join them.

But here the sun is shining, and somehow, in spite of the leaden weight upon our spirits, there is something in this health-laden air that stirs the spirit and sets the pulse of life flowing as in its first springtide; and, though we know the autumn of life is upon us and the winter may not be far off, ready to sprinkle its last snows upon our heads and write *finis* to our life's history, yet our hearts grow lighter and rise, as though inflated with this brilliant atmosphere, till we feel like floating away in the sunshine. After all, the living must march ever onward, and leave the dead days mouldering behind them.

We loved the city which our new friends had made so pleasant to us, but we were not sorry to pack up and leave it for a while. We were going to spend the Christmas on a Californian ranche with some old friends who were closely connected with the "days that are bygone," but who had been living in the wild part of this Western world for the last five-and-twenty years. No doubt we each expected the other to be changed past recognition; for my part, I thought to find the dashing young officer, who had borne himself so bravely during the Russian campaign, developed, through agricultural association and pursuits, into a Californian farmer, somewhat lanky about the lower limbs, hollow-cheeked, and with the soft and by no means unpleasant drawl of the native Californian. I do not know why I was so strongly impressed with this imaginary portrait, for, since my advent into the State, my preconceived opinions concerning it had undergone a rapid transition; things were so different from what I had expected; even the Californian drawl had dwindled into a thing more imaginary than real.

We leave San Francisco on Christmas Eve, a brilliant, sunshiny day, and take our seats in the cars of the South Pacific Railway, with a protest against the heat, for December being a winter month according to the division of time, the stoves are lighted at either end of the car; the blinds are closed to keep out the burning rays of the sun, but they keep in the stifling hot air of the stoves till the crowded car becomes uncomfortably close and warm. The rest of the passengers sit and bake in uncomplaining calm; to us the suffocating air grows unendurable; we get out and sit upon the steps of the rear platform, and are whirled along through pretty home scenery at the not especially rapid rate of twenty miles an hour. We have not long been in possession of this position when a polite brakesman taps me on the shoulder.

"Sorry to interrupt you, ma'am, but you see what's written there," he said, pointing to a warning above the car door.

I look up and shake my head with the blank ignorance of the "heathen Chinee." "I can't read," I say.

He translates the sentence: "Passengers are strictly forbidden to stand on the platforms."

"Ah! but we are not standing," I exclaim, exultingly, "and there is no prohibition against *sitting*."

He smiles, vanquished, and leaves us in possession of the field.

After a run of about four hours, we steam into Salinas station. But few passengers alight. The generality are going to places beyond. We had scarcely time to step out upon the platform and glance round, when the only occupant thereof—a tall stately gentleman—came hurriedly towards us, and, in unmistakable British accents, welcomed us most cordially. The tones of the well-remembered voice came back to me like the melody of an old song that has slept in the memory for years and is awakened suddenly by a new singer in a new land. A bridge seemed to be flung over the gap of time, and we old friends met as though we had parted but yesterday. Yes; we had both changed. I had developed from a mere thread paper to—but no man (or woman either) is bound to criminate him or herself. He had grown from a rather languid, delicate young fellow to a strong, stalwart man, broad-chested, with muscles and biceps which warranted him to come off only second best in a tussle with a grizzly; the fine-featured face was bronzed and full, but the smile and the kind brown eyes were still the same. He pointed out to us the ranche as we bowled over the rough, uneven road. It is about three miles distant from

Salinas, and, being situated in the flat, extensive valley, it was visible from the moment we left the station behind us. The tall, substantial windmill which surmounts the water-works, and the numerous white adobe buildings gathered round the main dwelling-house, give it the appearance of a pretty rural village lying sleepily in the sunshine.

The Valley of Salinas itself is neither pretty nor interesting. It is about twenty miles long and proportionately wide. The land is rich and productive, and every rood is well under cultivation; but we miss the beautiful green hedges which divide the fields and border the pleasant country lanes in the old country. Here there is no such luxuriant landmark; not a bush, not a tree to be seen; nothing but the wide, level plain surrounded by a perfect amphitheatre of hills and mountains covered with dark pine or sombre fir trees. Occasionally, we are told, their bald heads are covered with snow, which is rarely known to reach the valley below.

The ranche stands some distance from the roadway, and is approached by a long, wide avenue. On either side are planted rows of trees, which don't seem inclined to grow; they look weird and sickly, and, though they have been coaxed and nursed in the best agricultural fashion, they will not put on their dress of luxuriant green; they look dismal and melancholy, as though they wanted to expand into respectable, shady trees, but have not the heart to do it; they seem to feel the cruel gopher feeding on their roots and sending the poisoned sap through their tender veins. This is the third year this experiment has been tried and failed, as it is failing now.

We drive through this avenue and through an old-fashioned, arched, adobe gateway into an open courtyard. On one side is a collection of adobe buildings, the dwelling-places of former inhabitants, but which are now used as barns or lumber-sheds, and are the sleeping-places for the farm-labourers. On another side is a low range of adobe rooms or houses, comfortably fitted up, where some of the male members of the family sleep. On the left-hand side is the family residence, a comfortable frame house, two storeys high, which was sent out from England years ago, and, after travelling half the world over, was planted in that far-away corner of the Western world. It is arranged and furnished in every way according to the requirements of a refined and cultivated English family. A large hall has been added to the main building, forty feet long by twenty wide, with a great, old-fashioned bay-window at one end, looking out in a sweet, wild wilderness of a flower-garden. A wide chimney, with andirons, whereon pine logs are plentifully laid, ready for kindling, is on one side, a piano stands opposite, cosy rocking chairs, and other signs of a comfortable home life are scattered round the hearth; a long table runs down the centre of the hall, which is generally used as a dining-room when the family is increased by guests who, like ourselves, find always a welcome at the ranche, and come not in "single spies, but in battalions." The laundry stands in a corner of the courtyard, opposite the gateway, and the dairy in a field beyond. We received a cordial welcome from the ladies of the family. A collection of pretty girls and fine, manly young fellows, the sons and daughters of the house, came out into the courtyard to meet us. It was a pleasant sight, that father and mother, still in the prime of life, with their unbroken circle of blooming girls and sturdy boys around them—children of the Old World taking root in the soil of the New. I found my host was more British than ever. So far from his interests and sympathies with the Old World languishing or lessening from his long sojourn in this far-away land, they were keener than ever; he marches side by side with us in all social questions, and is more thoroughly conversant with political matters, both at home and abroad, than many who are in our midst. Papers, magazines, pamphlets find their way from the heart of London to the core of the Western world. We found the daughters of the house purely English in thought, tone, and feeling, all their aspirations rising towards the old land, and their longings turning thitherward, while the sons seemed as purely American in theirs.

Behind the ranche, and, as it were, keeping guard over it, rises Gapilan Peak, the highest and loveliest of all that mountain range. It seemed so near to us that I proposed a morning scramble and luncheon on top, but I was speedily informed that it would take a long day, of pretty rough travelling too, to climb the rugged mountain sides, and would necessitate spending a night on the summit, from which, however, could be seen a most glorious sunrise. This sounded romantic, but I had no desire to taste the doubtful delight. We occupied the principal guest chamber, which had no actual communication with the house, but opened on to a wide verandah, which led down through a deliciously wild garden direct to the woods. As we lay in our beds at night we could hear the coyotes come howling down from the wilderness, but the deep bay of our good watch-dogs speedily chased them off the premises. We had no fear of tramps or stragglers, for we had gallant defenders near, with guns and rifles loaded.

On Christmas Day there was a frost, and the ponds were covered with a coating of ice. They said we had brought an English Christmas into the midst of the sunlands. Such a thing as frost and snow had not been known there for twenty years. A clear, cold, frosty air, blue skies, and a blazing sun roused us early in the morning, and on descending to the breakfast-room we found pretty souvenirs of Aballone jewelry, peculiar to California, beside our plates, and the Chinese servants had presented the members of the family with some native toy, according to their custom.

At dinner the large family circle was increased by the advent of some solitary friends and neighbours. We were merry and sad and glad together. We thought of those who were gone, but we talked of those who remained. Our host proposed "The Old Country." I think there was a tug at our hearts, and our voices were scarcely steady as we rose with one accord and accepted it. I presently whispered a name which was caught up and echoed from one end of the table to the other—"With love and greetings across the sea." Then somebody suggested that "Rule Britannia" would be appropriate for an after-dinner melody as we gathered round the blazing pine fire. Forthwith that lady commenced ruling "the waves," and I don't think she ever performed that ceremony with more true and loyal hearts around her. We were all feeling ridiculously patriotic. We grumble when we are at home, and are severe on the faults and failings of our Motherland; we pick holes in her best coat, and find flaws in her finest policy. But when we are away, and thousands of miles of land and sea divide us from her,—well, she might beat us with her trident and we'd forgive her!

We passed a delightful time with this interesting family. We all had our own opinions, and strong ones too. We drove about the country, or roamed through the woods all day, and in the evening gathered round the fire (for it was cooler here than in the city), and discussed ourselves and our American cousins. We picked one another to pieces, and put ourselves together again, amid much fun and laughter, and a tolerable amount of fairness on both sides.

We had often heard our host alluded to in the local papers as "the Big Bug of Salinas;" a strange phrase, which sounded to us of the offensively facetious order, but it was not so held by the inhabitants of the place; by them it is employed quite as a title of honour, and applied to one whom all the townsfolk held in the highest esteem. It is no wonder that the people of Salinas paid this tribute of respect to our host, for he was the founder of their city, and it is entirely owing to his enterprise and judicious management that it has grown to be the important place it is. Twelve years ago the Salinas Valley was a vast uncultivated plain, with two wretched tumble-down Spanish villages—Natividad and Santa Rita,—both of the most miserable description, which are settled in one corner of it. He chanced to be passing through this lovely tract of country, where a winding river trailed its silver waters; numbers of wagon trains and other traffic passed along this valley on the way to Monterey and other settlements on the coast, and he thought it would be an admirable site for a halting-place. To think was to act. He bought an extensive tract of land, consisting of many thousand acres, selected an appropriate spot, and staked out lots for streets, churches, public buildings, etc., and advertised them for sale in all the Californian and many other papers. His venture met with entire success; the lots were bought up and building commenced with great rapidity, and the place has now developed into a city of between three and four thousand inhabitants, with numerous aids to religion in the way of churches, a bank, a town hall, and even a prison, which was occupied on the occasion of our visit by a handsome horse-stealer and a predatory Chinaman. The former was stretched upon his straw pallet reading a recent copy of the *Atlantic Monthly*. The city of Salinas is in a most flourishing condition; building is still going on, and as the wind blows fresh faces thitherward it promises to double its present numbers before many years are past. The whole of the valley, as I have said before, is in a state of high cultivation. There are several flourishing farms and extensive fields of grain. Opposite our entrance gate is a cornfield more than two miles long.

We soon exhausted the beauty of Salinas Valley, but could not so easily exhaust the hospitality of our friends, who resolved to escort us on a tour to Monterey, one of the oldest Spanish settlements along the coast, where there are still the remains of a most interesting mission built a century ago. We are to start in the morning, and we go out to take a last evening stroll, escorted by all the young folk of the family, one of whom, a young gentleman aged seven, proves an heroic acquisition. He marches in front of us, runs after the squirrels, chases the gophers into their holes, pelts the pigs out of our path, and at last compels an advancing corps of cattle to turn tail and run, while we take shelter from their crumpled horns behind a gatepost.

The sun sinks rapidly behind the hills, and leaves the Western hemisphere aglow with golden light, with feathery plumes of crimson, isles of amber, and pale amethyst cloudlets floating therein, changing and amalgamating their gorgeous hues, till they form one brilliant cavalcade of coloured glory. Long after the sun has departed the skies retain their brightest blue; slowly the trailing skirts of the twilight cover them, and we take a last look at the mountains shrouded in the purple mist peculiar to the Californian climate, which for the time gives them a mysterious airy appearance, as though they were growing in cloudland rather than on this solid earth of ours. In the glowing daylight this airy drapery is invisible; it is only seen when the shades of evening begin to fall.

CHAPTER XX.

IN THE VALLEY OF CARMELO.

Monterey—The Ruins of the Mission—The Spanish Inhabitants of the Old Town — The Moss Beach — The Lighthouse—The Pebbly Pescadero—Good-bye.

E reach Monterey in the cool of the evening. A queer tumble-down Spanish town lying close along the sea-shore. One or two fishermen are trailing their nets on the face of the water, and some fishing-smacks, with their brown, patched sails, are anchored in the bay, and are rocked so gently by the waves they seem to be coquetting with their own shadows. Not much more than a century ago a host of Spanish vessels sailed into this now lonely and deserted harbour, their colours flying, their decks crowded with soldiers, sailors, priests, and nuns. Here they landed in search of a good site wheron to found a mission for their priestly labours. They stationed themselves on an elevated point about two miles from the sea; there the labour of love began. They built a *presidio* for the soldiers to protect the fathers from the native Indians. Every man who had hands to work devoted himself to the cause, and laboured till the church and mission buildings were completed. All that

part of the country was taken possession of in the name of the King of Spain, and the work of conversion began. The ceremony was performed with a blare of trumpets, beating of drums, and salvos of artillery, calling out an army of echoes from the surrounding hills and mountains. The poor Indians were at first dazed with the display of tawdry magnificence and frightened at the thundering sounds which shook the air and seemed to make the solid earth tremble beneath their feet; but by degrees they approached, and then learned that this wonderful expedition was organized expressly for their benefit. Peace in this world and glory in the next was freely promised them. The gates of Paradise were opened before them; they had nothing to do but to walk in and take possession. Scores were converted every day; they bowed down before the altar. The acolytes swung the incense, the fathers preached and chanted in an unknown tongue, the nuns, from behind their grated gallery, lifted their songs of adoration and praise, and the poor heathen souls were caught up in the great mystery and won to God.

From Mexico and Spain settlers soon came flocking into the beautiful valley, establishing themselves upon the sea-shore, building dwellings, grazing cattle, and growing fruits and flowers, increasing and multiplying themselves and their houses till the city grew and, for a time, flourished in peace and plenty, carrying on a thriving trade not only with Spain and Mexico, but with the inhabitants along the coast. The descendants of the first settlers, to a great extent, still occupy the now half-deserted, dilapidated town. The mission church, presidio, and other buildings appertaining thereto are on an elevated spot some two miles distant from the town overlooking the lovely and extensive Carmel Valley.

Only a century ago the church was filled with priests and converts, the presidio with soldiers, their clanking arms and breastplates glittering in the sun; vessels rode at anchor in the harbour, and crowds of Dutch and Spanish traders, with their bales of merchandise, swarmed upon the silver-sanded beach below. Now all is gone, like painted shadows fading from the sunshine.

The church, crowning the hilltop and dominating the landscape for miles round, is one of the most beautiful, picturesque, and perfect ruins upon the coast. Its exterior is complete, even to the rusty bell which still hangs in the belfry tower, and creaks with a ghostly clang when wind blows through; and we are surprised to find so much of the decorative masonry still intact. Dilapidated saints and cherubs, with broken trumpets and mouldering wings, still hold their places, while all around is slowly but surely crumbling to decay; and, though in places you may see the daylight streaming through the roof, you can still ramble through the nuns' gallery and look down upon the altar, where the broken font still clings to the wall.

On the occasion of our visit, a small side chapel or vestry was decorated with ivy, evergreens, and paper flowers, and tin sconces, with the remains of guttering candles, were left upon the walls. It had been evidently used very lately—by the villagers, perhaps, for some festive gathering. The extensive range of adobe buildings which surround the church and were occupied by the converts and day labourers, are still in a state of semi-preservation; the roofs are gone, but the walls are still standing. The whole of these sacred possessions were enclosed, and entered then as now by a massive gateway at the foot of the southern slope.

The town of Monterey is only interesting from its association with the past. It is dirty, it is dusty, it is utterly void of all modern improvements. Streets! there are none to speak of, except, perhaps, a row of slovenly shops which have been run up by some demented genius the last few years. The old adobe houses—and they are all made of that species of sun-dried clay—straggle about in the most bewildering fashion; it is much easier to lose your way than to find it. The people are all strongly characteristic of their Spanish origin; they are a dark, swarthy, lazy-looking race, and scarcely seem to have energy enough to keep themselves awake. Their houses have no pretension to architecture of any kind; there is no attempt at pretty cottage-building or rural decoration; not even a creeping plant is trained to hide the bare walls; they have low doorways—a tall man must stoop to enter them—and small, square windows set in the thick clay walls. I suppose the men *do* work sometimes, but I have seen them at all hours, shouldering the door-posts, smoking in sombre, majestic silence, while the wives sit on stools beside them, generally with bright-coloured handkerchiefs pinned across their breasts, huge gold hoops in their ears, and often thick bracelets on their arms. In her barbaric love of display the woman forms a picturesque and striking figure in the shadow of her majestic lord; she is a piece of brilliant colouring, from the full, red lips, rich-hued complexion, to the sparkling black eyes which illuminate the whole.

In the heart of the town there is a long, low range of deserted buildings formerly occupied by the military; the windows are all broken, the worm-eaten doors hang, like helpless cripples, on their hinges, and only the ghostly echo of the wind goes wandering through the empty chambers. In all quarters of the town you may come upon houses with windows patched or broken and padlocked doors, the owners having died or wandered away, and no one (but the rats) cares to take possession of bare walls. Nobody heeds them; they are left to natural decay. We passed some lonely, barn-like dwellings, with curtained windows and large gardens behind, where we could see the orchard trees, and flowering shrubs, and white winter roses growing; these were shrouded with almost monastic quietude. We go to the primitive Catholic Church on Sunday, and wonder where all the beautiful women dressed in their picturesque national costume have come from. They have a proud, haughty look upon their faces, and seem to resent our intrusion. These, we were told, are the aristocratic remains of the ancient dwellers in the city, who form a small exclusive society among themselves, and live in the secluded barn-like buildings above alluded to. Some are in the midst of the town; some scattered on the outskirts. The music was good and the service reverently conducted.

There are two or three old-established hotels, all of a

more or less indifferent kind. We went to the best, which is of quite a second-rate character, but it serves well enough as a resting-place for passing tourists. The inhabitants are strictly conservative—not with the true spirit of conservatism, which retains the best and improves or lops off what is bad in its constitution, but they carry out the conservatism of ignorance ; they will not advance with the age ; "what was good enough for their forefathers," they argue, " is good enough for them ; as they were in the old days, so they are now ; they plod along in the old groove, and keep to their old customs, and nurse their old superstitions with undeviating blind persistency. Why should they trouble about improving ?"

There is not a drop of water fit to drink in the whole city. The bright sparkling springs may be bubbling beneath their feet, but they will not dig for it. The tourist must drink aërated water, lager beer, or a poisonous decoction called *wine*. Even the visitors have hitherto been content with the meagre accommodation afforded them. The United States, which, as a rule, is quick to perceive and put its progressive ideas in motion, seems to have forgotten Monterey and left it, so far, to govern itself. But things are changing now. People are awakening to a sense of the importance of Monterey, which might, and most probably will, become one of the most delightful seaside resorts in the State ; it has every requisite to make it most attractive. It has excellent facilities for bathing, a magnificent sea view, and the walks and drives about the surrounding country are beautiful in the extreme ; there are wooded bosky dells, luxuriant green valleys, and undulating hills on every side, and it is in close proximity to points of great interest; the roads are pleasant and easy to drive along; in fact, the only want at Monterey is accommodation for visitors, and that want is being rapidly supplied. A monster hotel of quaint Swiss architecture is in course of erection within a short distance of the town; it is partially surrounded by a wood of scented pine and grand old forest trees, and a wide, magnificent sea view stretches before it; its appointments are to be of the most luxurious description; hundreds of busy workmen are employed upon it, and a promise is held out that it will be opened for this summer season.*

One clear, cool morning we pack a luncheon basket and start for a "cruise on wheels." We drive first past the old mission buildings to the Moss Beach, lying along the shores of the Pacific Ocean, and so called from the peculiar mossy character and beauty of the seaweed it flings so liberally along the pure, white sand, for the beach here is like powdered snow, and stretches far into the wild inland, its still, billowy waves sparkling like diamonds in the sunshine. A few miles farther on, and after a pleasant drive through pretty home scenery, we pass a Chinese fishing village, it being a mere collection of miserable hovels, and, as an Indian decorates his wigwam with scalps, these are hung inside and out with rows of dried and drying bodies of fish. The beach is covered with their bony skeletons and fishy remains in different stages of decomposition, and the whole air is

---

* Since these lines were written the Hotel Del Monte has been completed and is now opened.

redolent with an "ancient and fish-like smell." We are satisfied with an outside view, and have no desire to explore, but drive on as fast as we can till we reach the "pebbly beach of Pescadero," which is quite a celebrated spot. People come from miles round to visit it, and spend many hours in hunting for moss agates; for these, and many others of a beautiful and rare description, may be found in great numbers there. But apart from the chance of finding these treasures, the pebbly beach is in itself a great attraction for its rarity, as all along that portion of the coast there is only a sandy shore.

Thence we drive on to the lighthouse, which stands on a rocky eminence jutting out into the sea. We climbed the narrow stairway to the top, and enjoyed an extensive panoramic view of the wild sea and wilder land surrounding. A lonely, desolate place it was, and to some folk would be maddening in its monotonous dreariness, with the waves for ever beating round its rocky base, varied only by the screech of the sea-birds or howling of the wandering wind. Yet even in this bleak spot the keeper has coaxed flowers into growing, and hollyhocks, scarlet geraniums, dahlias, and other hardy plants are blooming round the lonely dwelling.

We are to take our lunch at Cypress Point, which we reach about three o'clock in the afternoon. This interesting and romantic spot which we had selected for our temporary festivity is an extensive grove, a miniature forest of cypress trees, covering and growing to the very verge of a lofty cliff which rises about two hundred feet perpendicularly from the sea. Their sombre forms, still and motionless, though a stiff breeze is blowing, turn oceanwards like dark-plumed, dusky sentinels keeping watch and ward over the rock-bound land. How many centuries have they stood there? Their age is beyond our ken. We feel the strange fascination of this gloomy spot. The ancient trees have grown into strange, fantastic forms. Some lie prone upon the ground, gnarled and twisted as though they had wrestled in their death-agony ages ago, and left their skeletons bleaching in the sunshine, for like the whitening bones of a dead man they crumble at the touch. Some have twined their stiff branches inextricably together, apparently engaged in an everlasting wrestling match. Here, like a half-clothed wizard, stands a skeleton tree with withered arms outstretched, and crooked fingers pointing menacingly at its invisible destroyer. On every side the weird strange forms strike the imagination, and though the sea is laughing and sparkling in the sun, and the soft wind fanning us with its cool, invigorating breath, the grim, silent congregation gives us an uncanny feeling, though we gather under their shade and eat, drink, and are merry. We shiver as we think what a spectral scene this cypress grove must be in the moonlight.

We drive through the beautiful Carmel Valley, with its wealth of picturesque beauty spread in rich luxuriance for miles round us. Wood and water, undulating hills and grassy slopes succeed each other, making a natural panorama, as we drive slowly on, taking in the dainty scene with unwearying eyes. Occasionally we passed a lonely farmhouse in the valley, or a chicken ranche half hidden among the trees on the hillside. These, we were told, are many of them occupied by English gentlemen of culture and education. Indeed, not only in this part of the country, but all over California and in Colorado, in corners farthest away from the sight and sound of their fellow-men, we find our countrymen have settled down as tillers of the land and cultivators of the soil. We are sometimes disposed to wonder what has driven them to these far corners of the earth. With some, perhaps, a love of adventure; a desire to form a part of the electric life of a new land. One gentleman informed us that he had been plucked at college; another had failed in a public examination. They had generally been crowded out of the Old World by failure of one kind or another, and wandered away to the New, where there is room for men to build up another life, and every facility for striking out "into fresh fields and pastures new." They appear prosperous, happy, and contented, but one and all seem to encourage a desire to return to the old land "when the children have grown up."

Our pleasant visit came to an end. I don't think any of us cared to say "good-bye," but we went through the ceremony with dignified calm. The wonder rose in our hearts, though it never reached our lips, " shall we ever stand face to face in this world again?" "Perhaps," whispers hope softly. We shake hands. "Good-bye," "Good-bye." With a shriek and a whistle our train steams onward. We carry away with us, and I hope leave behind, many pleasant memories of our Christmas in California.

CHAPTER XXI.

ON THE BANKS OF THE BAY.

New Year's Visits—The Gentleman's Day—Local Attractions—Berkeley College—Saûcelito—In Arcadia—Among the Woods and Flowers—A Fairy Festival.

HE streets of San Francisco are empty—that is, empty as regards the female population. Not a petticoat is to be seen; Kearney is deserted, and masculine humanity is left in full possession of California and Montgomery. Rank, beauty, and fashion is "receiving" to-day. Buggies, sulkies, rockaways, and every conceivable kind of vehicle, filled with gentlemen in evening costumes, are dashing frantically along the streets; hospitable doors are open, and a constant stream of the nobler sex flows in and out; they come and go in such quick succession it seems as though they were shot out of a catapult one moment and shot back the next. It is a sort of "go-as-you-please" visiting race, and he who pays most calls between midday and midnight rises to an imaginary place of honour. The 1st of January is essentially the "gentleman's day." Every lady—that is, everybody who is anybody, and many who are "nobodies," who hold neutral ground, and cling, like a ragged fringe, to the skirts of society—stays at home to receive New Year's

calls and friendly greetings from her gentleman friends. The advent of a lady on this occasion would be considered an outrage of all propriety. Sometimes ladies unite, two or three together, and hold their mutual receptions under one roof, generally choosing the most important and most central position, so as to simplify as much as possible the labours of their admirers. Their decision is generally announced to the world in this fashion: " The lovely Miss A. and the accomplished Miss B. will assist Mrs. So-and-so in receiving to-day." Although the sun is shining brilliantly without, the windows are closed, the gas lighted, the rooms beautifully decorated with choice flowers, and the ladies descend in their full accoutrement of charms and enter into this artificial night to receive the greetings of their several admirers. This custom obtains in all the great cities of America, but in San Francisco it is held in the fullest splendour and maintained with the greatest tenacity. The next day the press teems with a thrilling account of the day's proceedings. Whole columns of the *Chronicle* are devoted to details of the ladies' dresses ; the number of their visitors are duly chronicled, and woe be to the delinquent *he* who has failed in his duty ; the rest —well, I fancy there is a good deal of uncharitableness working behind a masked battery of smiles in the exchange of female confidences on the next day's meeting.

The time flies so fast in this beautiful, hospitable land that we are anxious to make the most of it, and, having fulfilled our engagements in the city, we decided to pay flying visits to some of the lovely resorts lying along the banks of the bay, which, as I have said before, is large enough for all the navies of the world to play hide-and-seek in. Oakland, perhaps, takes precedence, it being the most extensive, the most important, and certainly among the loveliest of these rural suburbs. It has a railway of its own dashing through the crowded public thoroughfares from one end of the town to the other, its engine bell cling-clanging, warning everybody out of the way as it charges onward. There are plenty of handsome shops, some very fine churches, banks, and a free mercantile library, presided over by an accomplished and efficient lady librarian, for female intellect is held at a higher premium, and is utilized to a greater extent in the New World than in the Old. Branching off from the populous highway are picturesque grassy streets, with quaint or fanciful dwellings on either side, all detached and surrounded by blooming gardens, stretching away on all sides, till the busy, bright little town, with a series of coquettish manœuvres, touches the green slopes of Berkeley, the seat of learning, the fount of knowledge, whence the youth of California draw their mental sustenance. There stands Berkeley College, presided over by Professor John Le Conte, one of the most eminent classical scholars of the day, of European reputation. The professors are all chosen from the foremost rank of whatever branch of study they adopt. The college is formed upon the principles of similar institutions in England, and, if they take proper advantage of the benefits to be acquired there, the Californian youth should be second to none. The building itself is of handsome red brick, massive and simple in its architecture. It lies at the base of the foothills, surrounded by a luxurious growth of green, and it forms a principal feature in the landscape for miles round. Oakland and Berkeley seem to run hand in hand till they are lost and buried in the green hillsides. Many of the citizens of San Francisco make their homes in those attractive suburbs, which lie about eight miles across the bay. Magnificent ferry-boats, decorated with mirrors, carving, and gilding, with luxurious lounges and velvet carpets, ply to and fro every half-hour during the day. Alameda, St. Quentin, and many other sylvan retreats are settled down in cosy nooks scattered round the bay, all being equally attractive and easy of access.

One bright February morning, when the bay is as smooth as glass, and a score or two of vessels with sails all set to catch what little breeze is stirring are floating like white birds on the face of the water, and the sky wears its Californian livery of intense blue, we start to spend a long day at Saucelito, which lies in quite an opposite direction across the bay. We watch the steep streets of the city (the people passing to and fro, the vehicles crawling up and down are dwarfed to the size of dolls and toy carriages) recede from our view. We pass by "the silent guns of Alcatras;" they are muzzled, masked, and silent now, like lions couchant and asleep, but should danger threaten that city of the sunland they would rouse up and roar as loudly as in days gone by. Small green islets, some sparsely inhabited, others the solitary home of the waterfowl, are scattered round the fortified island. These, with the richly wooded hills surrounding this part of the bay give a picturesque beauty to the scene. The briny breeze, laden with three thousand miles of iodine, sweeps through the Golden Gate, and as we breathe this health-giving air our pulse quickens and we feel we are taking a lease of a new life, and as though lassitude of limb or weariness of heart could afflict us never any more. There is a glorious sunshine overhead, and we look out through the Golden Gate at the silvery Pacific stretching away and lying like a bar across the distant sky, while behind us a chain of soft green and purple hills embrace the peaceful Bay. The fresh invigorating wind sets our cheeks aglow, and our spirits seem to rise on invisible wings. We feel it is a glorious thing to live. Life *is* worth the living while there are such days and hours to enjoy, and our hearts sing their voiceless song of thanksgiving, which only God can hear.

The boat slackens speed. We have been so occupied by the extensive land and sea views that we have failed to cast our eyes towards the sheltered nook we are now fast approaching. We seem to have come suddenly upon a delicious bit of Italian scenery transplanted to this far corner of the Western World. The richly wooded land rises before us, clothed in its glory of luxuriant green. A few tiny cottages are strewn along the bay shore, and we catch glimmerings of white-faced, red-tiled dwellings, hidden here and there among the trees on the sloping hillsides. Two or three drowsy officials are lounging about the landing-stage, and a shabby-looking vehicle, with a skeleton steed, stands baking in the hot sun, waiting for passengers. But there is no one else about, no sign of humanity abroad, everything is quiet and peaceful everywhere ; it seems as though nature had taken all her living children in her arms and lulled them to sleep in the sunshine.

We climb into the vehicle aforesaid, and begin slowly ascending the undulating hillside. It is a lovely, winding road, with luxuriant trees, flowering shrubs, and sweet-smelling wild flowers sloping away from us on the one side, and climbing up the gradual ascent on the other. The brisk breeze which had swept so keen and invigorating through the Golden Gate dies away here into a murmuring soft and low, making music in the tall tree-tops, stirring the leafy branches, and coquetting with the wealth of wild roses. Here and there we come upon some quaint, fanciful dwelling peeping out from a bower of green, the gardens running out in unconfined loveliness, as though they were proud to show their blooming progeny to the passing world outside.

There is no such thing in America as hedging and walling in private grounds for the solitary gratification of the owner only. Everything is liberally and lavishly thrown open for all the world to see, and in so much, the poorest tramp trudging along the road, or the poorest labourer in the field, shares his more fortunate neighbour's wealth, and may enjoy the luxury of the rich man's pleasure-gardens, even as the rich man shares with him the sunshine God freely gives to all. Although, according to the division of time, it is early spring, it might be blooming summer-time, for here it is the very carnival of flowers ; they are everywhere growing in such glorious profusion, too. The dainty plants, such as geraniums, fuchsias, myrtles, roses, etc., which we are accustomed to see flowering in pots or perhaps growing two or three feet from the ground, here expand into monstrous bushes or tall graceful trees. We have stood under a geranium tree and looked up, through its wealth of scarlet blossoms, at the blue sky beyond. Camellias, orchids, and other delicate plants and shrubs bloom out in the open air, laden with a gorgeous display of dainty flowers. We counted one hundred and ten waxen white camellias on one tree alone, and were lost in admiration of the California Acacia, which flung out its golden banners on every side, its soft fluffy blossoms, like plumes of fairy feathers, hiding every trace of the green leaves which gave them such fostering shelter only a few weeks ago. We found our way slowly through this romantic Arcadian scenery; there were no wanderers, no tourists, no tramps astir; the narrow winding road was solitary enough, except for once or twice, when we overtook a batch of women, in short petticoats and sun-bonnets, trotting along singing, in not unmusical voices, to beguile the way. Our skeleton steed, jingling his bells as though to advertise to the world how much work he was doing, suddenly pulled up at the foot of a rugged green bank, broken with rustic steps, leading up to a kind of "Glen Eyrie" or eagle's nest, half hidden in the rugged hillside. This was our destination; we climbed up the rough-hewn steps and found ourselves at the entrance-gate of the pretty white cottage with a verandah literally covered with creeping plants running along in front of it.

Our hostess came out to greet us—a sweet, grave-looking woman, whose smiling eyes had a shade of something in them, as though, in some invisible part of her nature, there was

> "A feeling of sadness and longing
> That is not akin to pain;
> Which resembles sorrow only
> As the mist resembles rain."

She formed a pretty picture, standing there beneath her trailing vines to welcome us wanderers from the Old World. We followed her into a long, low-roofed, comfortable room, with chairs and lounges covered with the skins of animals; cases of rare birds, and butterflies, and natural curiosities of all descriptions were arranged on all sides; gatherings of great rarity from the bowels of the earth, realms of the air, and the depths of the sea, spoils from the very heart of nature were arranged in every nook and corner. Both within and without the house everything was quaint, picturesque, and suggestive of Old World fancies.

Our hostess was one of those women to whom Pope alludes as

> "Mistress of herself though china fall."

It appears we had mistaken our day. We should have put in an appearance the day before, when all preparations had been made for our entertainment. Now the lady was alone, absolutely alone in the house. Her Chinese servants (they all employ Chinamen here) had gone to participate in some national festivity, and the sudden irruption of half a dozen unexpected guests must have been trying to the nerves of our solitary hostess. We ought to have grovelled in the dust, but didn't. She was equal to the occasion, and, in a genial, pleasant way, made us feel quite at home—as though, indeed, we could not have come at a better season. We all enjoyed the idea of a general picnic, improvised on the spot, and, amid much chatter, laughter, and the mildest of mild jokes, there was a stampede towards the larder; but the idle drones and butterflies of the party (whose offers of assistance in the culinary department were wisely declined) went wandering about the wilderness of a garden and strayed out into the sweet-scented woods beyond, looking down through the tangled branches upon the shining bay below. A perfect paradise this Saucelito seemed to us, made up of flowers, and peace, and sunshine ; a fitting birthplace for romance ; the cradle of poetry, where fine thoughts are nursed till they burst out into full-fledged phrases, and fly abroad, and stir the soul of the world with their wise philosophy or tender song. Presently the melancholy voice of the horn came moaning through the woods, calling us to return. We knew what that meant, and were not slow in obeying the summons, taking with us such healthy appetites as would have digested the sole of an old shoe if dressed to taste.

We found our way into the kitchen, where the feast was spread. It was not a commonplace kitchen, where the whole culinary battery is unmasked and its mysteries are carried on before your very eyes, and clatter of pans and frizzle and frying take away your appetite without opposition on your part. This was a poetical kitchen, with no signs of prose about it; coppers bright as mirrors reflected you from the walls, multiplied you by scores, till the room seemed full of your shadows. Quaint old china decorated the dressers; bunches of the beautiful pampas grass and vases of wild flowers were ranged upon the shelves. The most useful articles were of an ornamental character. Standing in one corner was a shining black, quaintly designed stove, with bright brass knobs and decorated scrolls, polished to the highest point of polishing, like a black prince with "gilded honours thick upon him." His fiery eye was closed; he had done his work and was at rest. From the bowels of this gnome had been conjured the dainty repast which awaited our attack. A table spread with fine linen, rare glass, and quaint old china, such as would have made a collector's mouth water, was ranged along one side of the room. As for the repast, it was a *recherché* thing, that might have tickled the palate of an epicure. There were broiled chickens, crisp salad, mayonaise, and such rich, luscious fruit and cream, with lovely flowers and trailing smilax nestled among them. The very wine, as it was poured out into the Venetian vine-stemmed glasses, seemed to bubble and sparkle and cream over, as though it quite enjoyed being drank out of such rare prettiness. We kept the door which led into the garden wide open. The tall calla lilies bent their fair heads, and the saucy red roses, blushing at their own beauty, sent their perfumed breath wandering towards us, fluttering their tender leaves as though to frighten away the droning bees, who would rifle their sweets before our eyes. A whole squadron of familiar shrubs and flowers were gathered thickly round them, and they shook out their rustling leaves, nodded their fragile heads, and stared in at us with their white and violet eyes. We stared back and thought how lovely and refreshing it all was.

Our day in this modern Arcadia passed quickly, too quickly; we would fain have put on the drag and kept it for awhile. The purple mist began to fall over the mountain-sides as we started on our way homeward through a beautiful wide cañon, fringed with graceful ferns and tall stately trees, screening from our sight the light of the setting sun; a poor little wandering stream crept in and out among the broken boulders, as though it was tired and wanted to rest somewhere, and was trying to find its way to the great sea; once absorbed in the everlasting waters there would be peace, or it might chance to filter its way down to the hearts of the dead men who lie there shrouded in weeds waiting for eternity. We were late in reaching the boat, for we had been tempted to linger by the way; the bell was ringing and we had scarcely stepped on board the boat, when the engine gave a great satisfactory snort, swung round and started.

The sun had already sunk behind the hills, and the shades of twilight were rapidly closing round us, but the red clouds were still floating in the west, and ragged banners and broken bars of gold still streamed through the darkening skies. It was quite dark when we reached San Francisco; we saw the lights in her steep streets, and the fiery eye of the dummy dashing up and down, and the red and white car lights flashing hither and thither like fireflies; truly she looked like a queen gorgeously arrayed, flashing her diamonds of living light in the face of the sombre night.

CHAPTER XXII.

IN THE FOREST PRIMEVAL.

Pleasant Retreats—Californian Trees—Cañon and Forest Scenery—Duncan Mills—A Stormy Evening—The Redwoods—Farewell to the "Golden City."

HERE is so much that is beautiful, and of a most varied kind of beauty, from the magnificent and sublime to the pretty and picturesque, all along the wonderful Pacific Coast, and reaching inland to rivers and mountains, you might spend many months there and not have time to exhaust, nor even to thoroughly enjoy them all, but to those whose time is limited it is difficult to know what to do with it; but there are some places which must be visited, some things which must be seen. There are the orange groves of Los Angeles, where you wander for miles through forests of golden fruit, which, in this month of February, have just reached perfection, and are ready for the gathering. Men, women, and children are busy at their work, piling the dainty fruit in bushel baskets, with such delicate handling that not a bruise shall fleck the smooth gold skin, while the air is literally laden with the pungent perfume. Some of the fruit grows to an immense size, as large as melons, but

what they gain in size they lose in flavour; in fact, it is so with the generality of Californian fruits, which are magnificent to look at, both as to size, form, and colour, but they seem to have outgrown their strength and weakened their flavour, for it is very inferior to that of the same kind of fruit which is grown in the Eastern States. Of course there are exceptions, but I refer to the rule.

San Joaquin and San José are the most wonderfully prolific wheat-growing countries, perhaps, in the world. The grain grows so tall, so heavy and full, that the tasselled ears droop and seem toppling over from their own weight. These miles of fair fruitful lands lay rolling out from the foot of the mountains, catching every gleam of sunshine, absorbing every breeze that blows. Thriving farms are scattered throughout these valleys; on all sides there are vineyards, grain fields, orchards, and extensive cattle ranches; signs of thrift and prosperity are evident everywhere. It is very pleasant to pass through these highly cultivated lands, where civilization has left her mark in such unmistakable characters; but Nature in her wilder stages, amid her kingly rivers, her lakes, her unapproachable mountains and untrodden forests, is more sublimely impressive.

We were anxious to visit Yosemite Valley and the Mariposa Grove of big trees, but that was impossible, the valley being still snowed up, and the roads leading thereto rough and almost impassable. In order to be thoroughly enjoyable a pleasure excursion to the Yosemite Valley should be taken from early June until late October; during these months the magnificent scenery of this wonderful valley is seen in the highest perfection. Of course there are many adventurous spirits who make the tour at all seasons of the year, and force their way into the valley when it is clothed with icicles and crowned with snow. As we must, perforce, miss the Yosemite for this year at least, we decide on a visit to the Redwood Forest in Sonoma County. Once more we cross the bay, pass on the other side of Alcatraz, and thread our way through the green islets surrounding it till we are landed at St. Quentin; thence we take our tickets for Duncan Mills—the railway station is close to the landing stage. It is a narrow-gauge line; the carriages or cars are long and narrow; we can only sit three abreast. It looks like a train of tiny toy carriages, but our bright little engine is up to its work, and carries us on in a swift, spirited way, as though it was taking a holiday on its own account, not at all on ours. It looks like a serpent winding its way through a paradise of luxuriant green. We run alongside of Tomales Bay, nay, run into it, and cross its long arms more than once. Scores of wild ducks and geese are skimming along the face of the water. On one side of the bay is a range of low-lying hills, while our little train is puffing along on the other close under the shadow of massive gray rocks, with skeleton trees and stumpy bushes growing out of their broken sides. We pass the pretty fishing village of Tomales, and some few queer-looking hovels, on the edge of the bay, inhabited by Indians, for the squaws and little brown children are grouped under the eaves mending nets or making willow-baskets. We soon leave the bay behind us, and pass by picturesque villages nestling peacefully among the foothills, and here and there a half-ruined deserted dwelling at the mouth of a deep cañon, which leads hundreds of miles away into the wilds where the brown bear feels safe from the hunter and the young wolves bay the moon at night. We cross deep ravines upon narrow trellis-work which would have made us shudder in the old days. Presently we find ourselves running along the base of thickly wooded hills, with their wealth of strangely beautiful trees, which were new to our eyes. Here are a group of Madroño trees, with their orange-coloured bark, sometimes deepening to crimson, but always shining and smooth as polished ivory, their red veins running like graceful lacework through their leaves of tender green. These lovely trees will flourish nowhere but in their native woods. All known methods have been tried to raise them in ornamental grounds, but they obstinately refuse to take root; in spite of the tenderest care they droop and die. Then comes the Manzanita, with its pale-green leaves and delicate pink blossoms, drooping in bunches so close to us we could reach out our hands and pluck them as we pass. We are going now at only the rate of ten miles an hour, and the conductor occasionally gets off the train and runs alongside, gathering flowers or specimen leaves for us till we are overladen. Higher up the hillsides stand whole families of ash and popular, looking as fresh and green as the hand of spring could paint them. Here, grim and hoary, rise a company of live oaks, their ragged mossy robes scarce covering their long straggling limbs, but hanging all over them like a jagged fringe or gray beard matted and falling from its bald head, twisting and writhing round it as though to strangle the little life that lingered in its gnarled and knotted trunk. The scene changes, and, glancing across on the other side of the bed of the Russian River, we see the fir and pine trees growing in dense dark masses, with here and there a clump of golden trees, like yellow islands in a sombre sea of green. Presently we reach the forest, drive into it and through it for many miles; the dark trees, grown so straight and tall and strong in their native solitudes, close round us on every side. Looking upward we can scarcely see the sky, and the sun tries hard to fight its way down through the branches, but only succeeds in sending a bright lance here and there to smite the ground we are rolling over. Then the forest on one side at least, falls back and climbs the sloping hills on our left. On our right lies the Russian River, which has followed us all along, winding its way through the dense forest, playing hide-and-seek with the sun; sometimes with silent, secret persistency forcing its way through broken boulders and other natural impediments which hinder its progress; then, dividing its forces, creeping stealthily through narrow crevices till it unites again with double strength, and storms its way onward till it reaches a low-lying rocky ledge, and sweeps over with a thunderous roar and falls into its bed below. It is all right now, and its swirling waters roll on, leaping and laughing in the sunshine, on their smooth and pleasant journey towards the sea. Here and there we pass a wooden house lying upon its side in the bed of the river. Some of these capsized cottages are entire, as though they had merely toppled over; some are dilapidated and broken like match-boxes. We wonder how they got there, and are told that a few months ago the river rose fifty-four feet, overflowing its banks, and, rushing in its mad, headlong course through the country, swept all before it, leaving the *débris* where it still remained, some lodging on the banks and some lying in the bed of the river. The wreckage of homes and lands is strewn for miles along the river's course. We had but one fellow-passenger through all this journey, and he was shrouded in self-complacency and a linen-duster. He sat with his hat pulled over his eyes, and his nose buried in a book; he never once looked out on the grand scenery we were passing through; but that was Nature's book, perhaps he couldn't understand the language. He had been a candidate for Congress, we were told, and failed; if he had been a candidate for Napa Asylum, I think he'd have got it.

Duncan Mills is the terminus; the train goes no farther; it lies in the very heart of the forest. It is a mere station; it cannot by any stretch of fancy be called a village. It consists of one handsome residence, the home of Mr. Duncan, the owner of the great lumber mill, whence the station takes it name. The wood, cut down some miles away, where they are clearing the ground, is floated down the Russian River to its destination here. There are also some half-dozen cottages for the lumbermen, a livery stable, where excellent horses and carriages may be had for excursions in the surrounding country. Of course wherever a train stops there must be a hotel; here is one, a pretty rural-looking place, two storeys high, with a verandah running all round it, externally most pleasant to look at, and the interior arrangements render it a most delightful place for a temporary residence. In summer it is crowded with tourists, who are sometimes so charmed with the picturesqueness of the place as to settle there for many weeks, and season after season visit it again. Its surroundings are lovely and romantic in the extreme, mountain, river, and forest scenery lying close round you. It was the off season, the tourists had not yet begun to arrive, consequently we had this charming primitive hotel all to ourselves; there were no chambermaids, no Chinamen.

"We arrange things on a different plan when the real season begins," said our hostess, a pleasant-mannered, sensible-looking woman. "We have plenty of waiters and that kind of thing, but till then my daughter and I manage the work between us."

We were glad to have arrived at a season when there were no "waiters or that sort of thing;" it was pleasanter to be waited upon by our landlady and her charming young daughter than a pig-tailed "Chinee" or the supercilious white, who looks as though he was doing you a favour every time he hands you your soup. A violent storm arose on the evening of our arrival. There was a kind of haze over the sky, and the sun set with a heavy mist circling round it. We looked out and watched the gathering shades of evening creep down the sable-skirted pine forest, and were struck by the intense silence; the invisible insect world seemed suddenly to have sunk to rest; there was not a sound on the earth nor a tremulous motion in the air. A black darkness by degrees overspread the heavens, and big raindrops began to fall faster and faster, splashing on the verandah outside. The wind, from a low sullen murmur, swelled to a perfect gale ; we heard it sweeping down the defiles and hurrying along the hillsides, shrieking like a company of fiends, surging round and battling with the big trees till they groaned and reeled and shivered beneath the assaults of its fierce, strong breath. The rain increased to a perfect avalanche of water, as though it would drown us and send us floating down the Russian River. A dimly lighted room in a strange hotel was not a comfortable location for a stormy night. Our landlady invited us into the family sitting-room, where there was a big blazing wood fire ; we drew our chairs round it and sat rocking in a lazy, listless way, listening to the storm without and enjoying the comfortable scene within. The mistress of the house sat sewing by the light of a softly shaded lamp, while her daughter was busily engaged arranging some dried ferns and flowers. Presently the door opened, and a tall brown-bearded man, a perfect type of the strong stout-hearted frontiersman, with top-boots, frieze coat, and leather breeches, strode into the room. He glanced at us with a pair of sharp bright eyes. Mrs. W——, with a half-introductory smile, said, "Mr. G——, our express agent; he lives here all the year round." He drew his chair to the fire, "hoped he didn't intrude." *He* apologized for his presence, *we* apologized for ours, and in the course of a few minutes found ourselves engaged in an interesting conversation. They knew we had come from England, and were deeply interested in all concerning it. We would rather have gathered information of this wild Western world, teeming as it is with new interests, new life; but their thoughts were directed to the grave Old World across the sea. Their lives were saturated, filled to overflowing, with the adventurous, restless spirit that permeates their beautiful land; they seemed to enjoy the distant contemplation of the settled dignity and steadfast institutions of the mother country. They talked of the political aspect of to-day contrasted with that of the past, and argued that one had grown out of the other. In the course of conversation there were allusions to the repeal of the corn laws, the passing of the Reform Bill, and such bygone matters, with all of which they were perfectly conversant. They discussed Lord Palmerston's foreign policy as contrasted with that of the present, and were strong upon the ministerial difficulties of to-day, insisting that the then Conservative Government would go out, having made so many and such disastrous mistakes, and the parliamentary ribbons must fall into Mr. Gladstone's hands. They watch our political movements at home with as much interest as their own elections. We are not petticoat politicians, and occasionally found ourselves floundering out of our depths; it is as much as we can do to swim on the surface of the smoothest political waters, and were not sorry when politics went down and literature came up. They were familiar, the handsome express agent especially so, with our old dramatists and popular prose writers, and discussed their works with a propriety of expression, appreciation of subject, and judicious criticism that one could scarcely expect to find in these latitudes. There was a strength and originality in his thoughts and expressions, which we seldom find in what is called "cultivated society," where originality of any kind rarely comes to the surface. Towards the end of the evening our host entered the room quietly and gingerly, as though he were treading on eggs; he seated himself on the very edge of his chair, clasped his hands stiffly on his knees, and was dumb; if anything struck him as "funny" he opened his mouth, let a laugh escape, and shut it again with a snap. Long before we parted for the night the storm was over.

The morning broke calm and fair; no sign of the last night's tempest lingered on earth, in air, or sky, and we started on an excursion to Austin Creek, a beautiful romantic spot, about four miles on the other side of the forest.

On first starting from Duncan Mills we had to ford the Russian River, which was somewhat swollen owing to the heavy rains of the previous night. The horses plunged in, and before they had taken many steps the water was up to their bellies and surged over the axletrees of the carriage. Instead of crossing the river direct, our driver turned and drove towards the sea. I say "drove," but he merely let the reins lie on the horses' necks and allowed them to follow their own devices. To our eyes, looking over the sides of the carriage, it seemed as though we were being carried away by the strong tide that was flowing seawards. We glanced at our driver's face; it was perfectly serene; he was evidently master of the situation. In answer to our anxious eyes he said, "There's no danger, ladies; these horses have swum this river when it was sixteen feet deep."

"All very well for the horses," I replied, "but the carriage couldn't swim too." After going about a hundred yards down the river, he turned the horses' heads, and we were thankful to be once more on dry land. Almost immediately we plunged into the narrow forest paths, which are rough and uneven, and by no means pleasant to travel over, especially when we come to a piece of corduroy road, which consists of the felled trunks of trees, laid across, and partially sinking into a muddy Slough of Despond.

We are so bumped and bruised, and jolted from one side to the other, we can scarcely breathe,—we clutch the carriage sides,—we cling to each other, and when we are safe over, we feel our limbs to see if there is not a case of dislocation somewhere. For nearly two hours we drive through the solemn redwood forest, the tall straight trees growing like an army around us; there is no gentle swaying or fluttering of branches here; they rise high above our heads, and twist and turn their dark masses together, shutting out the light of the sun. We presently come to a part of the forest more densely populated with its silent multitude, where the trees grow larger, taller, and their gnarled roots force their way upward, and lie, like writhing serpents, petrified on the ground. The sound of the woodman's axe has never echoed through this solitude; it is a wild, virgin forest, vast, and in parts almost impenetrable. The roughness of the roads detracts somewhat from the pleasure of this excursion, though on arriving at Austin

Creek you are well repaid for your trouble. It is a most delightful spot, dreamy and romantic; you feel inclined to sit there by the bubbling water, and dream the long day through. An old backwoodsman,—quite a character in his way,—lives in a pretty rustic cottage near the creek, and is always ready to refresh his visitors with a good supply of lager beer, tea, coffee, the whitest of bread, and yellowest of butter; and, perhaps a salmon trout, fresh from the stream, to add flavour to the simple meal.

We made sundry other excursions in the beautiful neighbourhood of Duncan Mills, and left on the third day. The household turned out to walk with us across to the station, which is not fifty yards from the hotel door; the women with bright-coloured kerchiefs thrown over their heads; our solemn, silent host carrying our valise; a fat sow, with a young litter of grunters; two huge setters, with whom we had made great friends, and a pig-tailed Chinaman bringing up the rear. Our kind hostess handed us a dainty basket of fruits and sandwiches as we shook hands all round, and said "good-bye." Our gallant expressman, too, put in an appearance at the last moment; he had just time to wave his sombrero and wish us "God speed," when our smart little engine gave a snort, a jerk, and started on her way.

Beautiful as the redwoods are in this locality, they are not so fine as the redwoods in the neighbourhood of Santa Cruz, which is one of the loveliest seaside resorts on that part of the coast. The road to these redwoods is a most attractive one, through cañons filled with trees, all stretching their long arms upwards ready to clutch you as you pass by ; sparkling streams, whose waters are ever flowing round spurs of timbered hills, broken with gorges and deep ravines, scars of an earthquake or sabre-cuts of time ; then we wind along the steep mountain-side, looking down upon the boiling river, which is rushing among the broken boulders below. At last there is a sharp turn, and rapid descent into the forest, where there are some magnificent redwoods, second only to the world-famous "big trees" of the Calaveras and Mariposa groves. We are soon in the midst of them ; they grow so smooth, so straight, and high, like the columns of some great cathedral, outspreading and uniting their leafy crowns like a groined green roof, more than a hundred feet above our heads. We wander through these symmetrical, silent aisles,—the triumph of nature's architectural grandeur,—and feel inclined to bow our heads and lift our hearts heavenward.

It is difficult at first to realize the dimensions of these giants of the forest, all being of an immense size and height. There is no contrast ; but when some of our party went to measure one we speedily realized its magnitude, for the men and women looked like animated dolls parading slowly round the huge trunk. They measured it about four feet from the ground, and ascertained that it was more than seventy-five feet in circumference. This was considered one of the largest. We entered into one hollow trunk where General Fremont had taken a fortnight's rest during his arduous expedition westwards. After he had vacated this sylvan retreat a man with a wife and two children took possession and lived there for two years, while they were gathering together money and materials to build themselves a home on the fringe of the forest about three miles eastward. On one side they had inserted a glass window, which is still there, and, strange to say, unbroken; in another place they had cut a huge round hole, evidently for a stovepipe to carry off the smoke. One very fine symmetrical tree was clothed to the height of six feet with visiting cards, stuck on with tin-tacks! We wandered for some hours through this sacred solitude, and left it with much regret, feeling it was perhaps the last excursion we should make on this side of the Rocky Mountains.

We return to San Francisco, and somewhat dolefully make preparations for our departure from this glorious sunland; but our time is up, and the longer we stay the greater will grow our regrets. We spend our last few days in paying farewell visits, and go through that melancholy ceremony with satisfactory calm. We keep our lugubrious feeling deep down in our hearts, and say "good-bye" with smiling faces. We had entered San Francisco at sunset; we leave it in the rosy morning, when the sun is shining and flooding the beautiful city and its purple hills with golden light. A host of our kind friends escort us across the bay. Our hearts are too full to talk much, so with eloquent hand-clasps and brief "good-byes" we part.

The huge ferryboat bears them back to their Golden City, which fades from our sight in a mist,—a mist that blurs it in our eyes only; then the great yellow cars of the Central Pacific bear us eastward. We pass through the Sacramento Valley, climb once more the grand Sierras, and California fades from our sight, and is fast becoming only a memory and a dream.

To all those who are in search of health, of novelty, and who are able to enjoy the noblest, grandest, and most varied scenery this world can boast, I would say, "Go Westward," go over the sea, across the Rocky Mountains, the glorious Sierras, and sit down at the Golden Gate and rest.

CHAPTER XXIII.

THE SILVER STATE.

Snowed in—Indians—Journey to Denver—A Forage for a Supper—"Crazed"—Domestic Difficulties—Colorado Springs—Cheyenne Cañon—The "Garden of the Gods"—Ute Pass—Glen Eyrie.

ONCE more we are travelling eastward. It is early April, and in the land we have left the earth is wearing her gorgeous spring robes, embroidered with the loveliest and brightest of wild flowers; they are everywhere, they cover her like a jewelled mosaic of crimson, violet, white, and gold. Nowhere is there such a luxuriant growth of wild flowers as in California. We soon begin to feel that we have left the land of the sun behind us. The weather grows cool, and the blue skies are filled with floating islands of leaden clouds. At Colfax, which we reach about six o'clock in the evening, there is a general bustle and confusion. There is something wrong ahead; everybody worries everbody with inquiries "What is the matter?" and we learn, to our chagrin, that the weight of snow has broken in a thousand feet of snow sheds on the summit of the Sierras. We are shunted on to a siding where we are to

remain for the night, while fifty men are told off to clear the road. They come swinging down upon the platform, a crowd of strong, weather-beaten fellows, while the moon, shining like a white ghost amid the thunder-clouds above, lights up their swarthy faces. An engine and truck is soon prepared. They swarm into it, loaded with pickaxes and shovels; they overflow and cling wherever they can find a foothold; and the engine, with a huge snow-plough as big as a house, goes snorting and shrieking on its way, the men shouting and hurrahing as it bears them out of sight. We go to bed somewhat disconsolately; the idea of being "snowed in" at the foot of the mountains is not pleasant, and we look forward anxiously to what may await us at the top. At six in the morning it is telegraphed "All clear," and we recommence our journey. A gray mist has rolled over the Sierras, and shrouded the magnificent forest in a gray cloud mantle; we look down on a weird world of shadows; here and there a gleam of sunlight breaks out from the gloomy skies and is gone in a moment. It is dreary travelling for a while—a gray sky above, a gray world below, and a gray cloud mist falling over us on all sides; but our living street moves slowly with slackened speed through all. We settle down in a comfortable palace car, and with a chosen few of our fellow-passengers form quite a pleasant coterie. We visit each other's sections, passing freely from one car to another; we read, chat, tell anecdotes (some of us had quite a gift that way), and keep the ball of conversation rolling pretty briskly; when our wits are exhausted we take refuge in the inevitable fifteen puzzle.

In the evening we had our section lighted, and played a solemn game of whist, or were initiated into the mysteries of euchre, or watched the rollicking game of poker being carried on by a merry party in the opposite section.

The weather changed, the clouds lifted, and the next morning we found ourselves once more ascending the Rocky Mountains, which struck us with an idea of even greater sublimity, now that the novelty of our first view had worn off. The sun shone brilliantly, and an intense blue sky bent over us as we slowly wound our way through the lovely God-created world of stone where no man dwells. At Elko, and sundry other mountain stations, the Indians came down to see the trains pass. There were braves of all ages, with their squaws and pappoose staring in silent stolidity at the bustling scene. They were evidently got up for effect. The women wore striped blankets pinned round their bodies, and bright handkerchiefs or shawls over their heads. Their long matted hair streamed over their shoulders, sometimes over their eyes; and they had added to their natural attractions by blotches of coarse red paint daubed on the dark faces. The men were, on the whole, more gaily dressed and painted than the women. One especially attracted our attention. He was evidently a "buck" of the first water. He wore a blue blanket wrapped round him, and on his head a broad-brimmed ragged felt hat, with a mass of blue feathers drooping on his shoulders. The men stood in groups, solemnly regarding us with their big black eyes, still as statues; the women squatted on the platform or peeped at us from round corners. It was not exactly pleasant, but very interesting to find ourselves amid a score or two of this savage race, the men all armed with guns and knives. Some of them got on to the train (all Indians are allowed to ride free, getting on and off as they please : they never ride in cars with the other passengers, but on the steps or in the baggage van) and went with us to the next station.

After a run of five days we reach Denver City, capital of the Silver State of Colorado. It is near midnight as we roll through the silent streets and stop at the Grand Central Hotel, whose doors are hospitably open to receive us. We are tired and hungry. We had reserved a good appetite, intending to dine at Cheyenne, where we knew we should get a luxurious meal ; but as we desired to push on to Denver that night, and there was no connecting train at Cheyenne proper, we turned off at the junction, and having missed our dinner reach Denver in a semi-exhausted state. A solitary black porter, all smiles, relieves us of our hand-baggage, and shows us to a clean comfortable room on the third floor, the only unoccupied room in the house. It was fortunate we telegraphed, or we should not have had that. The house is crowded, the town is crowded ; people are pouring in and out every day on their way to and from "Leadville," a city that has grown up in two years, and has churches, banks, waterworks, stage roads cut out of a wilderness, and thirty thousand inhabitants. Mines are open, shafts sunken, and thousands of workers are digging in the bowels of the earth, searching for gold and silver—finding it, too. We ask for supper. We cannot have anything till the morning. The cook has gone; the larder is locked up. We stand aghast, but not cast down. We insist that we shall die of exhaustion before the morning, and we "*must* have something—anything, we don't care what." He grins, shows his white teeth, scratches his woolly head, and shakes it in the teeth of our distress. At last, by dint of prayers and entreaties, we induce him to go on a foraging expedition into the town. He returns presently—I believe he knocked up the doctor—with some roughly cut sandwiches of rancid butter and tough leathery beef in one hand, and a bottle of lager beer in the other. With this we are forced to be satisfied, if not content.

The next morning we have a capital breakfast, and are most anxious to go on a reconnoitring expedition through the town, but a blinding snowstorm confines us to the house. Still it is not cold; although there is a stove in the room we do not need a fire. It clears up in the afternoon; we wrap ourselves in our warmest clothing and prepare to sally forth. As we cross the hall we hear our name uttered in a familiar tone, and we encounter an old friend whom we had last seen in a London drawing-room. He recognized *us;* we should never have recognized *him*, in his frontier dress, with top-boots, broad sombrero hat, and clean-shaven face, bronzed and brown with the "bright sun's kiss." He had just returned from a seven-hundred-mile ride through the Indian territory, and still had his knives and pistols in his belt. These he now deposited in a huge box, which the office clerk proudly opened for our inspection.

"See here, ladies;" he said; "when the gentlemen come down from the hills they leave their arms here. Ours is a peaceable town now; there is no need to go armed. A dozen years ago every man carried his life in his hand—the air was full of pistol-shots; in foul weather it rained bullets. *Now* it is altogether different. You are as safe in the streets as in your own houses." He slammed the lid down with a clang.

Our Chicago friend volunteered to escort us about the town if we would give him time "to refresh himself." He was a long time refreshing, and when he made his reappearance he was refreshed out of all knowledge. He had discarded his top-boots, frieze jacket, and broad sombrero, and now appeared white-shirted and frock-coated, fit for a lounge in Bond Street. He had dug out the insignia of civilization from the depths of a huge trunk which travelled ahead of him "in case of being wanted." He had destroyed his picturesqueness, but looked respectable. With this renovated being we paraded the streets of Denver. Its ancient rowdyism is dead; its bowie-knived, swaggering, swearing population of ten years ago has departed; it is now a peaceful, law-abiding city, with long streets or boulevards planted with fine trees, which in summer-time must form a delightful shade, but in consequence of the great altitude, I suppose the summer is very backward here, for at present there is not a single green leaf to be seen. There are numbers of handsome dwelling-houses, mostly occupied by families who have flocked from all parts of the world, and settled here in consideration of the beautiful climate, which is genial and pleasant at all seasons, and especially beneficial to those who are in the least affected with any chest or lung disease. I have met here many hale, strong, hearty men, who the moment they leave the city and descend to the valleys below become suffering invalids. It is the same throughout the entire State of Colorado; the pure rarefied air has a surprisingly healing effect upon the lungs, and the asthmatic sufferers breathe like healthy men; they only recognize their afflictions when they leave these mountain heights. There are numbers of very handsome shops of all descriptions, the jewellers making a specially brilliant display; they are the best patronized, perhaps, of any here, for the miners, when they have made their "pile," come down from the hills and invest their gold in diamonds and jewellery for their wives or sweethearts. There are substantial banks; plenty of churches and chapels for all denominations and creeds; very fine public buildings—town hall, library, police courts, etc. The inhabitants are especially tetchy, and take seriously to heart any observation concerning the respectability of their city, and are greatly scandalized by any allusion to its former delinquencies. It is like a reformed rake in broadcloth and fine linen, and resents any allusion to its days of bowie-knives and buckskins. There is very good, though not exactly luxurious, accommodation for travellers in the way of hotels; but there is a monster hotel now in the course of building, which promises a combination of luxuries and comforts to tourists of the future.

The city is built on a wide plateau five thousand feet above the sea-level. A few streets and houses cover a wide area; there is plenty of room to build and breathe in. Some of the streets, two miles long, have scarcely fifty houses in them, but these are surrounded by gardens and pleasure-grounds; they are very wide, and planted with rows of cotton trees. The roads in all directions are beautifully smooth; it is a delight to drive over them. It is now the 12th of April; there is a bright blue sky, warm balmy sunshine, and a crisp invigorating air, but there is not a flower to be seen, not the twitter of a spring bird to be heard anywhere. Ranges of hills and mountains arise on all sides of it, some far away over the plains, some near, but mostly covered with eternal snows, their icy peaks flashing in the sunshine in striking contrast to the blue foothills below. Glancing on one side we see a wide endless plain; it seems bounded by the horizon. This, by mild gradations, unbroken by hills or mountains, leads through towns, forests, and cultivated prairie lands to the Mississippi river six hundred miles.

Having promenaded the streets of Denver for some hours we return to our Grand Central Hotel. On our way up to our rooms we meet a young, pretty-looking girl with an intensely preoccupied look upon her face. She hurries past us. We are inclined to ask "if anything is the matter?" but before we have time to think she is gone. We meet her several times during the after part of the day, running up and down the stairs, or roaming along the passages, still with the same strange, intent look upon her face. Late in the evening, while we are sitting chatting previous to retiring to rest, the handle of our door is very quietly turned. We step forward and throw it open.

There is no one there, but this girl is hurrying along the corridor, wringing her hands and moaning pitifully, "I've lost a pair of little baby's shoes!" and throughout the long night she was wandering about the house, along the passages, and up and down the stairs, uttering the same pathetic cry.

The next morning we were roused by a succession of piercing shrieks, and on our hurrying out to learn the cause, found the poor girl being dragged through the corridor by two sturdy, rough-looking men, who certainly did not "do their spiriting gently." All the visitors had turned out of their rooms, alarmed at the tragic disturbance, and though every one deplored what seemed to be the unnecessary violence of these petty officers "dressed in their brief authority," no one spoke to prevent it, well knowing that any interference with the "police" is dangerous, and followed by dangerous consequences. In spite of her heartrending shrieks, and appeals for help, the unfortunate creature was dragged down the stairs uttering the one piteous cry—

"I've done no harm. I was only looking for my little baby's shoes."

"She's crazy," volunteered the head waiter. "It is very sad. She's a stranger, too, in these parts; nobody knows anything about her. She drove up here yesterday morning in the station fly, and engaged a room, but she behaved queer, roaming about the house all day and all night. We were forced to send for the police to take her away; we could not have crazy folk hanging round here."

We returned silently to our rooms, all of us, I think sad at heart—the men looking especially downcast, evidently feeling that they might have done *something* for this solitary distressed woman. But what? They all knew that authority once acknowledged in these mountain cities must be held unquestioned and supreme.

It is quite a common thing in Denver for families to take up their residence entirely at hotels. Only two classes of people can enjoy the luxury of a home, viz., those who possess great wealth, and are able to keep large establishments, and pay princely wages for very indifferent service; and those who are able and willing to do their own housework, cooking, etc., without any extraneous help whatever. People of modest means, who in the old country might enjoy a cosy home and neat-handed maidservant, must not look for it here. An English lady resident in the hotel gave me her experience in the matter. She took a pretty house, furnished it, engaged a "help," and prepared once more to enjoy the luxury of home: the "help" had laid down the law what she *would* do, and what she would *not* do. All preliminaries being satisfactorily arranged, she entered on her duties. The dinner-hour came; the table was laid for three.

"There will be only the Captain and myself to dinner to-day; we seldom have company," said the mistress.

"But there's *me!* I'm to dine with you, I suppose?" replies the "help."

Upon its being mildly suggested that their conversation would not be particularly interesting to her—besides "they preferred dining alone"—she flounced out of the room. An hour afterwards the mistress ventured into the kitchen to learn the cause of the dinner's delay, and discovered that savoury meal flung into the scullery sink, the fire raked out, and the irate "help" departed!

Household labour is at a premium. The social aspect of affairs seems to be turned upside down; it is the *employée* who dictates terms, not the employer. There exists a kind of female domestic guild, whose members seem eternally "on strike." They decide who shall be served and who shall not be served; the scale of wages, and the rules to be observed by the household they condescend to enter. Woe be to the mistress who rebels against her maid!—she shall be maidless ever after. In spite, however, of this trifling drawback to domestic bliss, many ladies are brave enough to face the difficulties, and accompany their lords to the fields of gold, as in the old days they did to the field of battle. Denver is, and will long continue to be, crowded with adventurers from all parts of the world, for it is a place where fortunes are easily made,—perhaps as easily lost. It is a paradise, they say, for men, dogs, and horses, but no heaven for women.

The next day we bid adieu to our friend, who is starting for Leadville, while we take the train for "Colorado Springs," about four hours' run from Denver City. We reach the depôt early, and take our seats in an empty car; throngs of people begin to arrive, some on foot, some in ramshackle vehicles of all descriptions; the hotel omnibuses dash up one after the other and empty their living freight upon the platform, which is speedily crowded with an array of masculine humanity; but there is not a woman to be seen—not one!

A dark, swarthy, rough-looking set of men they are, with stern, impassive faces; they are mostly armed, and are evidently bound for the hills hundreds of miles up the country. One after another they swarm into the cars, exchange silent salutations; a nod, a smile, perhaps a few low-voiced words, and that is all. There is no laughing, no handshaking, no jesting, no geniality; they are thoughtful, energetic men, and all seem bent on the world's most serious business; each bearing the weight of his own concerns. Some read the *Denver News*. Nobody seems to be sociably inclined towards his neighbour; occasional scraps of conversation are floated to our cars; but they are mostly silent and preoccupied. We are the only ladies on board the cars, but that is not an embarrassing fact. No one takes any notice of us; they don't even seem to glance our way, though the fact of two ladies travelling in these regions without an escort must have been a novelty. Occasionally, if the sun incommoded us, a hand belonging to an invisible body arranged our blinds comfortably: by this token only was our presence recognized.

We reach Colorado Springs about midday, and as the train stops, a bearded giant in top-boots addressed us in lamb-like tones—

"You get out here? Strangers, I guess?"

We admitted both facts.

"Know what hotel you're going to? No? Well, I guess you'll find the National about the thing."

In another moment we find ourselves and our hand-baggage deposited in the omnibus of the National Hotel, and our depositor, with a profound obeisance, stands bareheaded as we drive away.

Colorado Springs (so called, I suppose, because the nearest spring is five miles off) stands on a sandy plain, six thousand feet above the sea-level; the Rio Grande Railway has a station here, where there is clean, comfortable, though not luxurious accommodation for tourists desiring to explore the attractions of this wonderful State, with its boundless plains, ice-crowned mountains, and great rolling uplands, sweeping away till they are broken up by the low, rugged foothills, or lost among eternal snows. Colorado Springs is a bright, lively little town, which during the last five years, has risen from the wild prairie land, and has now a population of three thousand residents. There are two other delightful resorts in the neighbourhood—the old Colorado city, sedate, solemn, and picturesque, but much neglected by tourists generally, who prefer the brisk, bustling "Springs," or the more aristocratic "Manitou," about six miles off, which is most romantically situated, and has luxurious hotel accommodation. In the immediate vicinity are several soda and iron springs, at which any passing traveller may stop and drink. Any one who tastes, as we did (we did more than taste, we drank draughts of it), the sparkling soda water bubbling up from its natural source, will forswear the manufactured article ever after.

On the afternoon of our arrival we start on an expedition to Cheyenne Cañon, some half-dozen miles from the

"Springs." We feel the full magnetism of this rarefied mountain air as we speed over the wide, rolling plain, which spreads in billowy waves of short gray-green grass on all sides of us. The skies are intensely blue, the air flooded with sunshine. Not the twitter of a bird is to be heard, not a tree is in leaf, not a flower in blossom, and it is late in April. The white bare branches of the cotton tree stand out like silvery lacework, traced in fantastic patterns upon the bright blue sky. There is nothing of soft, pretty picturesqueness here ; it is all grand, wild, and bare.

"You should have come here in June," says our driver ; "there will be plenty of greenery and flowers then. Of course everything is looking dry and thirsty now ; we haven't had a drop of rain since last August. It's due now, though ; we're expecting showers every day."

We get out of the carriage at the mouth of the cañon, and make our way through this wonderful chasm on foot as best we can, climbing over the rough, broken boulders crossing and recrossing the creek, now on felled tree-trunks, balancing ourselves on stones or stumps, climbing up slippery banks, beneath the shadow of the great gray rocks which lift their rugged heights five hundred feet above our head. Looking up we see a band of blue sky. We are wandering through a twilight world ; not a gleam of sunshine ever strays into these mysterious depths. We are surrounded on all sides by these dark, jagged rocks— above, below, everywhere—as though they would crowd round and crush us. Here and there a gnarled skeleton tree starts from some deep fissure, as though it had wasted its life trying to get out; and the gurgling waterfalls, gliding down from their home in the mountains to join the brawling stream below, makes a pleasant plashing music to our ears. We spend two hours amid the gloomy grandeur of Cheyenne Cañon, and return to the hotel in time for dinner.

The next morning early we start for the "Garden of the Gods," which is no paradise of shady groves and blooming flowers, but a collection of bright red rocks of most curious formations, covering an area of about fifty acres. At the entrance to the garden stand two tall red sandstone cliffs, rising sheer up from the ground to a height of three hundred feet. Glancing through these gigantic gates, and framed as it were within them, we see "Pike's Peak" flashing its icy crown in the face of the sun. It is seventy-five miles away, but it is so clearly outlined it seems quite near. We fancy we can distinguish the cattle grazing among the blue foothills below. We enter between these gates and find ourselves amid what might even be the ruins of some grand God-created cathedral, created and ruined before the age of man; the tall straight columns still stand crumbling in the deserted aisles, and the "garden" is spread like a panorama before us; the bright red sandy ground, rising and undulating in all directions, is embroidered with silvery sage brush and tufts of gray-green prairie grass; here and there the straggling evergreen trees struggle into a dwarfed, half-barren life. Their scanty verdure is, however, a relief to the eyes, for the intense blue skies and the golden sunlight, shining on the red rocky world round us, form a mass of brilliant colouring that is dazzling to the sight, and contrasts strongly with the massive white rocks which stand outside the garden gates. Weird, strange figures and half-formed fantastic shapes are on all sides of us, sometimes grotesque, like things seen in a dream, but always realistic and impressive. Local genius has classified these wonderful formations, and given to them familiar names; but the glib guide's chatter is wearisome. We prefer to wander at our leisure through this marvellous locality, and let our imagination run riot amid this warm glow of brilliant colouring and world of petrified wonders. It is easy to fancy that this must have been the playground or workshop of some athletic gods of old, who were disturbed in their work or in their play when the thunder of the Almighty Voice rolled down the mountain-side and called them home. The laggards were turned to stone; the warrior, with his broken club, is half-buried in the ground; and the tall figure of a veiled nun and hooded friar are rooted to the earth, where they are doomed to stand for all the world's wonder till the judgment day.

We cast many a long, lingering look behind us as we leave this fascinating spot, this veritable region of enchantment, which holds our thoughts chained long after it has passed from our sight. We drive on to Glen Eyrie, where there are some curious rocky formations of various colours—green, purple, and a dull dead gold; and, rising amid a very wilderness of cotton-wood and fir-trees, stands a group of gigantic needle-rocks—tall, straight-pointed shafts, which might be used to sew a broken world together. There are various other grotesque formations, grouped in harmonious confusion amid a luxuriant growth of evergreens, which flourish here in greater perfection than in the wide open plains above. A stream of sparkling water runs gurgling through the glen. Clinging, as it seems, like an eyrie-nest to the face of the cliff on the opposite side, is a lovely villa, the residence of General Palmer, the owner of the glen; from this spot the view of the surrounding scenery is unequalled for its extent and picturesqueness.

On our return journey we drive to the Ute pass, which, for the grandeur and sublimity of its scenery, is second to none. Not the ghost of an Indian is to be seen now on this their once favourite hunting-ground; its narrow winding paths—with steep precipice and brawling river running below on the one side, and the tall gray cliff rising on the other, sometimes overhanging above as though they might fall and crush us—are crowded now with wagon-trains, cattle, lumber-carts, and squadrons of men, women, and children all plodding their way to the Leadville mines near a hundred miles away. We could not abandon ourselves wholly to the beauty of the scenery, for we were occasionally diverted by the cries and shouts of the men as they extricated some little staggering calf from between our horses' hoofs or carriage wheels, while the poor mother lowed piteously in at the window, her horns in unpleasant proximity to our faces. We went as far as the Rainbow Falls, and then drove back through the pass, and thence to Manitou, where we pulled up for a few minutes and drank some delicious draughts from the sparkling soda springs. During the whole of this route our attention was constantly directed to some lovely homes, built sometimes on the hillsides, sometimes nestling at their feet, but always on some choice picturesque spot. These, we were told, are generally inhabited by English gentlemen, and one or two exceedingly pretty villas were pointed out to us as the residences of some American ladies of literary and artistic distinction.

It was late in the afternoon as we rattled over the breezy uplands and across the bleak, bare plains, back to Colorado Springs. We caught many a glimpse of the gigantic gates, which guard the bright red garden of the gods; in fact, they form the chief point in the landscape for many miles round. We regretted bitterly the compulsory shortness of our stay in this wonderful region; but we must "move on," leaving the utmost grandeur unseen. We had heard so much of the beautiful valleys, verdure-clad ravines, gloomy gorges, and almost inaccessible mountains, rugged and ice-bound with eternal snows. Among the most regretted of these unseen wonders is the mountain of the "Holy Cross." This most remarkable mountain is nearly fifteen thousand feet high, and the ascent is so difficult that few attempt it. A contemporary describes it thus :—

"The characteristic which gives it its name, is the vertical face, nearly three thousand feet in depth, with a cross at the upper portion, the entire fissures being filled with snow. The cross is of such remarkable size, and distinct contrast with the dark granite rock, that it can be seen nearly eighty miles away, and easily distinguished from all other mountain-peaks. The snow seems to have been caught in the fissure, which is formed of a succession of steps, and here, becoming well lodged, it remains all the year. Late in the summer the cross is very much diminished in size by the melting of the snow. A beautiful green lake lies at the base of the peak, which forms a reservoir for the waters falling from the high peaks. The perpendicular arm of the cross is fifteen hundred feet in length, and fully fifty feet in breadth, the snow lying in the crevice from fifty to one hundred feet in depth; the horizontal arm of the cross averages seven hundred feet."

Although Colorado is a rainless land, water is plentiful, rivers and streams are abundant enough, and the system of irrigation is perfect. In no other part of this vast continent are there more fertile, flourishing farms, or such a production of gigantic fruits and vegetables; they tell of cabbages weighing forty pounds—potatoes, apples, grapes, in fact, fruits and vegetables of all kinds, in similar proportions.

July and August are the best months for a tour in Colorado; then the mountain-passes are open, the snow has almost disappeared from the higher regions, and the beautiful parks and valleys lying among the mountains are easy of access, while the gloomy gorges and marvellous cañons, inaccessible at other seasons of the year, may be fully explored. There are some curious laws in Colorado. Any man who may be found spending his time in public-houses, saloons, gambling-houses, etc., and who is without any visible means of support, is liable to be arrested as a "vagrant," and upon being convicted by a justice of the peace, he is handed over to the sheriff's officer, to be sold at public auction to the highest bidder, for his services, for a term not exceeding three months. The proceeds of the sale to be given to his family, or, if he has no family, the money is added to the city treasury. I have just read a case in a Leadville paper: "Charles Green, having been convicted of vagrancy, was ordered to be sold at auction, and was placed on sale in front of Justice MacDowall's court yesterday forenoon, and auctioned off by Marshall Watson. Either his services were not considered valuable, or the principle of buying at auction was not favourably entertained, for the vag only fetched two dollars. Mr. Wyman was the successful bidder."

CHAPTER XXIV.

BRICKS AND MORTAR.

The Road to St. Louis—The Kansas Brigands' Exploit—Picturesque Population—Mississippi River—Washington—The Capitol—Public Buildings—Society—A Monument to a Lost Cause—Mount Vernon.

WE rest one more night in Denver, and start early next morning for St. Louis, *viâ* Kansas City. We soon feel as though we have left all the beauty and brightness of the world behind; for anything more dreary than the road thither cannot well be imagined. The whole day long, from morning till night, we look out upon the dull, uninteresting prairie land; the icy peaks, snow-clad mountains, and verdant valley have all disappeared, as though the magic plains had collapsed with all their wonders. We see nothing but the dreary dead level covered with short tufts of buffalo grass, so much beloved and so nutritious to the beasts of the plains. The road is strewn with the bones and bodies of dead cattle, some seeming to have dropped but yesterday, others bare skeletons, their bones bleached dry and white in the crisp rarefied air. No loathsome flies or birds of prey are hovering in the air; for the bodies do not decay, they simply dry up, and in time the bones crumble into atoms, like pulverized stone. It is a pitiful scene. The poor brutes have wandered from the herded numbers, to freeze and starve on these bleak plains. It is dull gray weather, the blue has faded from the skies, and for the greater part of the time a drizzling rain is falling. We buy a paper of the perambulating newsboy, and read the startling intelligence that only yesterday, on this very journey, two swaggering ruffians, armed to the teeth, had boarded the train at a small wayside station; the conductor recognized them at once as the two notorious brigands, Jesse and Henry James, whose illustrated "Lives and Exploits" were at that time, by a strange coincidence, being sold on the cars for twenty-five cents.

"For God's sake, keep quiet—take no notice, whatever they do," whispered the anxious conductor to the rather alarmed passengers; but they were evidently "off duty," neither robbery nor murder were on the cards that day. They swaggered about the cars, talking and laughing loudly, their very aspect creating alarm, as no one knew what might come next. They presently selected a table, ordered "supper and a bucket of champagne—quick as greased lightning, too."

Their order was obeyed promptly as might be; they flung their six-shooters on the table before them, enjoyed a hearty meal, becoming quite hilarious towards the end; then readjusted their arms, stopped the train in the middle of the wilderness, stepped off the platform, saying—

"Charge two more suppers to the Government."

No such adventure befalls us; we have a mere commonplace journey, with no genial companionship to brighten the way. So, for nearly eight hundred miles, we journey through this interminable desert land. During the last hundred miles, however, signs of cultivation begin to appear. The first sight of green fields is blessed and refreshing to our eyes. Herds of cattle, thousands strong, are feeding on these wide Kansas plains, and presently homesteads and farmhouses are dotted here and there, lying in the laps of their own cultivated lands. Soon, among the gathering twilight shadows, there looms upon our sight a wide-spreading city, rising from the level plains. This is Kansas City. We steam into the station; there is a general hubbub and confusion on the platform, which is crowded with a heterogeneous mass of humanity. There is the half-breed, clothed in a flour-sack or blanket; the cattle-dealer, in his quaint-cut fustian; and a scanty few western tourists going eastward. There is a great pushing and struggling, everybody rushing in search of the right train, often getting into the wrong one; engines are whistling and dashing in and out of the station, going to or coming from all points of the States. We wait here half an hour for refreshments; there is a capital buffet, where you may get anything you require at a moderate price. For any one who is not professionally interested in agricultural progress, there is no temptation to stay in Kansas City. We change carriages, having secured our sleeping-car, and proceed on our way. Next morning about eight o'clock we reach St. Louis.

Once more we are in a land of bricks and mortar; the air is close, warm, the atmosphere what is best understood by "muggy." We breathe the air with a sense of depression, both physically and mentally, and in the course of twenty-four hours our energies had left us so completely, we thought they would never come back. The city is a fine, large, substantial one, with long streets and fine houses, with the usual amount of public buildings, churches, theatres, and other places of amusement. It is full of bright, bustling life, flourishing trade, and thriving manufactories; there is a look of settled solidity about it that contrasts strongly with the Western cities we have been lately passing through. In some respects we might almost fancy ourselves transported back to London. Here are the omnibuses, tramcars, the gas-lamps, the long rows of tall houses, the hazy atmosphere, and the suffocating air of a damp July day; a gray, cloudy sky above, and the glorious Mississippi rolling sluggishly through the town in a state of far more muddy impurity than our own much-maligned Thames. An extremely light and elegant bridge, both for foot-passengers or carriages, spans the river and connects one part of the city with the other. There are pretty little parks or pleasure-grounds breaking out in all parts of the crowded town for the people's benefit. On the outskirts there are two very beautiful and extensive pleasure-grounds — Tower Grove and Forest Park; the former having been presented to the city by an English gentleman who has been a resident there for many years. It is beautifully laid out in shady walks and drives; great taste has been used in the arrangement of the rare shrubs, trees, and flowers, which are everywhere displayed to the best advantage. Forest Park is farther away from the town, and is on a wilder, larger scale, and rich in natural beauties. There are grand old forest trees, bosky dells, green slopes, and shady nooks and corners, with a rich luxuriant growth of green everywhere. So far St. Louis reminds us of our native land; but on closer observation, as we ramble through the streets and round about the town, we realize the fact that we are in a strange country. We explore the markets, and they abound in all quarters of the town, and street stalls, which are likewise plentiful. Here are bushels of cocoanuts, yams, sweet potatoes, egg and oyster plants, rich gold and red bananas a quarter of a yard long, and all kinds of tropical fruits and flowers, and crowds of coloured people everywhere, engaged in every possible kind of business—a bright, busy, industrious population; groups of curly-headed coloured children, slates and satchels in hand, hurrying to or from school, chattering and fluttering round like so many magpies. Little brown babies are paddling about, making mud-pies in the gutter, with a mingling of white babies joining in the fun; women flash about with their short cotton skirts, big gold earrings, and kerchiefs of all the colours of the rainbow pinned across their breasts, or bound turban-like round their heads. The weather had partially cleared, and a lurid red sun looked down through the murky clouds on this semi-tropical city, as we took our last stroll through the busy kaleidoscopic streets.

We stayed just long enough to get a glimpse at the outer aspect of the city, and to test the hospitality of one of its most prominent members, which was characterized by all the hearty cordiality of our friends at home. St.

Louis, I believe, is justly proud of its cultivated and refined society, of which Judge H. J—— and his charming wife are most attractive representatives. We spent a brief but pleasant time in their genial society, and only regretted our inability to stay longer and enjoy more of it.

Another two days' railway travelling through the populous Eastern States; through manufacturing towns and agricultural regions, with signs of prosperity and well-doing everywhere; through straggling villages and grassy meadows—no wild, unkempt lands, gloomy cañons, or weird ravines flash past us now—we reach Washington late in the evening, and drive through the brilliantly lighted streets to our hotel, the Ebbitt House, one of the most luxurious and delightful resting-places. In the morning we begin our usual campaign, and issue forth to reconnoitre the city —the finest and fairest of all the modern cities we have ever seen, or I believe we ever shall see (San Francisco excepted: *that* stands unique and alone). Its situation is most picturesque; it stands at the head of the beautiful Potomac river, a chain of low-wooded hills forming a kind of amphitheatre behind and around it. The city was planned by George Washington during his early days at Mount Vernon, and his design has been carried out in every particular, and has resulted in the production of one of the finest residential cities in the world; for Washington is by no means a busy, money-making, mercantile city. It is one of the most aristocratic quarters—if we may use that term in this republican land. Here is the seat of Government, and thither flock the diplomatic corps with their wives and families. The army and navy, the medical and legal professions, are also largely represented; for the pulse of the nation seems to require constant regulating, like a Brummagem watch with the mainspring out of order; and the legal machine is always at hand, well oiled, and in good order, ready to right the wrong, or wrong the right, as the case may be. There is society here, too, which keeps rigidly to its own lines, and allows no doubtful outsider to set foot within its magic circle. You must have your credentials ready, and well attested, for delivery at the doors. There are gradations of society here as elsewhere, from the *élite* and fashion of the White House, to the lowest rung of the social ladder. Each forms its own circle; one rarely touches the other; each keeps distinct and to itself. The equality and fraternity system, if indeed it exists anywhere, certainly ends here, and Madame Etiquette holds sovereign sway. No fear of meeting a man-milliner in her domain; everything is exclusive and select; everybody as a rule knows "who's who," and if they do not they take the quickest and surest means to find out. A visit to the consul of any special nation is generally satisfactory in such personal matters.

It is a positive pleasure to walk about the streets of Washington; they are all wide, beautifully clean, and paved with tiles as red as cherries, with rows of shady trees on either side—a luxuriant regiment keeping guard over the quaint, old-fashioned-looking brick houses behind. There are no ragged edges, or jagged fringe of squalid homes, clinging to the skirts of the town. It is all neatly finished up ; there are no dilapidated sidewalks, or rugged roadways; it is everywhere smooth and pleasant, either for driving or walking. There are wide streets of handsome shops, as well stocked and tastefully arranged as those on the Paris Boulevards.

The public buildings are generally of fine white marble, or of sandstone painted to resemble it, and most impressive and massive structures they are. The Patent Office is really a splendid edifice—a fine specimen of Doric architecture, most striking for its simple, majestic grandeur; the body is of sandstone painted white, but the wings are of pure marble. The Treasury is also remarkably impressive; it has a colonnaded front 330 feet long, supported by thirty elegant Ionic columns, and is flanked on either side by extensive buildings of massive granite masonry, which breaks the monotony of the long colonnaded front of the chief building; it has several magnificent porticoes, and on either side of the platform or steps leading thereto are masses of beautiful shrubs and flowers. About the centre of the city, and dominating the landscape for miles round, stands the Capitol, high and mighty in its pure architectural glory, crowning a gently swelling hill, and surrounded by a garden of velvet lawns, and shrubs, and flowers, sloping down to the wide park-like streets, which radiate from all sides of it; its white wings spread on either side. Lofty flights of marble steps lead to the colonnaded galleries which encircle the building. The beautiful white dome (which is only four feet lower than St. Paul's, and, standing on a cleared space of elevated ground, appears higher and more imposing), with its graceful spire, is silhouetted against the bright blue sky.

The architecture is purely Corinthian, and in every particular it is most elaborately finished. The view from the portico of the Capitol is very fine. The city's self spreads a wide panorama on all sides, melting away into the softly swelling hills and wooded valleys beyond; while the silvery streak of the Potomac seems to creep out from between the distant hills, gliding and wending its serpentine way till it meets and merges into the shining waters of the bay. To give the briefest description of the rest of the public buildings, schools, etc., of this beautiful young city would fill more pages than I dare devote to the subject; they are all specimens of architectural beauty of various kinds. The Smithsonian Institute is perhaps one of the most striking; it makes no attempt to trench on classic ground, and is of no special style, but a mingling of many. Some, who will accept nothing without a name, call it Romanesque, or Byzantine, or Norman; it is neither, but a fanciful rendering of all, and the result is most striking and effective. The Botanical Gardens, comprising ten acres of land, lies by the West Capitol Park, and the elegant conservatories and beautifully laid out grounds form a prominent feature in the landscape. Rare trees, and shrubs, and flowers of every clime are flourishing here; among them is one of rare significance, the *dumb*-cane of South America. If man or woman taste the sap from the root of this tree, it destroys their powers of speech.

We could not be in Washington without paying a visit to the Senate Chamber and House of Representatives, to which the public have free access, even when the House is sitting. Of course the floor of the house is occupied by members of Congress. A gallery, three or four seats deep, runs round the building for the use of visitors. As we entered, Mr. Thurman was speaking on the Alabama indemnity. He has a fine presence, a good delivery, and spoke most eloquently upon the subject. I don't know whether he was much listened to. A good deal of parliamentary eloquence is flung to the wind. Each member had a desk before him. Some were writing, some were reading the news, some were dozing, others looked extremely bored, while a few were having a genial conversation. The floor was strewn with papers. Boy-messengers were flashing hither and thither, larking by the way as though they were just out of school. The whole scene was wanting in that grave decorum and order which characterize our own parliamentary assemblies. On going from one Chamber to the other—the Senate which represents our House of Lords—we heard loud talking, it seemed of many voices. We glanced through the half-opened door at the crowd within, and inquired of the thin, loose-jointed individual who was lounging about on the threshold taking his duty easily, "if there was anything interesting going on?"

"They're doing nothing," he answered with supreme contempt; "they're always doing nothing—and they take a long time about it. They've been a-filibustering and a-filibustering all day, and I suppose they'll go on all night. I'm sick of 'em."

There are lovely drives all round Washington City, some of historic interest. Our first visit was to Arlington House, the home of General Robert Lee; it is but a short drive from the city, and stands in a most prominent position on Arlington Heights, surrounded by lovely scenery, and in the distance, looming out of the city's midst, stands the Capitol "with white dome lifted." At the close of the war the estate was confiscated, and a great portion of the beautiful grounds was set apart as a burial-ground for the Union soldiers. On every side, stretching away into the dim distance, are graves—graves everywhere ; thousands upon thousands of them, not raised in mounds, but under the smooth turfed ground. Each one is marked by a stone about a foot high, setting forth the name and age of the sleeper below. It seems a strange fatality that the home of the grand old rebel soldier should be the resting-place of the federal dead. In one part of the grounds stands a massive granite sarcophagus, which is placed over the bones of two thousand one hundred and eleven unknown soldiers, gathered from the battle-field of "Bull Run" and the route to Rappahannock after the war. The house is dismantled now, and our hollow footsteps echo through the vacant passages and empty chambers. As we wander through the deserted dwelling, we scarcely feel we are alone. The ghost of the dead days seems to be an ever-haunting presence there. Arlington House, in its isolated lonely state, stands there as a most melancholy monument to a lost cause.

Outside, at the back of the house, are the kitchens, stables, and slave quarters—all empty now, dilapidated and falling fast to ruin, like ghastly skeleton homers, scarred with many memories, and mutely eloquent of the days that have been. On our way homeward we drove through the beautifully picturesque grounds of the "Soldiers' Home," which consists of about five hundred acres, tastefully laid out in lawns, meadows, gardens, and lakes, and about seven miles of drives winding now by the lake side, or under the shady trees, or through the blooming "garden of roses."

Our next visit was to the home of Washington, the founder and father of the Union. Mount Vernon is situated about fifteen miles from Washington, down the Potomac river, passing through the pretty home scenery, and some highly interesting spots by the way. We have splendid views of the Arsenal grounds which run along the banks of the river, and the Government home for the insane, a magnificent building standing on elevated ground east of the city. Presently we pass Fort Foote and Fort Washington. Every rood of ground on either side of this lovely Potomac is marked by the footprints of the war, and is historied and enriched with its many memories. At length we reach Mount Vernon—a spot dear to American hearts of every degree, however one man may differ from another in social, political, or sectarian matters. Whatever tumult may rack the State, or tear at the spirit of the Union, all unite in their reverence to this one noble dead. When the horrors of war ceased for an hour, thither came men from both armies, with hands red with their brothers' blood; but here all was peace. The bitter enmity and hatred which convulsed the land was forgotten here; and the men in blue and the men in gray stood side by side, bared their heads, and bent reverently as before a shrine, by the grave of the father of their country.

General Washington is laid to rest in the grounds of his own home; we pass his tomb on our way to the house. Everything here is kept in perfect order; the quaint garden, designed and laid out by Washington himself in the fashion of the old days, with odd-shaped beds, and thick box borders about a foot high, is filled with gay, sweet-scented, rather than rare, flowers; on the lawn there are several trees, and a hoary old-hedge four feet high, and four feet thick, all planted by the beloved General's own hand, nearly a hundred years ago; and they are all green and flourishing, as though they meant to live another century at least. Here also is a superb magnolia tree, reared from a slip brought by the hand of Lafayette from St. Helena. The slave quarters, gardeners' cottages, laundries, stables, etc., are all ranged on the lawn at the back of the house. These are still occupied by coloured people, the direct descendants of those slaves who were raised on the place in the old days; and they are as proud of their race, and their connection with the Washington family, as though they had descended from a line of kings. They are a very superior and obliging class of people, and provide an excellent lunch for visitors, at a very moderate price.

Mount Vernon, though very beautifully situated, and surrounded by fine views, sloping away from all sides of it, is not so imposing an edifice as Arlington House. It is built of wood to imitate stone, and has a long, wide verandah running along the front. The rooms are small, with the exception of the banqueting hall, which, in comparison with the rest, is a large, handsome apartment. Here are some fine old oil paintings, and portraits of

Washington and his family, with some few miscellaneous curiosities; among them the key of the Bastile, presented by General Lafayette.

So much loving reverence surrounds the name of "Washington," that every room in the house is named after a particular State, which holds it in special care. The rooms are all furnished after the fashion of the old time; many still contain the Chippendale furniture that was used by the Washington family; there is the General's own escritoire, with its numerous pigeon-holes, and cunning secret drawers, the chair he sat in, and the bed he died on, in exactly the same position, and with the same coverlid and fast-fading hangings as when he left it. There is not a speck of dust to be seen anywhere. The house and grounds are the property of the Mount Vernon Ladies' Association, and everything is arranged and carried on under their personal supervision and care. Every relic having the remotest connection with General Washington is gathered together here, and most carefully preserved. A sweet scent of the old dead days lingers everywhere; even the roses that climb round the verandah have a perfume all their own—different, it seems, from other roses. As we retrace our steps through the quaint garden, down Washington's favourite path, between the thick box hedges, in our mind's eye (which sees so much more than mortal sight) we see him walking before us, in his cocked hat and periwig, with head bent down, and hands clasped behind him, exactly as, we are told, he used to walk there, to and fro, a hundred years ago.

CHAPTER XXV.

THE QUAKER CITY.

Baltimore—Its Stony Streets—Druids' Park—A Stroll through the City—Aristocratic Quarters—Washington Monument—Philadelphia—General Aspect—Picturesque Market Street—Fairmount Zoological Gardens.

TWO hours' drive and we are at Baltimore, one of the busiest and brightest of Southern cities, with miles of streets running in all directions, in a state of labyrinthine uncertainty, as though they did not know which way to turn, or where to go next; some are straight and wide, some narrow and crooked. The houses are of many colors; they scorn to be bound to the common-place rules of mere bricks and mortar; you may see a pink front blushing near a sombre gray, a creamy white or chocolate, picked out with amber, elbowing a bright blue, or olive-tinted green; the side-walks are paved with cherry-red tiles, and all this varied coloring, together with the quaint style of street architecture, gives the city a gay, picturesque appearance.

The business thoroughfares are overflowing with the hurry and bustle of life, and at certain hours of the day the side-walks are crowded with a jostling multitude, fluctuating to and fro, while the roadways are alive with many-coloured cars, dashing hither and thither. It is pleasant enough riding on tramways, but you cannot enjoy the luxury of a private carriage—without running the risk of dislocation, at least ; for the roads are of the roughest cobble-stones. The vehicles, driven at reckless speed, lurch and plunge from side to side, and bump you up and down. You hold on to the sides breathlessly, feeling they *must* topple over. But they don't ; they land you at your destination alive, though with splitting head and aching bones. You are disposed to patronize the humble cars in the future ; and the cars go everywhere, and one bright morning they landed us at Druids' Park.

You enter through a lofty pair of handsome iron gates, into a wide avenue, flanked on either side by stone vases fifteen feet high, filled with evergreens in winter, and in summer with showy flowers. The Baltimore folk are very proud of their Druids' Park ; and well they may be, for it is a most lovely spot, consisting of about five hundred acres of land beautifully laid out, their natural attractions being supplemented, not overwhelmed, by art. There are clumps of grand old forest trees, grassy slopes, and shady dells, filled with evergreen shrubs, feathery ferns, and sweet wild flowers, and a silvery lake, winding like a glittering white serpent through a paradise of green. Groups of coloured folk, with their wives and rollicking little piccaninnies, and young men with their swarthy sweethearts, all sprucely dressed in broadcloth and fine linen, with flowers in their button-holes, light-gloved, and patent-booted, their faces shining, as though they had been extra polished by Nixey's patent, are strolling under the trees, or sit chatting beneath their branches. The women, as a rule, wear less gaudy colours than their sisters at St. Louis, and altogether seem of a better-educated class.

Any lady desiring to enjoy the luxury of shopping, should postpone that pleasure till she gets to Baltimore, where there are plenty of shops, well stocked, and well arranged with every possible kind of fancy articles, as well as the necessary articles for daily use, and at certainly one-third less price than she would pay in most of the Eastern cities; besides this advantage, she will be treated with respect and civility, which does not seem indigenous to the nature of the American shopkeeper or his subordinates.

The residential part of the city, viz., Monument Square (and such-like fashionable localities), has a quiet, dull, deserted appearance, like a country town on Sundays when the shops are shut and the good folk are all at church, undergoing their spiritual ablutions. The houses in these aristocratic quarters of the city are more uniform and monotonous than the buisier portions, and yet there is a picturesqueness in the monotony of the long rows of tall brick houses, picked out with white, the white steps projecting on to the red-tiled pavement, while rows of green trees stretch their green arms before them. In every city throughout the United States statues of their beloved founder, George Washington, abound—some execrable, some well enough to look at; but that which occupies the centre of Monument Square is a finely conceived and splendidly executed piece of work. There is no exaggeration, no attempt at ornament or decoration about it—a tall, fluted column rises from a square stone platform, surmounted at the top by an effigy of General George Washington; it is no theatrical figure of an impossible athlete in an attitude of patriotic ardour or military devotion. He stands in the position of a simple gentleman, as he may have stood many times in the flesh, with folded arms, looking out over the city to Chesepeake, where the stars and stripes of the Union he founded are streaming now from scores of vessels in the beautiful bay.

The hotel accommodation is comfortable enough, and no doubt answers all the requirements of the mercantile population who are constantly passing to and fro this busy trading city, for the river is filled with shipping from all parts of the world, and the wharves swarming with a working population, loading and unloading the vessels; the visitor who runs down for a glimpse at these characteristic localities gets bewildered in the tangled collection of cranks, cattle, and the surging mass of pushing, shouting humankind. The hotels are wanting in some of those luxurious arrangements to which the tourists through the great cities of America have grown so accustomed as to regard them as necessities.

Our next point of attraction was Philadelphia, which delightful city we entered under most favourable auspices: the atmosphere was bright, warm, and cloudless. We caught our first glimpse of it from our car-windows, and beheld it afar off lying in the sunshine, its shining domes and cupolas outlined in the broad blue skies, and its myriad spires lifted lance-like in the air. On arriving there and first driving through the long, stately streets, we were struck by the number of magnificent buildings we passed on our route—marble fronts, marble columns, marble steps, marble everywhere.

The city is clothed with architectural beauty on whichever side you look. The public buildings, academies, churches, etc., are all, without exception, magnificent structures, some most striking from their grand simplicity, others from their varied and fanciful picturesqueness. Mr. Lippincott has published a guide to "Philadelphia and its Environs," profusely and beautifully illustrated with woodcuts of many important private dwellings and all the public buildings, the centennial erections in Fairmount Park, and some of the lovely scenery surrounding it. When you have "done" the city, you will not throw aside your guide, but keep it as a pleasant refresher to your memory in after days. It is a pleasure to walk up and down the clean, pretty streets, with their quaint old houses. Every window has an outside protection from the summer sun; some have the thick wooden shutters rarely seen in these days, others have green venetians, which make you feel you are in a semi-tropical region.

The streets running one way across the town are named after different trees, which at one time were supposed to have flourished on their site—such as "Chestnut," "Pine," "Spruce," "Filbert," etc.; those running in an opposite direction are simply numbered on the same plan as that followed in New York. Market Street, one of the great trading thoroughfares, runs straight across the city from one river to the other; it is a splendid street, a hundred feet wide. In Penn's time this was the High Street of the city. Some of the houses have gaily striped awnings, stretching across to the roadway; some have flags or banners flying, and adopt other fanciful means of calling attention to their special attractions. A full-length figure of Pocahontas, or some other savage celebrity, generally stands at the door of the retail tobacconists, offering a pinch of snuff to the passer-by. An eagle spreads its wings over one Art Gallery, while a lion in a cocked hat paws the air on the opposite side. Altogether, the streets have always a gay, festive appearance.

The great thoroughfares are crowded with pedestrians and vehicles of all description. Wholesale and retail trading we know is being briskly carried on; but there is no skurry or confusion anywhere, no pushing and jostling; the living stream flows evenly to and fro; business seems to be conducting itself in a quiet, orderly fashion. Taken altogether, Philadelphia is a sedate city; there is an air of severe respectability and old-world solidity about it; we fear it would take a great deal to stir its substantial self-possession. It lies between the Delaware and Schuylkill rivers, and covers an area of great extent; it is nearly double the size of New York, with a population considerably less. There are no overcrowded quarters here, no narrow courts or gloomy alleys, no tall tenement houses, like rabbit warrens, swarming with human creatures, sheltering hundreds within its reeking, dilapidated walls, where there is scarcely room for a score to live and breathe in. Everywhere in Philadelphia there is room " to turn round in, to breathe, and be free."

No grim poverty parades the streets, no sickly faces turn to the wall, no wolf-eyed hunger lurks in corners; the working population looks healthy, strong, and self-respecting, free from that communistic element which is agitating the far Western cities. Every man, from the lowest rung in the ladder, can rear his family in a home of his own if he pleases; rent is cheap, and the smallest cottage has its bath-room, wash-house, and patch of garden-ground. The city is confined within no limits; it has overflowed the river on either side, where there is plenty of room for it to stretch its limbs and grow, as it has grown, with its beautiful suburban branches, Kensington, Southwark, Germantown, etc. It is growing still; elegant villas, substantial squares, and meandering streets are springing up as fast as they can, clinging to the skirts of the great city, which is like a monstrous body, with arms as long as a gigantic octopus, reaching away on all sides, seizing all it can, or like a loadstone attracting all to itself.

Philadelphia is rich, too, in historical associations, and has preserved many interesting relics of the old times; for a century acquires the dignity of age in the New World, and anything that is hundred years old is considered worthy of a pilgrimage. Penn's cottage, occupied by him in 1701, is still extant; so far it has escaped the improving mania which swept so many of the old landmarks away. It is a small, unpretentious brick building, two storeys high, situated in Letitia Street, near the market, and quite overshadowed by the fine buildings which have sprung up round it. Indeed, many of the old interesting homes of the earlier settlers have wholly disappeared; others are elbowed away out of sight, to make way for the elegant villas and marble palaces of the present generation of wealthy Philadelphians, who form a nucleus of the most refined and cultivated society to be found in any quarter of the world. The oldest inhabitants of the State have still their representatives in Pennsylvania, though they congregate mostly in the city. Thither, in early days, came wandering branches from some of the best families in the old countries, and their descendants still occupy the land. We recognize a kindred spirit as we walk through the public streets, and feel the fascination of the Old World mingling with the vigorous strength of the New.

Philadelphia has not the cosmopolitan character of New York, and consequently does not present such varied fluctuating phases of life. It is a sedate matronly city, with nothing fast or frivolous about it, and its inhabitants uphold its dignity in a manner worthy of themselves. The most beautifully picturesque scenery lies round the immediate neighbourhood; few cities contain so many attractions within their grasp. The views on the winding Wissahickon are especially lovely, with a warm glow and romantic loveliness which makes one inclined to " linger long summer days " beside its banks. But Fairmount Park is, however, Philadelphia's greatest pride; its position and its natural beauties are indeed unsurpassed. Lying along the loveliest part of the Schuylkill river, it occupies three thousand acres of land, and is one of the most extensive parks known, being three times larger than the Grand Central Park, New York—and that, with its twelve miles of driving roads, strikes every one with surprise; but Fairmount has double that space set apart for driving and riding exercise.

At certain hours of the day the streams of handsome equipages and regiments of fair equestrians, driving and riding along the wide curving road by the river, presents a kaleidoscopic scene of great brilliancy; it is like a living panorama, which breaks up and fades like a dissolving view, as one by one they turn out of the main drive. Some disappear in groves of shady trees, or are lost among the romantic hills or pleasant winding ways which lead, between banks of blooming flowers, to the more secluded parts of the ground. But to thoroughly enjoy and appreciate the beauties of Fairmount Park, you must go on foot, ramble among its leafy dells and sunny slopes, its placid lakes hidden away in the heart of the woodlands, amid the tangled masses of a luxuriant growth of green, lichen-covered boulders and moss-grown banks, left to flourish in their natural wilfulness and beauty. Magnificent fountains have been erected in different parts of the ground, and marble monuments to deceased statesmen, philanthropists, and heroes are gleaming white on every side. That to Abraham Lincoln is perhaps the finest of them all.

In no country in the world are there such extensive and

delightful public parks and pleasure-grounds as in America. Nature, in most cases, has laid so much material ready to hand—rocks, hills, wilderness, forest land, and rivers. Art has but to wave her magic wand, clear away or reject all she does not require, and utilize and lay out the rest according to her tasteful pleasure. Thus, many of the primeval forest trees, rocky mounds, and sparkling rivers of the dead ages beautify the recreation grounds of to-day. The Zoological Gardens, lying along the opposite bank of the river, promise to be second to none; they occupy a vast extent of beautifully laid out ground, and the different buildings already erected there are architecturally pleasant to the eye, and at the same time those best suited to the requirements, and for the exhibition of the remarkably fine collection of animals gathered therein. The society has agents in all parts of the world, being resolved to spare neither pains, labour, nor expense in their endeavour to make their collection the most perfect of its kind in all the civilized world.

CHAPTER XXVI.

SUMMER AMONG THE GOTHAMITES.

A New York Summer—How they meet it—Airy Customs—Coney Island—Rockaway and Long Branch—A Mountain Village—Ellenville—View from "Sam's Point."

PHILADELPHIA to New York is a pleasant three hours' journey, and we were glad to find ourselves settled down for a few weeks' rest in the "Empire City"—if rest can be obtained in that electric atmosphere, which quickens the pulse and fills you with its own restless life, whether you will or no. We arrived there in the middle of May. The season was over, their fashionable season being the reverse of ours, for their gaieties are at their full flood-tide during the winter months, when ours are ended—if such things ever do come to an end in a great city, but it seems to me that the general mass build up a tolerable palace of pleasure out of the *débris* the fashionable world leaves behind it.

Our friends, the few who remained in Gotham to battle with the fierce summer sun, regretted that we had come back at the dead season; but they managed to make it lively enough. What with excursions on the water, picnics on land, theatres, and social gatherings at home, the time passed only too quickly. The days were too short; if we could lengthen them as we do our skirts, by adding a flouncing of a few hours, we should have had engagements enough to fill them. The weather was unusually warm for May, the thermometer sometimes rising as high as 90° in the shade.

As the weeks passed on, the temperature became almost unendurable. The coolest place in all New York was the Madison Square Theatre. The thermometer had mounted to 100° when we received a box for an afternoon miscellaneous performance in aid of the Edgar Poe Memorial Statue. Among the many other things selected for the occasion was an abridged version of "The Taming of the Shrew," when Edwin Booth consented to play Petruchio. Nothing less than a desire to see this celebrated actor would have tempted us to stir. The sun, like a ball of burnished copper, filled the skies with a heat-created mist, and poured upon the earth a fiery atmosphere that seemed to burn as it touched you, and the very breeze might have issued from the mouth of a furnace; but we gathered ourselves together—all that was left of us, for we were gradually melting away—and, armed with fans, smelling-salts and sundry antidotes to fainting fits, panted our way from Forty-fifth Street to a Sixth Avenue car, which landed us close to the theatre. Immediately on entering, we felt as though we had left the hot world to scorch and dry up outside, while we were enjoying a soft summer breeze within. Where did it come from? The house was crowded—there was not standing-room for a broom-stick;

but the air was as cool and refreshing as though it had blown over a bank of spring violets. We learned the reason of this. By some simple contrivance the outer air, circulating through and among tons of ice, is forced to find its way through a thousand frozen cracks and crevices before it enters the auditorium; thus a flow of fresh air is kept in constant circulation, which renders an afternoon in Madison Square Theatre a luxury during the hottest of dog-days.

The death roll is terrible during these hot spells, sometimes amounting from sun-stroke alone to twenty in a single day. The New Yorkers, however, know how to make the best of their semi-tropical summer. The more sensible portion of the masculine population go about in their linen suits and panama hats, though some men cling to their beloved chimney-pot and swelter under a weight of broadcloth; but no man is above carrying an umbrella, white, green, or brown, as the case may be. Rivers of iced lemonade are flowing at the street corners, at two cents per glass. You may see a multitude closing round and pouring in and out of the "drug stores" (chemist's shops). You think there must have been an accident—somebody run over, somebody killed. No such thing; it is only the more aristocratic thirsty multitude, who eschew street corners, crowding in for their iced drinks. The "drug stores" have, every one, a neat white marble fountain, with a dozen shining silver taps, which pour forth streams of fruit-flavoured iced drinks—pine, cherry, strawberry, raspberry, and lemon cream soda, the most delicious of all. From early morning till late in the evening these fountains never cease playing; small fortunes pour from their silver mouths into the pockets of their owners.

In the summer evenings the whole indoor population of New York seems to overflow on to the "stoops" of their house. Walking through some of the best streets, you may glance in at the open windows, and see the elegantly furnished vacant rooms, with their luxurious lounges, paintings, mirrors, and gilded magnificence, mellowed in the low-burning gaslight, while the inhabitants are taking the air on their doorsteps. The white moon, shining down on the yellow gas-lighted streets; the elevated railroad, rushing with its living freight through the air, blinking its green-and-red fiery eyes upon the world below; the tall dark houses, with their dimly lighted, luxurious interiors and family groups, from paterfamilias down to the youngest-born, the ladies, in their pretty, fanciful toilettes, taking the air on the doorsteps;—all combine to form a pretty picture, quite like a theatrical scene on the broad stage of life. Rippling waves of low laughter and scraps of musical chit-chat follow you as you pass along. This is an old knickerbocker custom, which still obtains everywhere except on the sacred Fifth Avenue, which confines itself strictly within doors, shrined from the vulgar gaze; perhaps the *nouveau riche* element (being largely represented) is afraid of compromising its dignity by following old-fashioned customs.

As the weeks passed on the weather became more and more trying, and we made daily excursions to the numerous watering-places immediately surrounding New York, leaving home early in the morning and returning the same evening, which is easily done. Coney Island, one of the great resorts for the million, is reached from the foot of Twenty-third Street in about an hour. A few years ago it was a mere wide waste of sand, and was bought by a clever speculator for a mere song ; it is now worth millions of dollars, and is covered on all sides with a miscellaneous mass of buildings of all descriptions. Restaurants, shooting galleries, pavilions, and refreshment-rooms to suit all classes, and some monster hotels, of light, airy structure, lift their faces towards the sea. Culver, Brighton, and Manhattan Beaches, the one being a continuation of the other, spread their wide stretch of silver sand along the side of the island and down to the blue Atlantic waves below. There are no pleasant walks or drives, there exists not a tree, there is no shade from the fierce, blinding sun to be found anywhere. No gray rocks or picturesque battlemented cliffs ; nothing but the level island, with its wide stretch of silver sand and a world of sea. The hotels are crowded, every nook and corner of the island filled to overflowing during the season ; the beach is covered with a lively mass of holiday-makers, all bent on enjoying themselves ; gay bunting is flaunting and flying everywhere ; musicians are hard at work, beating drums, scraping fiddles, and blowing trumpets, as though their very lives depended on the noise they are making. Altogether, it is a gay, stirring scene. Coney Island is not a place where the fashionable or aristocratic multitude most do congregate ; it is a rather fast, jolly, rollicking place, and serves its purpose well, as the health-breathing lungs of a great city.

Rockaway Beach is about half an hour's journey off,

and is disposed to set up a race of rivalry with Coney Island. Its general aspect is much the same—flat, level land, and sand, and sea; it is less frequented, less gay, and certainly has not such good accommodation; but a very fine hotel is now in course of erection, which promises very superior accommodation to visitors. Rockaway is scarcely as flat and barren as Coney Island; in its immediate vicinity clumps of trees are making praiseworthy efforts to grow, but at present their long, gaunt branches are sparsely covered with green. Long Branch and Long Island are both of easy access from the upper part of the city, by ferry and rail; they are equally favourite watering-places with those already mentioned, though of a rather different character; they do not depend for popularity on a floating population, being the resort (Long Branch especially so) of the more fashionable public. There are whole legions of hotels, and squadrons of boarding-houses, together with numerous elegant villas or cottage residences, which are let by the season to such as prefer the freedom of their own household to establishing themselves in an hotel. Many build their own fanciful dwellings, and migrate thither in early summer, and remain till the chill autumn breezes drive them back to the city; others make it their head-quarters, and reside there all the year round.

Long Branch is a delightful place. You can choose your companionship, and join the coteries of pleasant society, and have as much gaiety or as much social seclusion as you please. Some of the first-class hotels, which are largely patronized by transient travellers, have been erected on the low bluff which rises behind the strip of sandy beach. A fine wide avenue runs between them and the sea. They are none of them grand, imposing-looking buildings, and have no pretensions to architectural beauty, being for the most part long, low, frame-houses, with wide verandahs and balconies running wherever it is possible for verandah or balcony to go. Smooth-shaven, well-kept lawns run along the front, where there is a delightful promenade extending for nearly two miles, overlooking the sea. Orchestral music of the best description is provided for the amusement of the guests; everything is arranged for the enjoyment of people of refined, cultivated taste. Ocean Avenue is the fashionable promenade, which at certain hours of the day is crowded with elegant equipages of every description; from the bachelor in his "sulky," to the light landau, filled with pretty, tastefully dressed women, who change their toilettes half a dozen times in the day, and do a great deal of dancing and flirting in the evening—too much, perhaps, for their own good.

Those who prefer soft inland scenery, and mountain air, to the keen, invigorating sea-breezes, may gratify their taste in any of the many beautiful rural districts which surround New York. There names are legion, but one of the sweetest and loveliest of them all is Ellenville, which lies in the heart of the "Shewangunk Mountains." It is a mere mountain village, pretty, and picturesque in the extreme. There being only one small hotel in the place, it does not lay itself out for visitors, but is very glad to see them when they come. The narrow, winding high street of the village is a picture in itself. Tiny toy-cottages lie in the midst of their little gardens, where cabbages and sunflowers, gooseberry bushes, dahlias, and wild-rose trees grow together in sweet companionship. Some break out into shop-windows, and your "butcher and baker and candlestick-maker" show forth from a bower of green, or hide themselves beneath luxuriant grape-vines, where you would least expect to find them.

There are some elegant villa residences nestling among tall trees, and broken rows of less pretentious, but equally pretty dwellings standing in their own grounds of blooming flowers, and peach and apple trees, with wide verandahs, where the ladies sit in their rocking-chairs and work, or lie in a hammock indulging in *dolce far niente*, amid the drowsy hum of bees, and perfume of flowers, reading or dreaming through the sultry noontide. Planted on either side of these rustic lane-like streets, are rows of tall, wide-spreading chestnut trees, whose thick umbrageous branches form a perfect shade. There are several excellent boarding-houses, and some private families, who are happy to receive temporary residents when they come with friendly recommendations. We were received by two charming young orphan ladies, who made their house a most idyllic home for us during our too brief stay.

The artist world is beginning to penetrate the seclusion of this beautiful valley, lying so peacefully within its green girdle of mountains, and are making rapid acquaintance with its varied scenery, which holds so many tempting pictures ready grouped for their brush and canvas. There are hills and river, green ferny dells, deep ravines cut in the steep mountain-sides, and rocky chasms, whose mysteries are still unexplored. Here and there you come upon some of the loveliest nooks in all creation, full of wondrous lights and shadows—so still and peaceful, you feel inclined to lie down with folded hands and be at rest: you could sleep so soundly there, hidden away from all the world, until the judgment day.

It was decided among us that "Sam's Point," a lofty peak of the Shewangunk, must be visited. We started one bright morning by a narrow winding road which is carried along the face of the mountain, climbing upwards through tangled brushwood, past banks of flowering laurel, their shining leaves half hidden by their luxuriant masses of delicate pink and white blossoms; up, still up, through forests of pine and fir, over broken masses of lichen-covered boulders, with fantastic rocks looming on every side, and on over sloping stretches of breezy uplands, till we came to a strip of table-land. The horses pricked up their ears and put on a "spurt." Poor, tired brutes! they had travelled that road often enough, and could find their way to the low-lying shanty, where they know they are to be stabled for the next hour or two, without any of our guidance. At this stage of our journey we came in close view of "Sam's Point," standing out in clear-cut lines against the sky.

Here, according to the general custom, we unpacked our luncheon-basket. It was filled with such good things, and so many of them, we hardly knew which to begin first. We spread our feast under the shadow of a belt of dark trees, the last of their line that can lift their heads and grow on the now barren, flinty soil. With much fun and laughter we got through a luxurious meal; then our general commanding for the season insisted that we must climb to the very top of "Sam's Point." We obey, and start on a scrambling expedition up the sloping stony path, where straggling thorny bushes caught us viciously at every turn. With the hot sun blazing fiercely upon us, and a high, warm wind almost blowing us off our feet, we struggled on to the top. No, not quite the top: we halted on a rocky platform, just below the extreme point, and looked down from its dizzy, precipitous height upon the lovely landscape below, lying in the peaceful smile of a glorious sunshine, rolling and spreading out hundreds of feet below, as far as the eye can see. Dark belts of forest trees outline the distant horizon, thickets and wild woods sweep down through the hilly defiles, reach out their green arms, and run like a fancy network of nature's cunningest pattern over the valleys, while the silver thread of a river runs round and about, lacing the green meadow lands together. Scores of white villages, dwarfed by distance till they look like collections of dolls' houses, are scattered over the plains or cling to the sloping hillsides. The colouring, and the lights and shadows falling everywhere, give an additional charm to the exquisite picture before us. It holds us like a magnet; we cannot tear ourselves away from it; we perch ourselves on the narrow parapet and gaze our fill. There is a mellowness and balm in the atmosphere, and slowly a soft pink mist falls over the landscape like a bridal veil, and covers everything with a tender mystery.

We turn and scramble down the stony path, and are

soon winding our way down the mountain road homeward, still feasting our eyes with delicious bits of scenery as we go along. We drive round among the foothills to get a view of the Nopanoc falls, which are only about half an hour from Ellenville. They are not grand or imposing, nor do they fall from any visible height, but they are beautiful from their wild surroundings, and come creaming and foaming down the rugged mountain-sides, till they reach the stony bed below, and flow on beneath our feet to their far-off watery home ; they seem arranged by nature for transfer to an artist's canvas. Tired though we were with our long day's outing, we enjoyed our homeward drive through the evening shadows. There was no moon, and the dusky air was full of fireflies, floating about like globes of living light ; and the "whip-poor-will" commenced his melancholy plaint, which he never utters till the day is done. The bird came to his curious cognomen something in this wise. A benighted sinner commonly called "Poor Will" was stumbling home late one night when the bird began to sing, and to his muddled ears the notes arranged themselves into the words, " Whip poor Will." .He knew he deserved whipping, and believed that an order for his future castigation was being despatched through some mysterious agency to the realms above. Thenceforth, whipped by the stings of an awakened conscience, he set to and repented as hard as he had sinned, and the name stuck to the bird ever afterwards.

The "whip-poor-will's" notes had hardly died away, when the frogs, huge green goggle-eyed monsters, commenced their croaking concert, which is by no means an unpleasant thing to listen to; it goes with a rather musical, monotonous swing, quite different from the harsh croak of their froggy brethren on our side of the water.

The next morning we returned to New York, to rest one more night, our last, in that city previous to our visit to Boston. We left Ellenville with much regret. I know of no place where one could so delightfully dream away the long summer days, as in that rural little village with its tempting and delightful surrounding. It is reached by the Erie Railway from Jersey City, and is about four hours' journey from New York.

CHAPTER XXVII.

THE "AMERICAN ATHENS."

Aboard the *Massachusetts*—A Perambulation—The Electric Machine—An Easy Way of committing Suicide—Boston—The Cars—The Common—The "Glorious Fourth of July."

HERE had been so many terrible accidents by the river steamers during the last few weeks, that we were half inclined to go to Boston by rail; but on reflection we determined not to yield to an imaginary evil. Judging by averages, we ought to have a safe passage, for one of the finest vessels had been destroyed by fire only two days before, and great disasters are rarely continuous. Because misfortune had happened to other people, it was no reason it should tread upon our heels also.

Accordingly, we started on one of the finest Providence boats, the *Massachusetts*, for Boston, leaving New York at five o'clock in the afternoon. We spent the few remaining hours of daylight in admiring the river scenery, as our majestic boat steamed towards the Sound, and enjoying the brisk sea-breezes. Never had the "briny kisses" of the great sweet mother seemed so fresh and invigorating. The captain, to whom we had been previously introduced, invited us into the wheelhouse, which, contrary to our home custom, is lifted high up above the deck, commanding a clear view of all surrounding objects. There we watched with great interest the steering and working of the vessel. The bell seemed always to be ringing its signal, warning the small craft out of our way, and informing the larger craft which way we would "keep her head."

Afterwards we descended into the engine-room, and found the huge monster well worth seeing—its black body bound in bright bands, and studded with polished decorations of brass and steel, like a grim warrior wearing his coat of mail. We saw him fed with his vast furnace fires. He seemed always hungry, opening his red mouth for more food. We watched its gigantic walking beam rise and fall, in its solemn march across the world of waters. The vessel in all parts is lighted by electricity; and we were allowed to go downstairs to inspect the generating apparatus. In order to reach it we had to go through the machinery-room, where the crashing, groaning, and thudding, the rapid whirling of wheels, and clanking to and fro of countless bars, and the up-and-down stroke of the piston, deafened our ears, dazzled our eyes, and bewildered our senses, while the walking beam above, the great propelling power of all, tramped steadily on.

We passed through this distracting place, crossed a narrow passage, and at the end of it found ourselves in an empty room—empty except for the electric machine, with its invisible wonders working before our eyes. We could not absolutely *see* the machine; its evolutions were so rapid, they might have been impelled by lightning. It was surrounded by scintillating sparks of weird greenish light, playing round it as though some fiery genie was confined therein. There was not much noise, only a whizzing, whirring sound, and the ground shook beneath our feet with a quivering motion like a living thing in mortal pain. Radiating from the machine were sundry thin wires, each conducting the illuminating power to the decks and saloons, both above and below. Two wires ran perpendicularly one on each side of the apparatus, one conducting the negative, the other the positive current. Each one might be handled singly with impunity, but a simultaneous touch of the two together would be fraught with instant death. This easy mode of committing suicide lay within reach of our hands. We shuddered, and beat a hasty retreat, lest a sudden impulse might tempt us to try the experiment. How many unintentional suicides have been hurried into eternity by the uncontrollable impulse of a moment!

About seven o'clock a capital dinner, *à la carte*, was served, and we had the double delight of enjoying a dainty meal, and watching the sunset from the saloon windows. There was no gorgeous colouring such as sometimes clothes the western skies with the barbaric splendour of crimson, amethyst, green, and gold; but the whole hemisphere where the sun went down was filled with floating islands of golden light, sailing hither and thither in the face of the pale-blue sky. But soon came the twilight, trailing her dusky skirts between land and sea, and shut the heavens from our sight.

After dinner we went on deck, but there was nothing

to tempt us to stay there. It was a cool gray evening; there was no moon, and not a star was visible; we therefore went into the grand saloon, which is gorgeously upholstered in crimson velvet, and decorated with much carving and gilding, while mirrors and looking-glasses reflect and multiply you by dozens on every side. A piano stood at the farther end, and there was already a man in possession. He was short, he was fat, he was bald, and wore an immense pair of green goggles, such as are rarely worn except when crossing the ice. He looked as stupid and stolid as an animated jelly-fish, and knew as little about music as an oyster; but he sang, out of tune and out of time, the most lugubrious ditties. He enjoyed them if nobody else did. When he got to the end of one, he began another. He might have seen the expression of disgust on everybody's face, but he was self-absorbed, he never looked; if any one attempted to talk within earshot, he glared round reproachfully and sang louder than before. It is strange, but painfully true: it is precisely those people who can neither play nor sing who attempt to do both for the torture of their fellow-passengers on those river excursions, and perhaps on some other occasions.

We were driven to our state-room early, and the first thing that met our sight was a huge pair of ominous-looking life-preservers. We tried them on, saw that they fitted and fastened correctly, then leisurely proceeded to plait our hair in long pigtails for the convenience of our escort, so that, in case of accidents, he might float us easily. We had passed the wrecked remains of the *Sea-*

wanhaka an hour before: it had been destroyed by fire, and scores of its passengers had met their death within fifty yards of the shore. These river boats are splendid to look at, luxurious to travel in, but if a fire once seizes on any part of the vessel, being made of wood, it burns like a matchbox; there is no hope for it. There was nothing left of the unfortunate *Seawanhaka* but the huge boiler and a few ribs of iron, lying like a mutilated skeleton on the shore. It was not a pleasant picture to possess our mind the last thing at night; but we went to bed, and, strange to say, slept soundly enough until six o'clock in the morning, when we were served with a comfortable breakfast, and left the boat at Providence, where the train was waiting, and in about an hour we reached Boston.

It was one of the loveliest of summer mornings. A kind of spiritual sunshine lay upon the silent land as we drove through the empty streets, for at that early hour few people were astir. We felt as though we were entering some solemn cathedral town of the Old World; everything is so different from any other American city which we have lately been passing through. There are no long, straight streets, no lines of tall stone houses, whose sameness wearies the sight; no dull monotony here. The streets are labyrinthine, they radiate from all sides and cross at all angles; they run up and down, round corners, curving or straight, wide or narrow. There is no irritating uniformity anywhere.

From the first glance we feel that this city has a character of its own, and that character is essentially English. There is a certain undefinable something in the general aspect of the place and of the people which makes us feel near home. Familiar names greet us at street corners, their nomenclature being similar to our own. No tubs of household refuse stand on the side-walks, or flow over into the gutter. The streets are beautifully clean; it is a pleasure to walk in them. Beacon Street, which is one of the most fashionable localities, reminds us forcibly of Park Lane; in fact, it is Park Lane, in miniature, seen through the wrong end of a telescope. The houses are all in good taste, though of different sizes and varied forms of architecture. Some have old-fashioned bay windows, others are flat fronted, some of white or gray stone, some of cherry-red bricks. One has its balcony and window-sills filled with bright-hued and sweet-smelling flowers; another is literally covered with Wisteria, all abloom with rich purple blossoms. It is the pretty floral decorations and varied style of building which gives it so quaint and picturesque an appearance. It stands on gently rising ground. At the top is the State House, a very handsome colonnaded building, crowned with a huge bronze cupola shining like burnished gold, dominating the landscape and visible for miles round.

In front, railed in with light elegant railings, and running the whole length of Beacon Street, is the "Common," as the Bostonians modestly call it, though it is in reality a very beautiful park; but a park without carriage drives, devoted entirely to pedestrian exercise. There is a fine growth of forest trees, which for centuries cannot have had an axe among them. There are fountains, too, and flower-gardens, and comfortable seats arranged under the umbrageous shade of the spreading walnut trees. On one mound of elevated ground is a handsome memorial in honour of their dead ancestors; in another part of the common, on a greater elevation, stands an equestrian statue of General Washington. No city is complete without a statue of the founder of the United States. The common is a delightful rural promenade and pleasure-ground, and when the band is playing presents a most brilliant and imposing scene.

The absence of the tobacco-chewing process and its disgusting results is another striking feature in Boston. You may walk through the public streets or ride in the cars the whole day long without once being subject to the nuisance to which we ought to have become accustomed. In the streets, on the cars, or among the people, you recognize a familiar Old-World look, and signs of refinement and cultivation everywhere. Even a Boston crowd is a well-behaved, orderly gathering. We were there on the 4th of July. In the morning, escorted by a friend whose name will remain ever green in our memory, we went to an entertainment at the grand opera-house, which we imagined would partake of a national character. We expected to hear martial music and the national airs sung with the enthusiasm of a people who "exulted to be free;" but we didn't. The concert was confined to a few everyday melodies—"The Old Folks at Home" and "Annie Laurie"—all well enough in their way, but hardly suited to such an occasion as the "glorious fourth." Then, for the first time in our lives, we heard the "Act of Independence" read, with great emphasis and distinctness. We felt we ought to have blushed—but didn't.

In the evening there was a grand display of fireworks, an open air orchestral concert, and other amusements. The people swarmed upon the common by hundreds and thousands of all classes, all degrees. There were no "reserved seats," and no possibility of enjoying any part of the festivity in "luxurious ease." Anybody who wished to see or enjoy anything must go on foot. It is this temporary incorporation of the refined with the rougher elements of humanity which makes an American crowd different from any other. There is no pushing, no horse-play, no practical joking; nobody hustles or tramples on you. It is essentially a polite crowd. Of course we never got into one from choice, but sometimes from necessity found ourselves in the midst of it, and everywhere, in other cities besides Boston, found the same orderly behaviour.

On the evening of the "glorious fourth" we went out, with a pleasant titillation of curiosity, mingled with a nervous notion that brickbats might be flying or squibs and crackers be fizzing about too freely, or, perhaps, some little patriotic pleasantry awkwardly demonstrated.

An American visiting in England had said on a previous "fourth," "Ah! in my country every man will be gloriously drunk to-night; not a single one will go sober to bed." This perhaps coloured our ideas of the "glorious fourth;" whereas it might have been the fourth of any other month. The concerts which took place on different parts of the common were by no means of a patriotic or exhilarating nature. The orchestras were excellent, the music well played, but ill chosen ; that is, ill chosen for such an occasion. It was chiefly classical. Occasionally it pranced off into a waltz, and encouraged the idea of frivolity for a moment, but was speedily recalled under cover of the big drum, and a more select fugue or fantasia took its place. Classical music is not fitting for an open-air promenade, when nobody's attention can be wholly absorbed by it, as should be the case when good music is being played. Fancy a running fire of chit-chat, or cannonade of laughter being carried on, while the solemn strains of Handel, the subtle harmonies of Beethoven, or sweet melodies of Joseph Haydn are filling the air! Merry catching tunes or patriotic airs are best suited to these occasions, but never the ghost of one was abroad that night. John Brown's soul might have marched to the end of his journey, and lain down to undisturbed rest ; there was no one to "rally round the flag," shouting the battle-cry of freedom. The star-spangled banner was folded away out of sight, but the stars and stripes fluttered faintly from a few windows, and that was all.

The fireworks crackled and fizzed, while the multitude looked solemnly on. Roman candles burnt blue, showers of golden light were falling, Catherine wheels were whirling in circles of brilliant colours, fantastic designs, and fine set pieces blazed on all sides. We made our bow to an illuminated President, and watched the American eagle light himself up with a golden body, bright green wings, and ruby claws, big enough to clutch the world by the throat. He was a gorgeous bird, and dazzled our sight for a few moments, and then faded from it. We went home to bed with a virtuous feeling that we had assisted at the celebration of the " glorious fourth."

The arrangements for street traffic in Boston are as nearly perfect as they can be. Cars are running everywhere every minute of the day. Most comfortable cars they are—a great improvement upon any similar conveyances we had seen in any other part of the States. Some are closed, some are open; the seats are placed so that every one sits face forward. They are splendidly horsed, and you can fly in the face of the wind from one end of the city to another for five cents ($2\frac{1}{2}d.$). It is well lighted, and the numerous cars, with their coloured bulls'-eyes behind and before, illuminate the streets, like the flashing of monster fireflies.

Here, as elsewhere, are handsome churches, museums, picture-galleries, etc. No one need ever pass a dull day in this intellectual and cultivated city. Like Washington and Philadelphia, Boston is exclusive in the matter of society. Its social laws are many, and strictly kept. Reserved and dignified in its everyday life, it is not overgiven to demonstrative rejoicing, even among its best friends. We have all our little weaknesses, and perhaps Boston may be a *little* vain of its intellect and refinement. " We don't do ' that ' in Boston," is a common phrase, and considered strong enough to condemn "that" when it is done elsewhere.

The rural surroundings of Boston are very beautiful; but the interest of most tourists centres in the city itself, which, besides its many attractions, is the home of two men who have made the genius of America known and honoured in every quarter of the civilized world—I mean of the Poet Longfellow, and the genial philosophical poet and essayist, Oliver Wendell Holmes.

CHAPTER XXVIII.

FAREWELL VISITS.

A Visit to Longfellow—The Poet's Home—Dr. Oliver Wendell Holmes—Newport—A Fashionable Watering-place—The Old Town—The "Cottages"—Homeward.

T is not admissible, as a rule, to turn the result of a private visit into public copy. To be received into a family circle on terms of social equality, and there gather up scraps of conversation, and turn the sayings and doings of the unsuspecting household into public property, is a most ungracious return for kindly hospitality; therefore I have hitherto avoided all mention of my private friends in these pages. But every rule has an exception, and as the general world is supposed to be interested in, and are kept fully informed of, the most trivial circumstances surrounding the royal rulers of nations, I take it for granted that a much livelier interest must cling round the monarchs of mind, whose names are "familiar to our ears as household words"—whose gentle genius, playful humour, or tender philosophy has coloured the lives and gladdened the hearts of thousands, and helped to make the ignorant wise and the wise happy. Their thoughts come to us over land and over sea; in-

visibly and subtly, as the sweet fresh air we breathe, they permeate our lives, and become a part of us, circulating, with a pure ennobling influence, from the cottage to the palace. These are the only true magicians, god-inspired workers of miracles; shrined in the sanctity of their own peaceful homes, they are working to give light to the blind old world, that it may be better for their lives when the Great Master calls them home.

We should have been sorely disappointed if we had been compelled to leave Boston without paying our affectionate homage to Longfellow, whose name is associated with our earliest awakening thoughts. He had been so often with us in spirit for this many a long year, that we longed to see him in the flesh; it was therefore with great pleasure we received an invitation to pay him a visit at his marine residence, Nahant, where he generally spends the summer months. Nahant lies on the shores of the Atlantic, just outside Boston Harbour. We had a glorious sail, for it was one of summer's loveliest days—earth, air, sea, and sky were all invisibly blended in one perfect harmony. Our brief, bright journey was soon over, and on turning a sudden point of the bay we found ourselves scudding along on the waves of the Atlantic. Nahant was before us. Longfellow's house was pointed out to us from the vessel; it seemed to be lying close on the shore, but in reality it stands on elevated rising ground, open to the sea, but about a quarter of a mile from it. A carriage waited on the landing-stage to convey us to the house—an attention for which we were grateful, as a walk uphill, even for so short a distance, in the face of a blazing sun, was not desirable. After a short breezy drive, the carriage stopped at a delightfully picturesque villa, or cottage *ornée*, though it was more like a Swiss chalet than either. A child was playing with its toys and dolls in the verandah which ran round the four sides of the house, and two gentlemen were seated in rocking-chairs facing the wide winding road. As we drove up, one of the gentlemen rose and came down the steps and across the small front garden to meet us. There was no mistaking the man—it was our host himself; we had seen him often gazing at us with stony photographic eyes from the shop-windows thousands of miles away, but no more like the poet's actual self than a stagnant pool is like the living sea. We observed him well as he came down the steps, with a gracious dignity born of a benignant spirit. He is tall, slight, and erect as a soldier on duty, with refined features, and a pale complexion, with a slight tinge of colour on his cheeks, almost as delicate as the blush of a woman, kind blue eyes, and wavy hair, which is more white than gray; he wears a beard, has long shapely white hands that any lady might be proud of; his voice is peculiarly soft, and his manners full of that gentle courtliness which is fast dying out. He is in his seventy-fourth year, but looks considerably younger. There is none of the physical feebleness or querulous spirit of age about him; he seems now to be in the full autumn-tide of a hale, healthy life. Time is dealing very gently with him, leading him imperceptibly (as it is leading us all) down the valley towards "the silent land" which he has told us of.

After shaking hands and exchanging the usual greetings, he presented us to his two brothers-in-law, who reside with him. The household was not entirely masculine, however; the poet's two daughters were out in their yacht enjoying a sail: the one is married, and, with her little child, is only on a visit; the other, a very charming young lady, lives at home with her father. We went through the house and sat on the back verandah. A tempting-looking hammock swung there, and wild roses climbed up the lattice-work and nodded their odorous heads at us, and showered their pink petals at our feet. The poet gathered us a bunch of the fairest blossoms; they lie faded and scentless in my album to-day, but the memory of that July afternoon at Nahant is fresh and green still.

We sat there chatting in a pleasant way of the Old World and the New; the gray Atlantic, scarcely wrinkled in the light breeze, lay before us. We watched the various vessels—light brigs, sloops, and schooners, all full-rigged to catch the breeze, and stately steamers on their march across the world of waters, and pretty yachts, some curtsying to their own shadows, others with their white sails spread, like gigantic swans skimming over the face of the ocean. Presently the one particular yacht we awaited came prancing over the tiny waves, like a steed that knows he is nearing home. The two ladies sprang ashore, and speedily made a pleasant addition to our party in the verandah. The time passed only too quickly. The pretty, fair-haired little grandchild sat in the lap of its blooming young mother, playing and prattling its baby prattle. It was an idyllic picture, with its pleasant home surroundings—a living illustration of three stages of life:

the dawn, the meridian, and the evening before the sun sets and the night closes in.

The conversation was never allowed to flag; somehow, the merest everyday chit-chat seemed to gather weight and pungency by the mode of utterance: a pointed word, a look, the turn of a sentence, gave to every commonplace phrase an attraction and a meaning it would not in itself possess. Mr. Longfellow is no egotist; he evidently does not care to talk of himself or his work. He is full of that modesty which generally characterizes great genius, but is lamentably wanting in the many poetical aspirants who are buzzing about the world, trying their wings to see how far they can soar into those ideal realms where true genius sits calmly crowned. Whatever he says it is pleasant to listen to.

During the few brief hours of a first acquaintance, it is rarely we get into a very deep or animated discussion on any subject; we must first get the key to each other's minds, and become *en rapport* with each other's feeling, before the spirit of either can give forth its fullest, freest tones. As a rule, it is enough to skim the surface of the current topics of the day.

We sat down sociably to a *recherché* little dinner, the first course of which was one of the national dishes, to which we were by this time well accustómed—clam chowder. The meal, gastronomically considered, was on strictly international principles; we sipped the vintage of Champagne, while we enjoyed the pork and beans of Boston, and washed down corn-cobs and hominy with mineral waters of Germany.

We were obliged to leave Nahant early, as the Boston boat was at the pier, and time and tide wait for no woman, even in this chivalrous land. Cordially and regretfully we said "Good-bye." The dear old man, with his delighful family group, stood in the verandah, shading his eyes from the setting sun, watching till we were out of sight. He is photographed on my mind; I shall see him often in days to come, as I looked my last upon him then.

The next day, according to appointment, we paid a visit to another celebrity, Dr. Oliver Wendell Holmes, who has made himself a name in the Old World as well as in the New. He, too, was residing at his country cottage at "Beverly Farms," another of those delightful rural retreats in the vicinity of Boston, being little more than an hour's railway journey from it.

We reached Beverly Farms about noon—the fiercest, hottest part of the day. We had no idea how far the Doctor's residence might be from the station, but trusted to find some conveyance to take us there, feeling that it would be an effort even to walk a hundred yards in the heat of the blazing sun. The train steamed away from the platform, and we looked round in search of some one of whom we might inquire our road, and then looked blankly at one another. We had no idea which way to turn, and there was not a creature in sight to tell us. We walked through the empty station; the ticket office was closed, and not a railway official was in sight. Only a big black dog was lying curled up under one of the benches; every other living thing had mysteriously vanished.

Some labourers were working in a field not far from the station, and we noticed a pretty white cottage close to the roadway on the opposite side—scarcely a stone's throw from us. A gentleman in a linen suit, a straw hat, and carrying a green umbrella, came out of the gate and walked quickly towards the station; we advanced to meet him, and inquired if he could tell us where Dr. Holmes lived?

"I am Dr. Holmes," he answered, "and you, I presume, are the ladies I was hurrying to meet?" We acknowledged that we believed we were. He turned back with us, and in another moment we all three entered the garden which we had seen him leave a moment before. It was a pleasant first introduction, and here we scored another delightful day. We found Dr. Holmes a most genial and agreeable companion—exactly, as from reading his books, we had expected he would be. He is neither tall nor short, but of medium height; a thin, wiry man, with iron-gray hair, and eyes twinkling with humour and philosophy. Age has not dimmed their lustre, nor taken the spring from his elastic spirit; he is as brisk in his movements as many a man at five-and-twenty. Mrs. Holmes, a gentle-mannered lady, just the wife necessary for such a man—one who would make his home a harbour of rest and peace—came out to meet and welcome us. It is always pleasant to see a genius and philosopher well matched in his life's companionship; unfortunately, we have so often to look on the reverse picture. The right woman is an inspiration to the one, a study for the other; but the wrong acts like an irritant and blister, his whole life through. We were presently joined by his daughter—a brilliant young widow, a feminine edition of himself. Altogether we made a very pleasant party, and soon floated off into a brisk conversation. I wish I could reproduce his spirited, quaintly-turned phrases and quick repartee, to which the expression of his face gave additional point and high flavour. I think the most dry-as-dust doctrine would quicken into life if passed through the alembic of his sparkling philosophy.

It is not often that poetry and philosophy go hand in hand together as in this case it does. Dr. Holmes seems surprised to find himself so much more famous in this country for his prose works and philosophical studies than for his poetical productions. Scientific research and semi-philosophical lectures and literature are the occupations of his daily life, but poetry is the darling of his heart, the beloved companion of his holiday hours, the airy architect who builds for his spirit a home we know not of. We retired to luncheon in a pretty parlour looking out into the flower-garden, where the bees were droning and the tall lilies and roses nodding sleepily in the sunshine. He seemed very much interested in our intonation, and frequently called attention to our mode of pronouncing certain words. He afterwards read to us some scraps and snatches of his new poems, which was a great treat to us, for he has a melodious voice, and reads with great emphasis and spirit; indeed, we were so deeply engrossed by his brilliant conversations that we almost lost our train. With much regret we bade him and his family a cordial adieu.

There was one more visit to pay, and that the last. Time, the great "whipper-in," was behind us, bidding us gather our energies together, for we must soon—too soon —bid adieu to the New World, and turn our faces homewards towards the old land. The next day we started to pay a visit to Newport, Rhode Island, whose fame as the most beautiful, select, and fashionable watering-place in America had long been familiar to us. It is only about four hours' rail from Boston. Our host and hostess met us at the station, and we were too much occupied in conversing with them to take much notice of the town as we drove through it ; we made closer acquaintance with it afterwards. A half-hour's drive took us through the lower part of the town, the business quarters, and past the "old mill" which stands in a wide, open square. Some say it is a relic left by the Norsemen who once overran the land, and others assert that it was built by the earliest colonists centuries ago ; but nobody knows exactly when it was built, nor what was its use. It is a massive stone tower, with no visible means of entrance ; it must have been entered by scaling-ladders from without. It is now a ruin, by no means a picturesque one, but it is the only ancient relic on the island, and the people are proud of it ; they seem to have a vested interest in its antiquity, and regard it as a sort of illustration of their history and of themselves. Past this ancient monument, through a pleasant winding road, with charming villa residences, and shady trees on either side, and we turn through a pair of handsome iron gates into some beautifully laid out grounds ; a miniature park, indeed, with clumps of fine old trees of the most rare and varied descriptions, and evergreens and shrubs of the choicest kind, all so arranged that the foliage of one should contrast artistically with that of the other. We roll through a long, curving drive, and in another moment stop before an old-fashioned red-brick mansion, with gabled front and pointed roof, which might have been lifted bodily up, and transplanted thither from some ancient English manor. The house in its general style and all its arrangements was purely English, and both host and hostess were simply perfect, and combined the refined courtesy of our country with the lavish liberality and genial hospitality of their own. It is the same in quality and degree in most American houses; there is no stiffness or formality, but that peculiar kind of good breeding and *bonhommie* which makes the transient guest feel most perfectly at home. There is nothing fast, frivolous, or shoddy about Newport; only the *crème de la crème* of American society congregates there; the fun-loving, vulgar herd, with their holiday squibs and crackers, hold no orgies on its sacred shores. The floating population is clothed (metaphorically speaking) in broadcloth and fine linen; it takes up its abode for a night or so at the one solitary and rather gloomy-looking hotel, and passes away.

Newport proper, that is the lower, older portion of the town, is a dull, ragged, out-at-elbows sort of place; it looks tired and worn out, as though it had had its day, and wanted rest. Indeed, it has been busy and bright enough in its time. A century ago it was a bustling seaport; scores of ships were riding at anchor in the bay;

the wharves were crowded with merchandise, and sailors from all parts of the world wandered to and fro, creating a confusion of tongues, and perhaps a confusion of morals at the same time. All is lonely and deserted now; the wharves are dilapidated, rotting away; a few broken boats are hauled up on shore, and children play hide-and-seek amid the ruins of the old dead days.

The fashionable Newportians reside in the upper portion of the town, which grows along the face of the cliff, and is held sacred to themselves. Lodging-houses or "genteel apartments" are things unknown. Only the aristocracy of the surrounding States gather here; people of culture, of refinement, and of wealth. There are no flashily dressed people or Brummagem buildings in Newport, but a solid, substantial dignity greets you everywhere. The road from the lower town winds upwards through a labyrinth of lovely cottages, covered with vines and trailing roses, past an ancient Jewish burial-ground, which has received no silent inmates for many a long year. It is kept in perfect order, and looks like a blooming flower-garden, funds for this purpose having been left by a deceased Rabbi. The old synagogue, gray and hoary, stands in the midst, deserted, haunted only by the echoes of departed days.

By this pretty winding way you reach the highway, if such a commonplace term can be applied to such a royal road. It is a fashionable thoroughfare and general drive, about two miles and a half long, bordered on either side along the whole route by tasteful villas. Some, indeed, are quite palatial residences; every one is a specimen of architectural beauty ; each bears a sort of family resemblance to the other, but no two are exactly alike. Never was such a wealth of architectural attractions gathered on one spot. Along the whole line one beautiful dwelling rises after another, till your mind becomes a jumble of points and arches, cupolas and towers ; and you don't know which to admire most. One part of the houses faces seaward, the other fronts the road, which during the season is crowded with handsome, well-appointed equipages, which would do credit to Longchamps or Rotten Row. The ladies sit in their verandahs, reading, chatting, or working, as the case may be, and watch their friends " go riding by." The air, laden with the salt sea-breeze, is soft and salubrious ; there is generally a sea-wind blowing inland, which tempers the heat of the sun, and renders Newport delightful when the cities are unendurable.

This is our last resting-place in America. Our holiday is over ; the time has come when we must turn our faces homeward. No more lingering by the way, no more rolling over prairie lands, or lounging by inland seas. Regretfully, yet not wholly regretful, we say good-bye to Newport, spend half a hour in Boston, then on through Canada, a twenty-four hours' journey to Quebec. We pass through long flat stretches of country, where Nature seems to have exerted herself to show how dull, dreary, and monotonous she could have made the world if she had only tried. Everything is brown, dusty, and parched with the hot thirsty sun, which seems to have drawn every drop of moisture from the poor old earth. Occasionally we catch a glimpse of a lazy, sluggish stream, creeping along as though it was trying to hide itself from the fierce blaze above. We were glad, when the night closed in, to get into our comfortable berth, and shut our eyes on the dreary landscape. At seven next morning we reached Point Levis, and were ferried across to Quebec, where our vessel lay at anchor.

The cathedral bells are ringing, and the sound of their musical chime comes to us pleasantly across the water; we look once more upon the shining roofs and gilded spires pricking the pale morning sky. We should have liked one more ramble through the quaint old streets, but the *Sardinian* lies at the quay, ready to start, the smoke coiling up from her great red funnel, her huge prow rising like the wall of a house from the sluggish water that splashes slowly against her sides. There is bustle on the decks, which are all swept and garnished in readiness for the advent of the coming passengers. Our good captain's genial voice hails us on the gangway; the well-remembered faces of the ship's officers smile a welcome to us as we pass along the deck; last, not least, our kindly stewardess meets and marshals us to our cosy little state-room. In the saloon—which is gay with ferns and flowers and polished plate and shining glass—the ship's canary, the pet alike of officers and passengers is trilling his loudest and sweetest. All is smiling, bright, and cheery, as we take up our quarters in the little floating world, which was so pleasant a nine-days' home to us a year ago, and is now to be so once more.

An hour afterwards, the shining spires of Quebec have faded from our sight, we are steaming down the mighty St. Lawrence, and our faces are set for England and for Home!

THE END.

www.ingramcontent.com/pod-product-compliance
Lightning Source LLC
Chambersburg PA
CBHW030322240426
43673CB00040B/1243